W9-BWL-351

DISCARDED
JENKS LRC
GORDON COLLEGE

SMALL WARS, BIG DEFENSE

SMALL WARS, BIG DEFENSE

Paying for the Military After the Cold War

A TWENTIETH CENTURY FUND BOOK

Murray Weidenbaum

JENKS L.R.C.
GORDON COLLEGE
255 GRAPEVINE RD.
WENHAM, MA 01984-1895

New York   Oxford
OXFORD UNIVERSITY PRESS
1992

UA
23
.W36943
1992

Oxford University Press

Oxford   New York   Toronto
Delhi   Bombay   Calcutta   Madras   Karachi
Petaling Jaya   Singapore   Hong Kong   Tokyo
Nairobi   Dar es Salaam   Cape Town
Melbourne   Auckland

and associated companies in
Berlin   Ibadan

Copyright © 1992 by Twentieth Century Fund

Published by Oxford University Press, Inc.,
200 Madison Avenue, New York, New York 10016

Oxford is a registered trademark of Oxford University Press

All rights reserved. No part of this publication may be reproduced,
stored in a retrieval system, or transmitted, in any form or by any means,
electronic, mechanical, photocopying, recording, or otherwise,
without the prior permission of Oxford University Press.

Library of Congress Cataloging-in-Publication Data
Weidenbaum, Murray L.
Small wars, big defense :
paying for the military after the cold war
/ Murray Weidenbaum.
p. cm. "A Twentieth Century Fund book."
Includes bibliographical references and index.
ISBN 0-19-507248-0
1. United States—Armed Forces—Appropriations and expenditures.
2. United States—Armed Forces—Finance. I. Title.
UA23.W36943 1992 355.6′22′0973—dc20 91-25509

2 4 6 8 9 7 5 3 1

Printed in the United States of America
on acid-free paper

To the memory of William M. Allen
Whose special combination of integrity
and accomplishment is a continuing inspiration

The Twentieth Century Fund is a research foundation
undertaking timely analyses of economic, political,
and social issues. Not-for-profit and nonpartisan,
the Fund was founded in 1919 and
endowed by Edward A. Filene.

BOARD OF TRUSTEES OF
THE TWENTIETH CENTURY FUND

Morris B. Abram, Emeritus
H. Brandt Ayers
Peter A. A. Berle
José A. Cabranes
Joseph A. Califano, Jr.
Alexander Morgan Capron
Edward E. David, Jr.
Brewster C. Denny, *Chairman*
Charles V. Hamilton
August Heckscher, Emeritus
Matina S. Horner
Madeleine M. Kunin

James A. Leach
Georges-Henri Martin, Emeritus
P. Michael Pitfield
Don K. Price, Emeritus
Richard Ravitch
Arthur M. Schlesinger, Jr.,
Emeritus
Harvey I. Sloane, M.D.
Theodore C. Sorensen
James Tobin, Emeritus
David B. Truman, Emeritus
Shirley Williams

Richard C. Leone, *Director*

Foreword

The economics of defense spending run a poor third in the debate about national security policy. The size and composition of the Pentagon's budget are the subject of considerable press coverage. And in the Congress and the nation at large, there is intense interest in where the money will be spent. Cutbacks, as well, cause an explosion of local press and political attention in the places affected. In contrast, the macroeconomic effects of the defense budget's billions are of interest only to specialists.

The end of the cold war has provoked a rare reconsideration of the economics of defense spending. In its simplest form, the discussion is focused on the size and impact of a possible "peace dividend" created by the potential for a significant reduction in U.S. armed forces. These speculations were muscled aside briefly by the American military expedition to the Persian Gulf. But with progress on new arms agreements with the Soviets and announcements of plans to halve the U.S. presence in Europe, questions about future defense spending are certain to once again occupy a key place on the nation's policy agenda.

The Twentieth Century Fund is fortunate, therefore, to have Murray Weidenbaum, former chairman of the Council of Economic Advisers, write about this issue for us. He clearly addresses such questions as, "What sort of military spending are we likely to need in the post-cold war world?" and "How should we manage the resources we devote to this critical public function?" Bearing in mind always the problem of providing economically for the long-run defense of the country, he extends our understanding of these issues well beyond today's headlines.

Weidenbaum tells us that we can afford to reduce our military establishment. Future military challenges must not be minimized; our ability to project power decisively the world over must not be allowed to deteriorate. Still, with the threat of a massive ground war in Europe all but eliminated, our military plans and therefore our military procurement and establishment must be changed. The share of our gross national product devoted to the military can be reduced by one or two percentage points, that is, by perhaps 20 to 30 percent. Such reductions, Weidenbaum is quick to point out, while economically significant—freeing up resources we can employ elsewhere—are not a fiscal treasure chest. The cold war peace dividend will be on the same order of magnitude as the post-Vietnam dividend. Not many chickens to count, even after they hatch.

Regardless of how much we spend on our military, we ought to get as much as we can for our money. On this issue, Weidenbaum provides us with the kind of detailed, expert analysis only a participant in the budget and procurement processes could generate. This book surely will become required reading for anyone within or outside of government who aims to rationalize America's military spending.

September 1991

Richard C. Leone,
DIRECTOR
The Twentieth Century Fund

Preface

This book is addressed to people who are concerned with the unique set of problems and opportunities that arise from major changes in the size and composition of military spending. Some parts are likely to upset both hawks and doves. After all, I advocate a strong national defense, but at much lower cost. I am anxious to see the civilian sector productively use the valuable resources released by the military, but I envision a minimum role for government in the process.

Having seen the workings of what my students call the military–industrial complex from both industrial and governmental vantage points, I believe that I have some special insights to offer. The readers will have to judge for themselves—and I hope that there is an adequate quantity of them to do so.

This book was completed while war was raging in the Persian Gulf. Yet, the central message relates to economic aspects of national security policy which are as relevant to peacetime adjustments as to war mobilization.

The work on this book was sponsored by the Twentieth Century Fund. I am grateful for the support and encouragement provided, and for the valuable counsel from John Samples, Bernard Wasow, Beverly Goldberg, and Carol Kahn.

The Center for the Study of American Business at Washington University provided the environment in which I could do the research and writing. Mark Jensen was my able research assistant. Christine Moseley transformed my peculiar brand of hieroglyphics into readable manuscript form. James Davis subjected himself to the special travails involved in reviewing the early drafts. To each, I am grateful.

St. Louis   M.W.
May 1991

Contents

PART I

MEETING TODAY'S CHALLENGES

CHAPTER 1

Matching the Military Budget to the National Security Environment

The military establishment of the United States resembles a heavily loaded, rapidly moving vehicle. The driver is trying to reduce the speed substantially, but without shaking up the passengers too badly and while keeping the car on the right side of the road. As the driver slows down, there are all sorts of noises in the engine. This reminds the driver that the vehicle is overdue for repairs and maintenance.

In that same spirit, the policy task facing the American people after the end of the Persian Gulf conflict is how to gear down the massive military effort that was under way since the early 1980s, but to do so while maintaining the capability to conduct demanding military operations. Events following the Iraqi invasion of Kuwait have made it clear that the United States must continue to be able to respond to rapid and substantial changes in the international environment— including changes for the worse. History shows that the nature and intensity of the threats to our national security change substantially and at times abruptly.

At the same time, the pressures to reduce the massive federal budget deficit make an often-postponed challenge more urgent: reforming the way the armed forces buy and operate weapon systems and recruit and retain servicemen and servicewomen.

To demonstrate how this galaxy of issues can be dealt with effectively, this book undertakes a double task. First, it shows how the American economy can adjust successfully to large (albeit constrained) defense cutbacks and thereby move to a more civilian-oriented economy. It then presents ideas for getting the most out of the lower defense budgets that are in the offing, while maintaining the capability to reverse course should that once again become necessary.

3

SETTING THE STAGE

With substantially improved relationships between the two nations, both the Soviet Union and the United States are making considerable efforts to reduce their military arsenals of weapons—especially those that would be used in a war between the two superpowers. Despite American concern over the harsh Soviet treatment of the Baltic republics, it is hard to conjure up any contemporary circumstances under which the two nations would go to war with each other. They share many common interests and lack any serious border disputes or similar aggravating relationships. The high level of cooperation shown in the Middle East in 1990–1991 is indicative of the post–Cold War world that is likely to emerge.

Although it is by no means a universally held position, this positive outlook has much support. Kremlin watcher Daniel Goure reports that a reassessment is under way within the top Soviet political–military leadership. They are increasingly embracing the belief that the modern world is interdependent and that security for one must mean security for all. He cites an editorial in *Kommunist* as capturing the essence of this thesis:

> [A] new spirit unparalleled in the past . . . rests on the fact that a world community united by . . . common interest . . . is being formed. The most important . . . is averting a nuclear catastrophe. Such interests are above any . . . class antagonism.[1]

A variety of analysts echoes this benign view of Soviet intentions. William Kaufmann of the Brookings Institution states that, "at a minimum, Gorbachev appears to be looking for a long respite from the Cold War."[2] Jeane Kirkpatrick goes further: "The abandonment [by the Soviet Union] of the Brezhnev Doctrine and of the effort to control Eastern Europe by force marks the end of the Cold War."[3] Arnold Horelick of the RAND Corporation provides a variation of that theme, "By every measure of conventional postwar scorekeeping, 1989 was the year in which the West won the Cold War."[4]

Michael Howard of Yale University arrives at a more positive view of the same phenomenon, "The Soviet Union . . . will continue to pursue its interests throughout the world; but those interests will be as likely to lie in cooperating with the West as in opposing it."[5]

Events have overtaken the traditional notion that the main potential threat that the U.S. military establishment must be prepared for is a Soviet invasion of Western Europe involving nuclear weaponry. With the crumbling of communism in the countries along the supposed invasion route to the West—East Germany, Poland, Czechoslovakia, and Hungary—that notion has become an anachronism. If anything, these nations are being transformed into a buffer protecting the West.

If the Warsaw Pact ever was an effective military organization, its role now has been consigned to history.[6]

Likewise, the possibility that the continental United States will be directly attacked by the armed forces of any other nation is also remote. However, other threats to our national security surely remain—to some degree, they are growing—and we will take those up shortly. Surely, the events in the Middle East are a constant reminder that force continues to be part of the system of competitive nation-states. Yet the essential nature of that competition is changing from the days of the Cold War.

Under these circumstances, it seems sensible to consider seriously the possibility of substantial reductions over the next several years in the existing military forces and in the defense outlays of the two superpowers. Indeed, the analysis that follows is based on the premise that there will be great pressure to lower the U.S. military budget in the period following the war against Iraq.

In retrospect, the moment at which it became clear that Washington opinion leaders accepted that the threat to the national security from the Soviet Union was greatly diminished was the March 1, 1990, testimony of William Webster, the director of Central Intelligence. Webster reported that, "There is little chance that Soviet hegemony could be restored in Eastern Europe." The underlying idea is that any hard-line successor to the present Soviet leadership would face the same severe economic and political pressures and would be deterred from engaging in a major military buildup or from taking a confrontational stance toward the United States. Webster went on to state that Marxist–Leninist ideology is now bankrupt and that communist parties will continue "to lose legitimacy and strength."[7] That now widely held view, bolstered by events in the Soviet Union since then, underscores the weakness of the Soviet system. Yet we should not be carried away by enthusiastic prognostications of the bright prospects for democratic, market-oriented societies to quickly emerge in what had been the Soviet sphere of influence.

In a general sense, we can approximate the outer limits to any process of mutual reduction of armaments on the part of the United States and the Soviet Union by acknowledging the obvious: each of the two military superpowers will still want to maintain overwhelming superiority over any third nation or other external force. Events in the Middle East in 1990 showed that such capability can be extremely demanding and far greater than was the case in earlier periods.

The present outlook is for a continued reduction of armaments on the part of the two military superpowers and therefore continued improvements in the overall state of their relationships with each other. Yet, in the light of history, some skepticism is always in order.

Thus, even though he believes that the Soviet threat has collapsed, Theodore C. Sorensen notes that the Soviet Union remains the only nation on earth capable of bringing about the physical destruction of the United States.[8] More specifically, Norman R. Augustine, chairman of Martin Marietta and a former undersecretary of the army, warns that the principal current reductions of Soviet military capabilities have been in obsolete systems rather than in first-line equipment.[9]

Universal peace is not a reasonable expectation. Indeed, it is likely that the United States will maintain a large military establishment for the indefinite future—although not necessarily at the very high recent levels of spending. If substantial, albeit fluctuating, levels of military outlays are here to stay, the sensible response is to try to understand that costly phenomenon and to make the best of it. The role of defense in the American economy clearly needs to be rethought in the light of a post–Cold War environment.

FEAST AND FAMINE IN MILITARY BUDGETS

When economists write about public policy, we usually succeed only in conjuring up images of Ebenezer Scrooge, green eye shades, detailed statistical tabulations, and arcane mathematics. In these pages, however, I hope to conjure a different line, using the approach of William Gladstone. The great nineteenth-century British prime minister wrote that financial issues "are not mere matters of arithmetic, but in a thousand ways go to the root of prosperity of individuals, and relation of classes, and the strength of kingdoms."

The pattern of defense spending over the past half century can be best described as a frantic stop-and-go (or rather go-and-stop) cycle, oscillating between aggressive calls for accelerated spending and periods of declining military budgets. The result is hasty planning of military force structures followed by cancellation or inefficient stretch-outs of expensive weapon systems, a waste of the vast resources devoted to national defense. The most recent outlook has been one of both feast and famine—generosity for Operation Desert Storm simultaneous with cutbacks in the rest of the military budget.

Since the beginning of World War II, the military budget has never experienced an extended period of stability. Eras of rapid growth have alternated with times of austerity. Often the change in the size and direction of military spending has mirrored the shift in the national security environment facing the United States. This was the case after the Vietnam War when the end of hostilities permitted a substantial reduction in military spending. At other times, the changing internal response to a relatively constant set of external factors has been more subjective. Witness the rapid buildup in the early 1980s and the abrupt decline starting in the middle of the decade, all of which occurred during a period when the threat to our national security remained relatively constant.

Some reflection on the past patterns is useful in developing policy for the future. The military buildup associated with the Korean War came while memories of World War II were still fresh. In turn, the end of that war was followed by a much slower pace of defense spending in the 1960s. It is easy to forget the uncertainty that existed during each phase of the stop-and-go cycle. For example, in 1969 John Kenneth Galbraith tried to explain to a congressional committee that large-scale military spending was a thing of the past: "Finally, it must be recognized that the big defense budgets of the 1950s were a unique response to the conditions of that time." Galbraith concluded that, "Then there were the deep fears generated by the Cold War, the seeming unity of the Communist world, and, at least in comparison with present circumstances, the seeming lack of urgency of domestic requirements. All this has changed."[10]

Galbraith went on to state, "We have a wide range of tacit understandings with the Soviets; we have come to understand that the average Soviet citizen . . . is unresponsive to the ideas of nuclear annihilation. . . . It is now even agreed as to where the first danger to American democracy—if there is one—lies. It is not from the U.S.S.R. . . . [but] from the starvation of our public services."[11] Galbraith's language does indeed have a very contemporary ring to it. In the light of subsequent developments, however, his point appears to be somewhat premature—at least two decades too soon.

Another start-and-stop cycle started in early 1981, when the newly elected Reagan administration developed a five-year defense program calling for spending $1.5 trillion in fiscal years 1982–1986. If all the requested money had been appropriated, then defense spending in real terms (after allowing for inflation) would have increased more than 10 percent per year and reached an annual level—again in real terms—higher than any other peacetime period in American history.

Actually, Congress was rather generous, granting $1.3 trillion or almost nine-tenths of the amount requested. Between fiscal years 1980 and 1985 the size of the defense budget doubled, rising more than 50 percent in real terms. By the middle of the decade, U.S. military procurement expenditures exceeded those of the Soviet Union for the first time since the late 1960s. That rapid buildup of weapon systems in the first half of the 1980s was greater than the peak pace of military production at the height of the Vietnam War.

In retrospect, many of the arguments used to justify the crash effort were weak: because, just before he left office, President Carter proposed an annual increase of 5 percent in military spending (plus an allowance for inflation), then the Reagan administration must do much more; because a preliminary estimate showed a 100 percent increase in proposed defense appropriations over the next four years, then any deviation from that—such as a 90 percent rise—would send the wrong signal to the Soviets. If I had not been in the room at the time these arguments were presented to President Reagan, I might be inclined to dismiss them as an implausible basis for decision making on national security policy.

Congress reversed direction in its action on the military budget for fiscal 1986, cutting the funds requested by 10 percent, and it continued on that downward path until the Iraqi invasion of Kuwait in 1990. The defense budget dropped in both real and nominal terms, ending an upward trend that began with the Vietnam War. Congress has reduced the real level of military appropriations in each fiscal year since (excluding the special costs of Operation Desert Storm).

According to former Assistant Secretary of Defense Lawrence J. Korb, " . . . this sudden and unprecedented shift in the direction of defense spending has created chaos in the Pentagon."[12] In perhaps excessively colorful language, Korb was referring to the tendency of the Reagan administration to ignore the intent of the congressional reductions in defense appropriations. Thus, the Reagan administration's basic reaction was to leave the long-term plans of the Pentagon unchanged and merely add the shortfall in a given year's funding to the amount requested in future years. Planned expenditures for hundreds of programs were each reduced slightly with the expectation that large increases would resume in the next year. The procedure was repeated each time that Congress reduced the military budget request. It served both to widen the gap between military planning and fiscal reality as well as to aggravate the relationship between the Legislative and the Executive branches.

When Frank Carlucci became secretary of defense late in the Reagan administration, he was faced with the challenge of reconciling the extremely expensive force structure imbedded in the Pentagon plans that he had inherited with the lower, albeit still substantial, sums being appropriated by the Congress. His main response was to "stretch out" the procurement of major weapon systems—an approach that has costs as well as benefits.

On taking over the Pentagon leadership in the incoming Bush administration, Secretary of Defense Dick Cheney made a series of budget changes, also trying to respond to the lower levels of congressional funding. This meant eliminating the construction of one new aircraft carrier and canceling or cutting back several major aircraft procurement programs, such as the navy's A-12. Nevertheless, the gap between plans and money remained. The General Accounting Office reported that President Bush's five-year defense plan for fiscal years 1990–1994 was almost $114 billion short of the money needed to carry it out.[13] Some private observers estimated the funding shortfall as much greater. A study group of the Council on Foreign Relations estimated it to be in excess of $200 billion.[14]

Simultaneously, the relative "famine" in the basic military budget was accompanied by a generous amount of funding for the U.S. effort to contain Iraqi aggression in the Persian Gulf region (the latter outlays were exempt from the congressionally mandated limits on defense spending). The one-shot cost of Operation Desert Storm was approximately $50 billion.

Of course, the stop-and-go approach to military budgeting has generated serious repercussions. During the "go" times, defense planners assume that rapid increases in military funding will continue indefinitely and plan accordingly. Then along come the austere years, when substantial cuts are made. There is natural reluctance, of course, to cancel the weapon systems that only recently had been approved.

Hoping that the time of budgetary austerity would soon pass, military decision makers respond by slowing down and stretching out the production plans for all the systems underway. They take that course of action even though it raises unit costs and, perhaps more important, it makes the full completion of all the production plans infeasible.

As a result of the inefficiencies resulting from the start and stop cycles since the end of World War II, the United States has gained far smaller enhancements of its national security than might have been expected from the vast resources devoted to defense programs. In the understated words of a team of researchers of the nonprofit RAND Corporation, " . . . such instability clearly affects the efficiency of weapons acquisition."[15]

Congress and the Pentagon have also attempted to adjust to lower military budgets by squeezing government contractors so severely that the results were counterproductive, as we will soon see. The reader should recall, however, that in the mid-1980s, a host of outrageous examples of waste and inefficiency (not all of them accurate) created an atmosphere conducive to imposing stricter requirements on the companies providing materials for defense.

THE UNFORTUNATE SIDE EFFECTS

As is inevitable when hundreds of billions of dollars are being spent in a fairly limited period of time, many shortcomings in military procurement emerged in the 1980s, ranging from outright dishonesty to unintentional inefficiency. Prosecution of the lawbreakers was clearly appropriate, but imposing more detailed and burdensome regulation also did little to reduce the overall cost of weapons acquisition. The immediate impact was what experienced observers of the Washington scene would expect: an increase in the expense of producing the goods and services ordered by the military establishment. A more basic—and unexpected—response to the increasingly onerous regulation was an exodus of defense contractors and especially subcontractors from the military market. Those firms that had attractive commercial alternatives left voluntarily.

Avtex Fibres of Front Royal, Virginia, was an example of the involuntary erosion of the defense industrial base. By 1988, Avtex was the only supplier of aerospace-grade continuous filament rayon yarn for the nose cones and booster rockets of nearly all U.S. strategic missile and space programs. All the other companies that could have produced this material turned instead to civilian markets and left Avtex in a monopoly position.

Late in 1988, this obscure sixth-tier supplier announced that it was closing its doors and filing for bankruptcy. Alarmed by the prospect that the production of an arcane although critical component of military production was to be halted, the Department of Defense quickly supplied $22.6 million—and NASA another $18 million—to get the 1,300-employee supplier back into production long enough to build up a rayon yarn stockpile and establish and qualify a second source.[16]

The Avtex case was more complicated than it appeared at first blush. In November 1989, the company closed its doors permanently because of its unwillingness (or inability—the point is now moot) to meet pollution control requirements. The plant was described at the time of closing as "one of the worst and most recalcitrant polluters in the mid-Atlantic region." The State of Virginia had sued Avtex for almost $20 million, but collected only $8 million by the time of closing.[17] Apparently, it did not make good economic sense for the company to modernize the half-century old facility and to stay in business as a government contractor.

A more subtle but far larger example of the impacts that arise from the squeeze on defense contractors is the case of the Boeing Company, traditionally one of the Defense Department's largest suppliers. Over the years, Boeing has earned a reputation for a combination of technological advance and economic efficiency—for designing and producing such successful aerospace products as the B-47 and B-52 bombers, the KC-135 tanker, and the Minuteman ICBM.

In 1989, however, the company reported that its government work incurred an aggregate loss of $470 million. At the same time, it had achieved the largest backlog of commercial airplane orders in the industry's history (by the end of 1990, that backlog exceeded $100 billion). To be sure, Boeing has not abandoned military business, but is it any surprise that its efforts are now mainly oriented to the civilian marketplace? (The company received the fifth largest share of defense contracts in fiscal 1981; by 1988, it was down to tenth place.)

The reader should be warned that, over a quarter of a century ago, the author served as Boeing's corporate economist. The only current ties are sentimental. Nevertheless, I suggest that government policymakers should be concerned when a strong, efficient company such as Boeing cannot operate profitably in the military market.

Far more than Avtex, Boeing may be a harbinger of what is in store for large portions of the defense industry if the Pentagon and the Congress refuse to conform the planned force structure to budget realities. It is impractical to resort to simply reducing the funds available to government contractors without cutting the tasks imposed on them. Given the $100–200 billion fiscal mismatch in the Pentagon, the key decision makers on national defense have only a few effective choices (none of them pleasant) to maintain a sustainable defense production effort: (1) reduce the number of aircraft, missiles, ships, and so on, to be bought; (2) reduce the operational readiness of the military force in being; (3) increase military budgets; or (4) some combination of the previous three.

The sensible approach is to tailor the military's demand to match the limited supply of fiscal cloth. Surely, the quaint notion of producing more weapon systems by paying defense contractors less must be classified as a futile exercise in wishful thinking. Meanwhile, the continued erosion of the U.S. defense industrial base is one of those quietly undramatic but strategically worrisome events that deserves more attention than it has been receiving.

According to a report by the Center for Strategic and International Studies, by 1987 the number of companies that provide "defense-critical" goods to the Pentagon had declined to 38,007 from 118,489 in 1982, a loss of 68 percent of the entire defense industrial base. This sharp drop, however, did not reflect the broader and positive trends in the national economy. The total number of firms in those same industries—including those who sold only to civilian customers—rose from 123,000 to 150,000 in the same five-year time period.[18]

For example, a large shakeout occurred in the airframe structural components business, with the departure of more than 4,000 companies. At the same time, 600 companies quit supplying antifriction bearings to the military and 668 of 834 vendors stopped supplying navigational instruments. The U.S. aerospace industry traditionally has depended on a wide array of subcontractors and suppliers. To replace the companies that have dropped out of the domestic military market, prime contractors have been establishing strategic alliances with offshore suppliers. The foreign factories tend to be newer and often more productive than their U.S. counterparts, further increasing the dependence on overseas sources.[19]

THE HIGH COST OF STRETCH-OUTS

Another popular way in which the military establishment has responded to lower budgets is to stretch out production programs over longer periods of time. Although it sounds harmless, this approach is a costly "quick fix." Producing 1,000 fighter aircraft over a five-year period does cost less in each year than producing the same number over a four-year time frame. This sounds like the easiest way of curtailing defense spending, but, as so frequently occurs in federal budgetary matters, easy answers are not ultimately satisfying.

The economic effect of stretch-outs is adverse: the total cost of producing those 1,000 aircraft will rise—and by far more than the rate of inflation. That is so because the aerospace industry (as well as other defense producers) is characterized by a "learning" or "improvement" curve in its production cycle. Companies and their employees learn how to improve the work they do as they do more of it.[20]

In addition, many specific reductions in unit costs are achieved through higher production rates. Labor savings are obtained by assigning more specific tasks to larger crews of workers. This greater specialization of labor allows them to become more proficient, and to avoid the delays that come about with shifting from one task to another. Similar savings are possible in the use of machinery, since a larger number of units can be produced once a machine is set up to perform a given task.

If the rate of production is high enough, it becomes economical to build special purpose machines to do tasks more efficiently than can be done with general-purpose tools. Economies also result when quantity discounts are obtained on purchases of parts and components. Other reductions in unit costs come from spreading fixed production costs (such as for tooling, test equipment, and overhead) over a larger number of units. Much of this benefit of mass production is lost when fewer units are produced in any given time period, especially below the economically optimum rate of output.

For example, the Department of Defense estimates that reducing the annual numbers of Black Hawk helicopters produced from eighty-two a year to sixty-one (a 26 percent reduction) increases the cost of each helicopter by 25 percent. Similarly, cutting back the production of the M1 tank by 25 percent raises the unit cost by 13 percent (see Table 1-1 for detail).[21]

The F-15 fighter aircraft program provides another striking exam-

Table 1-1 Changes in Unit Cost of Weapon Systems, 1987–1988

Weapon System	Percent Change in Annual Quantity Produced	Percent Change in Unit Cost
M1 Tank	−25	+13
Blackhawk Helicopter	−26	+25
Harrier Jet Airplane	−24	+25
EA-6B Electronic Warfare Plane	−50	+61
E-2C Warning Plane	−40	+45
Sidewinder Missile	−54	+163

Source: Derived from data contained in Congressional Budget Office, *Effects of Weapons Procurement Stretch-Outs on Costs and Schedules* (Washington, D.C.: U.S. Government Printing Office, 1987).

ple of the high cost of stretch-outs. The original plan for the air force's F-15 called for producing about 150 per year, a rate that was considered to be an efficient use of the available production capability. Because of budget cuts and cost overruns, the air force decided to stretch out the programs by almost three years and to produce fewer than 100 F-15s annually. The added cost due to the stretch-out (excluding the effects of inflation) was about $2 billion. This was equivalent to the cost of procuring approximately eighty-three additional F-15s. In effect, the United States lost more than a "wing" of aircraft because of the production stretch-out.[22]

The B-1 bomber program furnishes a cogent example of the high cost of program instability. After Rockwell International was awarded the contract, the company proceeded to build up a work force in the Los Angeles area. When the Carter administration cancelled the program, Rockwell laid off 17,000 employees and sold the plant it was using. Subsequently, when the Reagan administration revived the B-1, a new plant was built at Palmdale and 11,000 workers were hired in Rockwell's southern California division—in addition to 2,000 in the company's Tulsa facility and 7,000 in its Columbus, Ohio, division.[23]

Clearly, stretch-outs and program instability impose a cost penalty on procurement programs, as well as delaying delivery of weapons to the military forces.[24] Completing acquisition programs more slowly also increases the likelihood of technological obsolescence.

THE NEED FOR NEW POLICY APPROACHES

The cycles of feast and famine in military budgeting force executives within the Department of Defense to make unsound management decisions. The unpredictability and instability encourage Pentagon managers to procure as much as possible when funding is relatively plentiful, and avoid developing stable and realistic procurement plans. According to Comptroller General Charles Bowsher, "History shows that when too much money is pumped into the acquisition system over a relatively short period of time, we will have problems."[25]

Meanwhile, critics of the military establishment maintain that the still high levels of defense spending are needlessly provocative in international relations, and cause harm domestically. The negatives they cite include inflation, lower economic growth, less employment than if the money were used for domestic programs, and squeezes on higher priority civilian activities, notably the support of health and education. Ultimately, what are termed "excessively high" levels of military spending are seen as leading to national decline.

External Threats

Supporters of higher defense outlays, in turn, note both the continuing large size of the Soviet military establishment as well as the domestic benefits that flow from military outlays (especially in their own localities). The benefits of defense spending include important contributions to technological innovation, manpower training, industrial investment, and thus a stronger economy. Both sides make important points that, although often overstated, should not be ignored.

Serious problems arise, however, because of the rapid shifts in the political strength of the adherents of the two polar alternatives. Rather than a blend of the two viewpoints occurring, the result is a constant political battle that results in the frequent "starts-and-stops" in military budgeting. Over the long run, this unstable relation reduces both the effectiveness of military outlays and the efficiency of the civilian economy that provides the resources for the military establishment.

The attitude of decision makers toward defense spending needs to be redefined. The nature and intensity of the threats to national security do change substantially over time and so, reasonably, should the American response. We are currently witnessing a substantial and welcome decline in tension between the two military superpowers. The weak Soviet economy—weaker than most analysts anticipated— seems to be conducive to a more peaceful posture on the part of the Soviet Union.

The United States should take those actions that extend the new and more positive relationship, but should choose the approaches that are consistent with our national safety. It would be risky to cut U.S. defense budgets more rapidly than the declines in Soviet military capabilities. Surely the cyclical nature of international relations over the years provides little justification for either basing our defense plans on the assumption that an uninterrupted downward spiral in the arms race will resume after Desert Storm or the reverse—that the United States will invariably be engaged in active hostilities. The possibility of reversals in the state of international tensions surely remains, as does the need to be able to reverse our response to the changed external environment.

A steady movement to universal peace is not the most reasonable expectation. Historical experience tells us that such an eventuality should not be elevated beyond the status of pleasant possibility. A more realistic approach is that taken by historian-philosopher John Nef in his monumental study of war and progress:

> Let us not hoodwink ourselves with notions of perpetual peace and the millennium. These only increase the danger of war, for they rest upon a misunderstanding of human nature. Men and women are not angels.[26]

Just spinning the globe is instructive. The harsh crackdown by Soviet troops in Lithuania and Latvia is disturbing, especially as it indicates some shift in power relationships within the Soviet Union toward those who favor a harder line in military matters generally. Nor are China and North Korea areas of economic and political stability, and both nations possess substantial military power. Likewise, the most casual examination of the strategic and political situation in the Middle East following Operation Desert Storm confirms that the region remains an extremely dangerous area.

There is an especially perilous twist to recent developments. With the slowing of weapon system production by the two superpowers, the substantial pool of Western and Western-trained scientists, engineers, and technicians is being tapped by Third World nations eager to acquire their expertise for missile, nuclear, chemical, and other weapon projects. With the Soviet military threat receding, the spread of advanced weaponry to the developing countries has become the greatest danger to stability in the world.[27]

Many nations, developing and developed, now possess the capability to produce and deliver weapons of great destruction—nuclear, conventional, and unconventional. Experts estimate that at least sixteen—and perhaps as many as twenty-two—Third World countries own or are developing ballistic missiles. Some of them also possess the most advanced conventional military capabilities, such as the M-1 main battle tank, F-16 fighter aircraft, Exocet antiship missiles, SS-21 surface-to-surface missiles, and nuclear submarines.[28]

According to CIA Director William Webster, by the year 2000 at least six Third World countries probably will have missiles with ranges up to 5,500 kilometers. In addition, more than a dozen countries can now make chemical weapons. Moreover, most developed nations have the capability to use some of their nuclear energy generation and research facilities in weapons production with relative ease.[29] (See Table 1-2 for one such set of estimates.)

North Korea, for example, has continued to build up its military establishment. Its army, the world's fourth largest, reportedly has a manpower advantage of 370,000 over the South Korean Army. The North has some 50 brigades, with 3,500 tanks and self-propelled artillery, along the line of demarcation that separates the two countries (the DMZ).[30]

That is a particularly worrisome area of the world because there would be little warning time to prepare South Korea for an attack. Most of the latter's industrialization, located close to the border, could be destroyed in an initial attack from the north.[31]

Table 1-2 Potential Weapons Proliferation in the 1990s

Country	Short-range Ballistic Missiles	Intermediate-range Ballistic Missiles	Inter-continental Ballistic Missiles	Biological/Chemical Weapons Production	Nuclear Weapons Production
Argentina		X			X
Brazil	X	X		X	X
Cuba	X			X	
Egypt	X	X		X	
Ethiopia				X	
India	X	X	X	X	X
Iran	X	X		X	X
Iraq	X	X		X	X
Israel	X	X	X	X	X
North Korea	X			X	X
South Korea	X			X	X
Libya	X	X		X	
Pakistan	X			X	X
Rumania	X	X		X	X
Saudi Arabia		X			
South Africa	X	X		X	X
Syria	X	X		X	
Taiwan	X	X		X	X
Vietnam				X	
South Yemen	X			X	

Source: "In the News," *High Frontier Newswatch,* March 1990.

The U.S. Response

The United States has responded to the various threats to the national security with a high level of military strength. In the forty years from 1949 to 1989, the ratio of U.S. defense spending to gross national product (GNP) has rarely fallen below 5 percent. Slight exceptions occurred in 1978 and 1979, immediately prior to the rapid buildup of the early 1980s. The U.S. military ratio (some would say burden) is well above the 3 percent average for our NATO allies in Western Europe and the 2 percent for Canada.

If substantial albeit fluctuating or declining levels of defense spending are here to stay, then defense spending should neither be viewed as something to be abhorred vehemently nor embraced enthusiastically. Rather, the military budget can be seen as an important factor in the nation's economic development, whether or not it is a particularly efficient one. After all, military procurement shifts resources from public and private consumption to research and development and high-tech production (as will be demonstrated in Chapter 6). Whether we agree with them or not, decisions on the size and composition of defense spending have important impacts on the overall pace of innovation and, hence, on national productivity and international competitiveness.

Important policy conclusions flow from this line of reasoning. The investment process is a long-term affair and military budgeting is a case in point. Hence, both the military and civilian sectors would benefit by replacing the current practice of quick fixes in defense policy with fundamental, slower-acting reforms.

As a general proposition, the long-run effectiveness of the resources that are devoted to military purposes will be increased by lowering the peaks of military funding and raising the valleys. Wild fluctuations in the levels of defense budgets make it extremely difficult to carry out such desirable reforms as multiyear production contracting. In turn, the present state of affairs discourages private contractors from making the long-term investments in new factories and production equipment necessary to increase the efficiency and reduce the costs of procuring the weapon systems that are needed.

Much of the present array of regulation of military contractors results from attempting to alleviate short-term pressures on the military budget. Efforts to reduce the cost of defense purchasing should focus instead on an overhaul of the basic procurement system (as described in detail in Chapter 8).

True multiyear budgeting—not limited to twenty-four months—is only the most obvious example of the efforts needed. Compared to the continuous modernization of private industry, investments in new military production facilities have been neglected. This deficiency leads to high levels of costs and numerous quality shortcomings. The experiences with deregulation and privatization in the civilian sectors of the economy, both positive and negative, should be drawn upon.

Decisions in each stage of the extended production cycle for weapon systems should reflect longer-run factors. So should decisions on the numbers of weapon systems to be procured in each time frame. That is, given the combination of geopolitical and domestic factors that determine the size of military budgets, real stability in military expenditure levels is not always going to be the most likely outcome. The military establishment needs to learn how to capitalize on the "up" periods to build stocks of the high-priority weapons that are most likely to be needed during the coming "down" period. This approach would avoid the Department of Defense becoming committed to so many different weapon systems when money is very generous that chaos ensues during the inevitable downturns in funding availability.

In the light of these factors, lower-priority weapons programs should be identified expeditiously. The numbers of each to be produced should be reduced substantially or entire programs should be scrapped. The need to overhaul the cumbersome military procurement process remains a fundamental task. The focus should shift from meeting bureaucratic requirements to providing the incentives that characterize high-tech private industry. That approach would simultaneously raise the efficiency of the process and improve the prospects for strengthening the dual or civilian technology base so essential to international economic competitiveness.

Nor can we ignore the continuing efforts of members of Congress and the administration to saddle the military budget with costs of achieving unrelated civilian objectives by means of social requirements imposed on the military procurement process (a topic covered in depth in Chapter 8). The attitude that the Department of Defense should fund social objectives because it supposedly has the money is no substitute for sensible budgeting of civilian activities. In addition, old-fashioned political pressures too often override the choice of weapon systems—and of which contractors are to produce them. Use of the military budget as the premiere political gravy train is a luxury that this nation should abandon quickly.

In addition, the ineffective system of generous across-the-board pay increases for military personnel—alternating with penurious raises during periods of budget tightness—should be replaced. Instituting market-oriented pay scales would help attract and keep people whose skills are in short supply, while avoiding excessive salaries to others. Spending personnel funds more wisely both reduces the drain on the Treasury and enhances the quality of the military work force.

In sum, there is a compelling need to rethink the way in which this country finances the military establishment in the light of the changing long-term role of defense in the American economy.

A NEW CONTEXT FOR MILITARY SPENDING DECISIONS

Basic decisions on the size and composition of the military budget are now being made on the basis of a strong belief that a sea change is occurring at the heart of this nation's foreign policy—that is, in the U.S.–Soviet relationship. At one extreme, some proclaim that the Cold War is over and that arming against a Soviet military threat has become an anachronism as this nation faces the 1990s. Simultaneously, at the other end of the policy spectrum, there are those who react to the Soviet reform concepts of *perestroika* and *glasnost* as merely empty symbols devoid of substance: these analysts are concerned that a shift of power from the Soviet capital to the increasingly independent republics may eventually increase the likelihood of military action in that part of the world.

Most serious analysts of national security and foreign policy take an intermediate position. They note that many of the basic causes of the Cold War endure, although they often require different responses than were warranted in earlier periods. The Soviet Union is still the dominant military power in Europe, though its day-to-day utilization of that power has diminished visibly and its weak economy is a major deterrent to military adventures. The retreats from areas as diverse as Eastern Europe and Afghanistan notwithstanding, Moscow continues to possess the ability to follow an aggressive foreign policy; however, it is not now doing so. In any event, the United States and the Soviet Union remain the two unchallenged military superpowers on the face of the globe.

It is ironic that the Soviets appeared as the apostles of peace in the 1980s even though their military budget was continuing to rise—while U.S. military spending was declining. It is only since 1989 that the Soviet's military outlays have come down (according to our best measurements).

In that light, the Soviets' stated desire to reconfigure its forces to fit a "defensive" doctrine thus far has been more talk than action. The Soviet Union still deploys more than 12,000 strategic-nuclear weapons. It still maintains an increasingly modern navy of more than 700 submarines and surface ships. It is still expanding its fleet of nuclear attack submarines at a rate of five or six per year.[32] Even the reduction in armaments that the Soviet Union leadership has pledged will have only modest impacts. Retiring 5,000 of the more than 50,000 Soviet tanks in Eastern Europe is surely helpful in defusing tensions, but it does not change the fundamental balance of power. This will especially be the case if the tanks withdrawn from East Germany, Czechoslovakia, and Hungary are not destroyed, but merely parked on the Soviet side of the border, where they can be rapidly redeployed.

The Conventional Forces in Europe Agreement requires the Soviet Union to demobilize over 300,000 soldiers and destroy tens of thousands of tanks and other weapon systems critical to offensive operations. Yet, the Soviet armies that remain deployed in the Western Military Districts of the Soviet Union still dwarf those of any other army in Europe. They also constitute a force many times more formidable than the army that Nazi Germany threw across the Low Countries in 1941.

In contrast, recent reductions in the Soviet naval threat are far smaller and much easier to reverse. The Soviet Navy has adopted a more defensively oriented posture than it had been maintaining previously; nevertheless, after some preparation those ships could sail again in the open seas.[33] Moreover, its production of surface combat ships in 1989, measured in tonnage, was the greatest in more than two decades.

Soviet strategic nuclear forces remain the paramount military threat to U.S. national security. In the words of long-time Pentagon critic Richard J. Barnet, " . . . the military power of the Soviet Union to destroy the United States remains intact."[34] The Soviets have been pursuing a modernization effort that is improving their overall strategic capabilities. They continue to invest heavily in ballistic missile defense. Notwithstanding the political and economic crises facing the Soviet Union, the modernization of its strategic forces remains relatively unimpaired. The major exception is a cutback in their Blackjack bomber production that goes beyond the requirements of the START arms reduction agreement.[35]

On the bright side, most military analysts have long believed that a strategic nuclear war would most likely result from an escalation of a conventional war, particularly in Europe. As the likelihood of a conventional war in Europe has diminished, the probability of a nuclear exchange between the United States and the Soviet Union likewise has declined substantially.

Looking ahead, a more positive and optimistic attitude does seem to be justified. Robert Legvold, director of Columbia University's Harriman Institute for the Advanced Study of the Soviet Union, believes that a revolution is under way in Soviet foreign policy greater than any in the postwar period, "indeed, greater than any since Lenin . . . "[36] He discounts the concern with the limited specific actions that the Soviet Union has taken to change its military position, noting that "behavioral" revolutions precede "conceptual" revolutions.

One such behavioral revolution in international relations occurred in the first half of the nineteenth century and provides a parallel for today. The devastation wrought by the Napoleonic Wars convinced all the major powers that military conflict was too costly. They were sufficiently satisfied with Europe's new landscape that none desired to alter the status quo in a fundamental way. Each of the nations sought a nonthreatening international environment that would allow them to focus on domestic problems.

The resultant concert of Europe preserved the peace from 1815 to 1854.[37] That seems to be what its members had in mind when the NATO summit conference in July 1990 declared that, "Today our alliance begins a major transformation. Working with all the countries of Europe, we are determined to create enduring peace on this continent."

Soviet expert Arnold L. Horelick has developed a thought-provoking spectrum of alternative Soviet futures. At the most optimistic end, the Soviet Union completes the process of *Perestroika* and adopts a genuinely federal system. Under a far more pessimistic scenario, the Soviet Union as we know it today tends to disintegrate and faces chronic interethnic warfare. A Russian nationalist backlash drives out progressive economic reformers. Under this latter alternative, the Soviet Union could become the "sick man of Europe," the role that Turkey played when the Ottoman Empire was coming apart.

In practice, some intermediate position is more likely than either polar alternative. Horelick believes that the least plausible Soviet future is a return to the highly stable Soviet Union of the 1970s. Even if the Soviet Union is run by a much more assertive leadership than it is at present, the reconstitution of the old Soviet threat to the West, according to Horelick, "simply will not be possible."[38]

More basic to the new view of U.S. national defense requirements is the increasingly accepted notion that most threats to national well-being are not merely military, but contain major economic and technological elements as well. In this view, military power alone does not necessarily provide an adequate solution to those threats.[39] After all, the collapse of the Warsaw Pact and the reduction of the Soviet threat to Western Europe did not result from successful military action by the West. Rather, it came about from economic failure in what was then the Eastern bloc nations. In the post–Cold War environment, threats to a nation's economic interests are coming to be regarded as a grave danger. According to Martin McGuire of the University of Maryland, "Economic hazards are central rather than peripheral as before."[40]

This perspective underscores the vital need for more frugally allocating and carefully spending the still substantial resources that are likely to be devoted to national security purposes in the years ahead.

Even if the trend of defense outlays cannot be made more predictable, the way in which spending on equipment and manpower is allocated needs to be improved. Government regulation of defense contractors is so heavy-handed that it severely blunts the operation of market incentives. By better husbanding the resources of this formidable sector of the economy, we can improve both the productivity of our armed forces as well as the performance of the rest of the society.

Because military procurement shifts resources from consumption to research and development (R&D) and to a special form of capital investment, decisions on the size and composition of defense spending affect the pace of innovation and, hence, national competitiveness and productivity. Although many analysts have held that military and civilian research and development compete for the same resources, there is—as we will see—little evidence to support this opinion. Indeed, the resources devoted to civilian R&D are as likely to increase as to decrease when military R&D increases.

The positive correlation of military and civilian R&D expenditures must not be taken to mean that military-supported R&D should be expanded or that the Department of Defense can provide an American answer to Japan's vaunted Ministry of International Trade and Industry. As will be shown in later chapters, an enhanced military–industrial complex is not the way to promote efficiency and competitiveness in the American economy. This approach ignores the lessons of the past. The overregulated defense sector is a poor sponsor of innovation. Indeed, the pace of product improvement is much slower in the red-tape government environment. In fact, the military can gain by making better use of the competitive markets of the civilian economy.

There is a close connection between ever-expanding regulation and the rising dropout of defense contractors and subcontractors. The trivia of such military requirements as the fourteen-page specification for buying a fruitcake lends itself to ridicule. Far more important, however, in the aggregate this overregulated, bureaucratized procurement process leads naturally to politicized behavior by firms that have accommodated to that unique set of groundrules. Further, the politicization of defense contracting usually helps older industries at the expense of the newer firms. Long-established companies, by dint of their years of support of political candidates, have greater clout than do the newer growth industries. Ailing companies also have more incentive to devote time and effort to obtaining subsidies from government via political action than do healthy companies.

The time is appropriate to consider "deregulating" and "privatizing" much of the process. The basic reason for contracting out, rather than using the arsenal system, is to obtain the advantages of private initiative, entrepreneurial risk-taking, and competition. The current do-it-by-the-numbers approach virtually assures that a bureaucratic procurement process will result.

Reform of the military spending process—of budgeting and procurement and regulation of military contractors—will take time. The current practice of looking for quick fixes in defense policy must be replaced by fundamental, if slower-acting, reforms. The long-run effectiveness of military spending also will be increased if the Pentagon's outlays evidence more stability. Decisions at each stage of the extended production cycle for weapon systems should more fully reflect longer-run trends in the international security environment. In turn, this attitude will enable the organizations in the public and private sectors that serve the military establishment to do a better job.

NOTES

1. Daniel Goure, "Soviet Doctrine and Nuclear Forces into the Twenty-first Century," in William C. Green and Theodore Karasik, eds., *Gorbachev and His Generals* (Boulder: Westview Press, 1990), p. 10.

2. William W. Kaufmann, *Glasnost, Perestroika, and U.S. Defense Spending* (Washington, D.C.: Brookings Institution, 1990), p. 3.

3. Jeane J. Kirkpatrick, "Beyond the Cold War," *Foreign Affairs*, Vol. 69, No. 1, 1990, p. 4.

4. Arnold L. Horelick, "U.S. Soviet Relations: Threshold of a New Era," *Foreign Affairs*, Vol. 69, No. 1, 1990, p. 51.

5. Michael Howard, "The Springtime of Nations," *Foreign Affairs*, Vol. 69, No. 1, 1990, p. 30.

6. Phillip A. Petersen, a European Specialist in the Pentagon's policy planning staff, cited in Michael R. Gordon, "Aide Disagrees With Cheney on Extent of Soviets' Threat," *The New York Times*, March 13, 1990, p. A7.

7. Quoted in "Bush Is Reported Willing to Accept Big Cuts in Military Budget," *The New York Times*, March 18, 1990, p. 20.

8. Theodore C. Sorensen, "Rethinking National Security," *Foreign Affairs*, Summer 1990, pp. 1–2.

9. Statement of Norman R. Augustine before the House Armed Services Committee, March 21, 1990, p. 11.

10. John Kenneth Galbraith, "Military Power and the Military Budget," in Robert H. Haveman and Robert D. Harrison, eds., *The Political Economy of Federal Policy* (New York: Harper & Row, 1973), p. 115.

11. Ibid., p. 116.

12. Lawrence J. Korb, "The Reagan Defense Budget and Program: The Buildup That Collapsed," in David Boaz, ed., *Assessing the Reagan Years* (Washington, D.C.: Cato Institute, 1988), p. 86.

13. *DOD Budget: Comparison of Updated Five-Year Plan With President's Budget* (Washington, D.C.: U.S. General Accounting Office, 1990), p. 6.

14. Philip A. Odeen and Gregory F. Treverton, *Thinking about Defense Spending* (New York: Council on Foreign Relations, 1989), p. 7.

15. G. K. Smith and others, *A Preliminary Perspective on Regulatory Activities and Effects in Weapons Acquisition* (Santa Monica, Calif.: RAND Corporation, 1988), p. v.

16. Larry Grossman, "Industrial Base: The Supplier Bottleneck," *Military Forum*, May 1989, p. 40.

17. B. Drummond Ayres, Jr., "Jobs Are Lost in Plant Shutdown, but So Is Foul-Smelling Air," *The New York Times*, November 21, 1989, p. 10.

18. James Blackwell, *Deterrence in Decay: The Future of the Defense Industrial Base* (Washington, D.C.: Center for Strategic and International Studies, 1989).

19. Bruce Stokes, "Come Fly With Me," *National Journal*, March 31, 1990, p. 782.

20. An 80 percent learning curve is widely used in the aerospace industry. Thus, producing a second batch of aircraft requires only 80 percent of the resources used for the first batch—and 64 percent for the third batch (80% of 80%), and so forth. All sorts of variations arise in practice. For example, design changes require relearning. See *Underestimation of Funding Requirements in Five Year Procurement Plans* (Washington, D.C.: U.S. General Accounting Office, 1984).

21. Weapon system cost estimating remains an arcane art and pinpoint accuracy is not anticipated. The reader may thus wish to take with a grain of salt the conclusion implicit in these numbers that, in four of six cases, the elasticity of cost with respect to quantity is one or greater. Unit costs rise, but it is not likely that total costs rise when quantity is reduced; rather, the military establishment is using an opportunity to try to discourage cuts in its budget.

22. Jacques S. Gansler, *Affording Defense* (Cambridge: MIT Press, 1989), p. 124.

23. Ibid., pp. 249–50.

24. Congressional Budget Office, *Effects of Weapons Procurement Stretch-Outs on Costs and Schedules* (Washington, D.C.: U.S. Government Printing Office, 1987), p. 17.

25. Testimony of Charles A. Bowsher, Comptroller General, in U.S. Senate Committee on Armed Services, *Defense Acquisition Process* (Washington, D.C.: U.S. Government Printing Office, 1988), p. 6.

26. John U. Nef, *War and Human Progress* (New York: W. W. Norton and Co., 1963), p. 416.

27. Michael R. Gordon, "Greater Threats From Lesser Powers," *The New York Times*, April 8, 1990, pp. E1–E2.

28. C. D. Vollmer, "The Future Defense Industrial Environment," *Washington Quarterly*, Spring 1990, p. 103; Joseph Pilat and Paul White, "Technology and Strategy in a Changing World," *Washington Quarterly*, Spring 1990, p. 84; Baker Spring, *Meeting the Threat of Ballistic Missiles in the Third World* (Washington, D.C.: Heritage Foundation, 1989).

29. Benjamin Frankel, "Nuclear Proliferation Policy," *The American Enterprise*, March–April 1990, p. 10.

30. David Martin, "The Coming Decade in the Pacific Basin," *Law and National Security Intelligence Report*, May 1990, p. 2.

31. See Joseph S. Nye, Jr., "Arms Control After the Cold War," *Foreign Affairs*, Winter 1989/90, p. 52.

32. Jay P. Kosminsky, *Four Imperatives for Cutting the Defense Budget* (Washington, D.C.: Heritage Foundation, 1990), pp. 3–7.

33. Sam Nunn, *Nunn 1990: A New Military Strategy* (Washington, D.C.: Center for Strategic and International Studies, 1990), pp. 23–24.

34. Richard J. Barnet, "Defining the Moment," *The New Yorker*, July 14, 1990, p. 46.

35. Nunn, *Nunn 1990*, pp. 29–30.

36. Robert Legvold, "The Revolution in Soviet Foreign Policy," *Foreign Affairs*, Vol. 68, No. 1, 1989, p. 82.

37. Clifford Kupchan and Charles Kupchan, "After NATO: Concert of Europe," *The New York Times*, July 6, 1990, p. A11.

38. "Reflections on Some Possible Soviet Futures: An Interview With Arnold Horelick," *RAND Research Review*, Spring 1990, p. 6.

39. Legvold, "Revolution in Soviet Policy," pp. 83–85.

40. Cited in Leonard Silk, "National Security: New Priorities," *The New York Times*, June 22, 1990, p. C2.

CHAPTER 2

Cutting Back the Defense Sector

While visions of massive peace dividends no longer dance in the heads of politicians, we as a nation still have not yet decided what the stripped down military establishment should look like in a post–Cold War environment.

THE SIZE OF THE DEFENSE REDUCTIONS

It is pleasant to speculate about the size of any future declines in military outlays. A good starting point for calculating specific magnitudes is to take account of recent experience. Although the military budget has continued to grow in nominal terms, making an allowance for inflation shows that the level of "real" military appropriations declined at about 2 percent per year from fiscal 1986 through fiscal 1990. Ignoring the special costs of Operation Desert Storm, the decline is continuing. That steady shrinkage has been both quiet and real. The drop in actual military spending has been slower, because in part the Defense Department could live off its substantial backlog of unspent appropriations. (The special costs of Desert Storm more than offset cuts in the base of the military budget during recent fiscal periods.)

A scenario of minimum change is to assume that, following the Persian Gulf conflict, the downtrend in the military budget during the late 1980s will resume. That is, we can forecast that, over the five-year period 1991–1995, the military budget will rise in nominal terms, but not rapidly enough to offset the full effects of inflation. Thus, no substantial change would be made in the trend of funding for the military establishment. In real terms, defense spending would follow the pace of appropriations and decline at the rate of 2 percent per year. Over the coming five-year period, the Congressional Budget

Office (CBO) estimates that this policy would generate a nominal dollar saving of approximately $80 billion compared to a stable level of defense outlays. An additional saving of $11 billion would arise from lower interest costs because of the reduced budget deficit.[1]

In its understated way, the General Accounting Office illustrates the more optimistic view of potential defense cuts that prevails in the nation's capital: "Although the fiscal year 1991 budget proposed by the president reduces real defense spending by 2 percent, even deeper cuts appear inevitable."[2]

A second possible scenario is to assume that a lower overall level of military tensions is achieved with the end of the crisis in the Persian Gulf. As a consequence, Congress will refrain from voting any increase in the military budget at all, even in nominal terms. If the United States continues to experience an average inflation rate of approximately 4 percent per year, this would mean an annual decline at the same 4 percent rate when the outlays are measured in real terms, or double the scenario of minimum change. Over the 1991–1995 time period, this approach would generate a nominal dollar saving of $158 billion plus an additional reduction of $20 billion in interest on the public debt (see Table 2-1).

William Hyland, editor of *Foreign Affairs*, makes an important qualification: budget reductions should reflect a military strategy. Thus the end of the Cold War requires working out a new military strategy that supports new foreign policy goals and priorities.[3] That also could make much larger reductions in defense spending than are shown in the table more realistic.

Table 2-1 Savings from Alternative Defense Paths Compared with the CBO Baseline (fiscal years, in billions)

Category of Spending	1991	1992	1993	1994	1995	Total 1991–1995
2 Percent Annual Real Decline in Budget Authority						
Change in Defense Spending	$-4	$-9	$-15	$-22	$-30	$-80
Change in Interest Spending	a	-1	-2	-3	-5	-11
Total Change in Deficit	$-4	$-10	$-17	$-25	$-35	$-91
4 Percent Annual Real Decline in Budget Authority						
Change in Defense Spending	$-8	$-18	$-30	$-44	$-58	$-158
Change in Interest Spending	a	-1	-3	-6	-10	-20
Total Change in Deficit	$-8	$-19	$-33	$-50	$-68	$-178

a = Less than $500 million.

Source: Compiled from Congressional Budget Office data.

Spelling out the details of a new defense strategy is beyond the scope of this book (and is beyond my expertise); however, it is becoming clear that five principles should guide the United States in shaping a national strategy and the defense budget necessary to finance it:

1. The military force structure should be reduced to reflect the lessened threat from the Soviet Union and the demise of the Warsaw Pact.
2. The quality of the smaller military force that remains should be maintained. This permits forgoing some of the new weapon systems previously planned for and making do with the current generation of military equipment.
3. The cadre necessary to reestablish larger forces, should that become necessary, must be given priority.
4. A high level of research and development and a viable defense industrial base should be kept, so that enhanced military capabilities can be reconstituted should the need ever arise.[4]
5. Renewed attention should be given to the need to counter the threat resulting from proliferation of nuclear and other weapons, especially on the part of Third World and terrorist groups.

Substantial reductions in U.S. military spending are most likely if the United States and the Soviet Union actually begin to eliminate key strategic weapons. Along those lines, both nations have been working on a treaty to reduce their long-range nuclear arsenals to 6,000 warheads each—a 30 percent cut for the United States and a 50 percent reduction for the Soviet Union. The United States can also benefit from the increased warning times and reduced likelihood of surprise that will result from improved reconnaissance and surveillance technologies.[5]

With such an agreement, the United States—according to three former chairmen of the joint chiefs of staff—will be able to make large reductions in several expensive weapon systems currently being developed, particularly multiple-warhead, rail-based MX missiles. The United States could also avoid deploying the new single-warhead Midgetman missile.[6]

Prior to the invasion of Kuwait, retired General Andrew Goodpaster, former commander of NATO, had proposed a 50 percent reduction in NATO forces by 1995. The chairman of the Senate Armed Services Committee, Sam Nunn (D-GA), and former Secretary of Defense James Schlesinger urged planning on a residual U.S. military force in Western Europe on the order of 75,000–100,000 troops within five years.[7] Former Assistant Secretary of Defense Lawrence Korb has called for reducing the navy's fourteen carrier battle groups to the more traditional force of twelve.[8] If reductions of these magnitudes occur, some offsetting increases may take place simultaneously in weapon systems geared to an Iraqi type of confrontation.

The armed forces, when pushed for budget cuts, prefer to junk old equipment rather than to curtail the development and production of new weapon systems. Yet the urgency to build new weapon systems before the Russians come up with them has dissipated, at least for the time being. The emphasis can now shift to the far-lower cost task of modernizing the aircraft, ships, tanks, and missiles already built or on order. In the words of Chairman of the Joint Chiefs of Staff Colin Powell, "If the squeeze finally comes and you cannot do it all, then I vote in an instant for a smaller but ready force with the kinds of quality we have now."[9]

Forecasts of a massive reduction in defense spending—on the order of one-half or more over the decade—gained considerable currency in early 1990. Yet, in light of more recent events, such forecasts do not now seem to be realistic even if the Soviet military establishment were to cut back far more than reflected in the proposals currently contemplated. That is why we should also analyze an intermediate position—a larger reduction than we have been considering but short of a massive cutback—say a 10 percent annual reduction in real defense spending. For the United States, that would generate a cumulative budget saving of about $375 billion over the period 1991–1995. Cuts in military demand of that size, if they could be accomplished without significantly reducing the level of economic activity, offer the federal government the opportunity to reduce the annual budget deficit very significantly.[10]

Major savings from base closings, at home and abroad, will occur only if the people assigned to those facilities are discharged from the armed forces, and not just assigned elsewhere. The truly large dollar cuts in the procurement budget will only take place if entire weapon systems are cancelled or the numbers on order are greatly reduced. One new aircraft carrier is priced at $3–4 billion, with supporting ships and planes extra (but not optional). A new DDG-51 destroyer is estimated at $1 billion. Each B-2 bomber is priced in excess of $0.5 billion. Advanced Stealth fighters cost in the hundreds of millions of dollars each. A new LHX army helicopter is priced at $35 million.

Then again, consider the estimated price tag of $30 billion for the entire Midgetman mobile land-based missile program[11] and the even larger outlays still being planned for the Strategic Defense Initiative (Star Wars). Senator Nunn, one of the most knowledgeable members of the Congress on military matters, has identified eight key areas where two or more of the military services overlap in function. He

Table 2-2 Eliminating Duplication Via Competition

Mission	Potential Competitors
Control of the seas	Navy carrier battlegroups versus air force long-range bombers
Projection of tactical forces	Army and air force versus marine and navy forces
Close air support	Army attack helicopters versus air force fixed-wing aircraft
Tactical missions (close air support, air-lift, and submarine warfare patrol)	Active forces versus reserve components
Military satellites	Large air force satellites launched by massive vehicles versus electronically linked smaller navy and DARPA sat-ellites launched by smaller vehicles
Training and education (flight training, basic skills)	Army versus navy versus air force
Ongoing modification and support of weapon systems	Army depots versus navy depots versus air force depots
Central and support services	Army versus navy versus air force

Source: Adapted from Sam Nunn, *Nunn 1990: A New Military Strategy* (Washington, D.C.: Center for Strategic and International Studies, 1990).

urges "constructive competition" in each of these areas in order to obtain a lower cost mode of military operation.

For example, both the army's attack helicopters and the air force's fixed-wing aircraft could provide close support on the battlefield. The army and the air force together have the capability of fighting a local or "theater" war; so do the navy and marine forces. Military satellites are launched by both the air force and the navy. Table 2-2 contains these and other examples of duplication. Cynics, however, may recall the concern beginning in 1949 about the overlap between the air force's B-36 long-range bombers and the navy's super carriers. Notwithstanding the ensuing debate about duplication of the strategic mission—which dragged on for many years—the two services managed to obtain funding for both programs.[12]

Senator Nunn is persistent, pointing out many specific anomalies in the Pentagon's requests for funds. These, too, represent opportunities for budget cutting:[13]

1. *The army is asking for $112 million for the follow-on-to-Lance program, when German officials have made it clear that they will not permit the missile to be deployed on their soil.* Moreover, the commander of U.S.

forces in Korea, the alternate "customer," has said that he has no requirement for it. Such short-range nuclear weapons that cannot reach beyond the borders of Germany and Czechoslovakia would seem to have no mission in today's world.

2. *The air force is continuing to buy F-16 aircraft at a rate designed to support thirty-six tactical fighter wings, although the Defense Department is planning on eliminating five of those wings over the next five years.* This may not be the only such inconsistency (or "disconnect," to use Senator Nunn's term) in a military budget developed before the recent changes in the international environment.

3. *The army is proposing to spend $4 billion to develop a new heavy tank that will not see service for the next six to eight years.* This tank was developed to meet a threat posed by the Warsaw Pact that no longer seems to exist.

4. *The fiscal 1991 defense budget contains more than $1 billion for new military construction projects overseas.* Yet, at the same time, the level of our forces stationed in the same areas is being reduced substantially.

Senator Nunn is not alone in identifying large potential savings. The CBO has identified sixteen areas of the military budget that could be reduced substantially. Table 2-3 contains CBO's estimates of potential dollar savings in military personnel and procurement for the years 1991–1995. A fundamental rationale for massive cuts in the procurement of new weapon systems is the assurance that for some time the United States can rely on the powerful arsenal of modern aircraft, missiles, tanks and ships acquired in the 1980s.

An important limitation on the size and speed of reductions in the U.S. military budget is political—most dovish members of the Congress quickly become hawks when the bases or defense plants in their districts are threatened by budget cuts. An article in *The New York Times* on the congressional response to the fiscal year 1991 military budget is very revealing. Under the headline, "Plan for Closing Military Bases Alarms Capitol," the front page article sounds like a wartime communique:

> D-day in the battle of the military budget came to Congress three days early as lawmakers mobilized today to protect bases in their districts . . . [14]

In a more circumspect way, former Congressional Budget Director Rudolph Penner reaches a similar conclusion. He notes that, if improvements continue in Eastern Europe, the public will demand some very large cuts. At the same time, however, voters will be reluctant to lose defense-related jobs in their districts.[15] Jonathan Gaffney of the Center for Strategic and International Studies concludes that the fu-

Table 2-3 Potential Defense Savings (outlays in billions of dollars)

Item	1991	1992	1993	1994	1995	5-Year Savings
Cancel B-2 bomber	1.1	2.6	3.8	4.4	4.8	16.7
Cancel C-17 transport	0.6	1.4	2.1	2.4	2.6	9.0
Cut Trident sub production 50 percent	0.1	0.2	0.4	0.4	0.6	1.7
Limit SDI to research	0.5	0.7	0.7	0.5	0.2	2.6
Cancel national aerospace plane	0.1	0.2	0.3	0.3	0.3	1.2
Reduce procurement staff 10 percent	0.1	0.5	0.9	1.3	1.8	4.7
Retire 4 battleships	0.2	0.3	0.4	0.4	0.4	1.6
Reduce military personnel by 250,000	1.1	3.6	6.7	11.0	15.9	38.4
Reduce drills for noncombat reserves	0.2	0.3	0.3	0.3	0.3	1.3
Reduce procurement of F-16 aircraft to 72 yearly	0.1	0.2	0.5	0.7	0.7	2.2
Reduce procurement of DDG-51 destroyers to 3 a year	—	0.2	0.5	0.8	0.8	2.3
Cancel amphibious lift vehicles	0.1	0.2	0.4	0.5	0.7	1.8
Eliminate increase for supporting procurement	0.7	1.6	3.3	4.6	5.7	15.9
Eliminate dual compensation for selected reservists	0.1	0.1	0.1	0.1	0.1	0.5
Eliminate BAQ payments to reservists	0.1	0.1	0.1	0.1	0.1	0.5
Redefine reservists' pay for drills	0.6	0.6	0.6	0.6	0.6	3.0
Total	5.7	12.8	21.1	28.4	35.6	103.4

Source: Estimated from budget baseline computed by Congressional Budget Office.

ture military force structure will be driven by "politics, pork-barreling, and special interests . . . Turf wars will be chaotic."[16]

An alternative and seemingly more orderly approach, proportionally reducing each item in the military budget, may be expedient in terms of mollifying both the services and minimizing political pressures, but it also results in less efficient military procurement. Senator John McCain (R-AZ), a former naval aviator, warns against that traditional, and still current, tendency for responding to lower military budgets:

> You know how they are over there in the Pentagon . . . "You cut your tanks a third and I'll cut my planes a third." That's not a recipe at all for defense in the twenty-first century.[17]

USING THE "PEACE DIVIDEND"

Reductions in defense spending during the next few years are likely to be substantially less—in terms of economic importance—than the cuts made after either the Korean or Vietnam Wars. The American economy has grown substantially since then. After both of those wars, defense spending as a percentage of GNP fell approximately four percentage points, bringing that ratio to about 10 percent of GNP after the Korean War and approximately 6 percent after the Vietnam War. A swing of 4 percent in today's massive $6 trillion GNP would be awesome, but such a reduction in defense outlays from fiscal year 1991's projected level of 5.5 percent of GNP is unrealistic. To reduce U.S. defense spending to 1.5 percent of the GNP requires virtually dismantling the entire military establishment.

A more reasonable expectation is that any "peace dividend" in the 1990s will be in the neighborhood of one-fourth to one-half of 1 percent of GNP each year—accomplished by annual budget cuts upwards of 4 percent, as discussed earlier. A cumulative reduction of 1.5–2.5 percent of the GNP over a five-year time period would be substantial, yet it would constitute neither a great bonanza for the advocates of civilian spending increases nor the overwhelming problem of "conversion" to a peacetime economy feared by others. As Charles Schultze of the Brookings Institution put the matter, "We can clearly shift this modest amount of resources between military and civilian pursuits without any significant macroeconomic problems."[18] To state the matter bluntly, the list of the different ways in which a peace divided can be spent is "as long as the roster of Washington lobbyists."[19]

Moreover, the Federal Reserve System can be expected to act to offset the adverse economic effects of reduced defense spending. Such action is especially likely because other decreases in federal expenditures are being made in order to meet congressionally mandated targets for bringing down the federal budget deficit. A recession did follow the post-Vietnam military cutbacks; however, the general belief among economists is that the downturn in the economy resulted from a tight monetary policy, accompanied by sharp increases in the price of imported oil.[20] Nevertheless, we must note the coincidence in 1990–1991 of a defense cutback, a sharp increase in oil prices, and a downturn in the national economy.

It is fascinating to read the account of the massive post–World War II conversion written by Herbert Stein of the American Enterprise Institute and a 1945 alumnus of the Office of War Mobilization and Reconversion:

The conversion plans of the office . . . had little to do with the success of the transition. The reality was that government closed up the war effort quickly and left the conversion to the private sector.[21]

There are important lessons to be learned from the experiences of the "peace dividends" generated by ending the Korean and Vietnam Wars. The fundamental point is that nobody remembers any special use of those "dividends," and for good reason. By and large, the funds were absorbed by expansions of ongoing federal civilian programs, such as Social Security and Medicare. The concern that I am raising is not that of a reactionary opposed to shifting priorities from warfare to welfare. Rather, the worry is that of an ex-budgeteer who sees a one-shot saving in defense being used to justify a relatively permanent commitment to a higher level of civilian spending. That was the unfortunate fiscal approach that generated the intractable budget deficits that have bedeviled every administration, Democratic and Republican, since the end of the Vietnam War.

Public policymakers would do well to reverse their normal preconceptions. They should be modest in assessing the size of any peace dividend, and skeptical in approving new spending commitments whose major effect is off in the future. Perhaps the best way of viewing the decision-making process is to consider any peace dividend as finite and temporary and to avoid using the proceeds for commitments that are permanent and growing. If fiscal discipline is not restored in this decade when the elderly population is growing slowly, it is doubtful that it ever will be. The baby boom generation will start to retire early in the twenty-first century just at the same time as the number of working people to pay for those benefits slows dramatically.[22]

The way that the United States deals with the cluster of issues involved in the peace dividend–defense conversion debate will determine in large measure this nation's success in the global marketplace. Strange as it may sound, a seemingly "do nothing" policy is needed. Merely permitting lower future levels of defense spending to result in smaller budget deficits is the wisest fiscal policy. In helping to reduce the level of interest rates facing American business, such "inaction" will also turn out to be the most effective industrial policy to enhance the competitiveness of the private sector.

A traditional fiscal conservative prefers seeing any reduction in military outlays devoted entirely to bringing down the still massive budget deficit. When full account is taken of the expensive bailouts of failed savings and loan associations, the continuing tide of federal red ink is awesome. Dealing with that issue has the added benefit of not tying the hands of the next generation if it chose to shift to a different set of priorities. Moreover, smaller budget deficits lead to lower interest rates, more national saving, greater investment, and rising productivity. The result is a higher living standard for the average American with greater choice on future priorities.

If political pressures require civilian spending to offset the reductions in defense spending, one-shot investments are the most sensible approach. Examples include specific civilian R&D projects, rebuilding some badly battered bridges, overhauling several dangerous nuclear weapons plants, and constructing a few new airports to service the rapid expansion of air travel generated by deregulation. Such choices reflect a decision that some urgent civilian needs deserve a higher priority than reducing the deficit. Whatever our personal value judgments, that approach would not generate fiscal problems for the next set of government decision makers.

On the other hand, consider the situation where a five-year reduction in defense spending is used to justify establishing—or expanding—long-term financial obligations of the federal government. There is considerable support for that position. Senator Edward Kennedy (D-MA) urges that any peace dividend be used for domestic programs of the federal government. Moreover, an April 1990 opinion poll conducted by *The New York Times* and CBS News reports that 61 percent of the 1,515 adults surveyed want the money spent "to fight problems such as drugs and homelessness." Only 23 percent support deficit reduction and 9 percent favor lowering taxes.[23] The same long-term adverse fiscal effects would flow whether the peace dividend goes for aid to the homeless or subsidies to farmers or benefits to business—or even a reduction in income or Social Security taxes.

As a general principle, new government programs require time before they hit their stride. The first year or two is usually devoted to recruiting key staff, organizing an agency to carry out the program, and setting policies in place. Many of the outlays that do take place are incurred by contractors in the private sector. Very little actual government spending is involved at this stage, yet this is precisely the time that military spending would be declining. Is it any wonder that the Senate and House Committees become generous in making long-term commitments whose effects they can only dimly see? With most of the bills not coming due until somebody else is in charge, the temptation is very great.

CONTINGENCY PLANNING

Forecasting, one astute observer once said, is neither an art nor a science. It is a hazard. Yet forecasting is a hazardous activity that often must be undertaken. That seems to be the correct spirit in which to think about the future military environment facing the United States.

Given the vagaries of human experience, a modest amount of contingency planning is wise. Indeed, the highly cyclical pattern of this nation's past defense spending reflects the sharp and abrupt changes that can occur both in the international environment facing the United States and in our reaction to it. Predictably—and correctly—Secretary of Defense Dick Cheney warns that it is too soon to say that the Soviet Union will "never again" pose a threat to the United States or its Allies.[24]

The authorities cited earlier provide sobering second thoughts, somewhat along the lines of Cheney's concern. Jeane Kirkpatrick warns that the Soviets are still engaged in a concerted effort to develop some very high-tech weapons.[25] Michael Howard notes that, barring its total disintegration, the Soviet Union will remain a great power and will continue to pursue its interests throughout the world.[26]

Soviet specialist William F. Scott presents a cynical appraisal of the efforts of Gorbachev and other reformers in the Soviet leadership. He contends that *Perestroika* has many features in common with reforms initiated by previous occupants of the Kremlin. "His predecessors were seeking to maintain the power of the state," warns Scott. "There is no reason to believe that Gorbachev has a different purpose."[27]

French president François Mitterrand has raised the related concern that, in the event the current relatively benign leadership of the Soviet Union should fail, "nothing can guarantee that a new Soviet power—which might not be communist—would not still be military and totalitarian."[28] Marshall D. Shulman, a Soviet expert at Columbia University's Harriman Institute for Advanced Study of the Soviet Union, embellishes on Mitterrand's theme. The range of possible outcomes, he believes, includes a conservative, nationalistic, and perhaps militaristic regime intent upon resurrecting the order of the past.[29]

Nevertheless, such changes would not occur abruptly. Until recently, conventional military planning was based on NATO having ten to fourteen days of warning time of a Soviet invasion of Western Europe. The collapse of communist control in Eastern Europe and the Soviet Union's deep economic crisis have eliminated the Soviet Union's ability to launch a blitzkrieg invasion, one that could have brought the Red Army's tanks to the English channel in a matter of weeks.

Not only are the Soviets now denied the use of the armies of the other Warsaw Pact nations, they also have lost secure railroad lines and highways through Poland and Czechoslovakia to supply and reinforce their troops in East Germany. Now, if the Soviet Union wants to attack Western Europe, it has to reinvade Eastern Europe first.

According to Admiral David Jeremiah of the Joint Chiefs of Staff, it would now take on the order of two years for a full-scale mobilization

for a Soviet ground attack on Western Europe.[30] The change in warning time is very significant. It influences war plans and helps to determine the size and deployment of U.S. forces; however, threats from
other quarters now loom larger in American military planning.

Most studies of general and complete disarmament—which is hardly the situation envisioned here—assume that significant armed
forces will be retained by the United States and other nations. A
variety of reasons is offered, including the need to assure international order in the face of potential threats from nations that are not
parties to any general disarmament agreement. It is pertinent to note
that the Central Intelligence Agency identifies thirteen continuing
international land boundary disputes, ranging from that between
Bangladesh and India to the disagreement between Ecuador and
Peru.

The Hudson Institute lists twenty disputed frontiers in Eastern Europe alone, including the Transylvania area involving Hungary and
Rumania, and the Kosovo region, which pits Albania against
Yugoslavia.[31] A very different possibility is that nationalist or terrorist
forces could overrun a nuclear storage site in one of the Soviet republics.

In the case of most organized societies, a certain amount of national
force is deemed necessary to maintain internal order, especially in
periods of political upheaval or geological disruption (such as earth-
quakes). The experiences of the Soviet Union in Armenia in 1989 and
in Azerbaijan in 1990 are vivid cases in point. Even as communism
collapses in many parts of the world, the forces of democracy still face
many dangerous rivals. These include fierce nationalist hatred, long-
simmering religious disputes, deep class resentment, personal ambi-
tions of key leaders, and also the survival instincts of the endangered
regimes. However, many of the conflicts that arise may be peripheral
to the interests of the United States and we can be more detached
than during the period of superpower rivalry.[32]

It is intriguing to note that the public never shared the euphoria
expressed by many who wrote about large military cutbacks and peace
dividends. A November 1989 survey by Yankelovich Clancy Shulman
revealed that a clear majority would keep defense spending at least at
its present levels. Only 18 percent of the sample surveyed believed
that the Cold War had ended.[33] A poll by *The New York Times* and CBS
News in early 1990 yielded similar results. A little over 60 percent of
those surveyed believed that U.S. military spending should be kept at
current levels or increased.[34] Perhaps as a reflection of the expected
success of the national security policy of the United States, few Americans expect a nuclear war in the next ten years—18 percent in a May
1990 survey, which is down from 30 percent in October 1987.[35]

THE NEED FOR REVERSIBILITY

A skeptical attitude underscores the need for maintaining the capability of reversing rapidly the direction of military policy. As we have seen in the period following Iraq's 1990 invasion of Kuwait, effective reversibility requires a basic military force in being, which can be augmented quickly by calling up the reserves and national guard units. A period of sustained reductions in the level of defense spending, however, would underscore two other key aspects of reversibility: a healthy defense manufacturing base and an ongoing R&D effort focusing on the design of new and improved weapon systems. That does not require maintaining every weapon system or military supplier, but reversibility does point up the need to maintain an adequate industrial base containing an array of strong prime contractors and subcontractors that can compete effectively for the design and production of the equipment needed by the substantial military force that will be required for the indefinite future.

One veteran analyst of the international scene, William G. Hyland, warns that American policy cannot ignore the possibility that sometime in the future Soviet power will once again pose a threat to Eastern and Central Europe. Hyland suggests a policy of "reinsurance." This includes a strong Western alliance and a united Germany as well as a domestic military posture that can be rebuilt in fairly rapid order.[36] The Soviets apparently have adopted their own "reinsurance" policy. A General Yazov was quoted on the Moscow radio in February 1990 to the effect that only the oldest military equipment was being destroyed and that all of the new hardware will remain. He went on to state, "Moreover, any hardware that is still serviceable is not being withdrawn from the armed forces . . . it is being mothballed and, should the need arise, will be used."[37]

Some military observers also report that the Soviet General Staff is doing research on technologically advanced forms of military power that might be both nonnuclear and nonterritorial. The latter term relates to the notion that a new generation of satellite-based communications could be based almost anywhere; they could track the actions of other nations and then relay instructions to nonnuclear ballistic and cruise missiles to attack the designated targets.[38]

These futuristic weapon systems would require relatively small numbers of military personnel to operate, but a high level of supporting technology.[39] This development, in turn, has led some American analysts to suggest that, during a possible period of development in the decade of the 1990s it would appear sensible to devote more of the reduced availability of military funding to technological advance than to maintaining traditional production strength.

Thus, the notion of reversibility is consistent with closing down or converting defense plants that are no longer needed. The defense industry is coming off an all-time peak and a substantial reduction in its size is to be expected. Since many of its production facilities are ancient by the current standards of the competitive commercial economy, the opportunity to phase them out should be welcomed. Some defense plants may be useful in civilian endeavors, while a select few may have to be mothballed for contingency planning purposes. It is vital that the remaining defense suppliers in the aggregate be financially viable and that they possess the ability to meet the likely design and production needs of the military establishment in the years ahead.

NOTES

1. U.S. Congressional Budget Office, *The Economic and Budget Outlook: Fiscal Years 1991–1995* (Washington, D.C.: U.S. Government Printing Office, 1990), p. 66.

2. *NATO-Warsaw Pact* (Washington, D.C.: U.S. General Accounting Office, 1990), p. 3.

3. William G. Hyland, "America's New Course," *Foreign Affairs*, Spring 1990, p. 8.

4. This is based, with some variation, on *The Statement of Richard Perle*, before the European Affairs Subcommittee of the Senate Committee on Foreign Relations, March 7, 1990, p. 4.

5. Joseph Pilat and Paul White, "Technology and Strategy in a Changing World," *Washington Quarterly*, Spring 1990, pp. 82–83.

6. "Ex-Military Chiefs Urge Dropping of Missile Plans," *St. Louis Post-Dispatch*, February 3, 1990, p. 1B.

7. David Evans, "Budget Pressure, End of Cold War Bringing Changes," *Chicago Tribune*, October 29, 1989, p. 1; "Sen. Nunn on Vision of Military," *The New York Times*, April 20, 1990, p. A10.

8. Lawrence J. Korb, "How to Reduce Military Spending," *The New York Times*, November 21, 1989, p. 23.

9. Quoted in George C. Wilson, "The General and the Pendulum," *Washington Post Weekly*, October 9, 1989, p. 34.

10. *Summary of the Economic Effects of Reduced Defense Spending* (Washington, D.C.: U.S. Congressional Budget Office, 1990), p. 7.

11. Gregory F. Treverton, "The Defense Debate," *Foreign Affairs*, Vol. 69, No. 1, 1990, pp. 193–94.

12. John Newhouse, *War and Peace In the Nuclear Age* (New York: Alfred A. Knopf, 1989), p. 71.

13. Sam Nunn, *Nunn 1990: A New Military Strategy* (Washington, D.C.: Center for Strategic and International Studies, 1990), pp. 10–11.

14. Andrew Rosenthal, "Plan for Closing Military Bases Alarms Capitol," *The New York Times*, January 27, 1990, p. 1.

15. Rudolph G. Penner, *Federal Spending Issues of the 1990s*, a paper prepared for a conference at the American Enterprise Institute for Public Policy Research, January 16, 1990, p. 11.

16. Jack Robertson, "Defense Business Plan: Pray," *Electronic News*, April 30, 1990, p. 10.

17. Quoted in "Bush Is Reported Willing," *The New York Times*, March 18, 1990, p. 20.

18. *Statement of Charles L. Schultze before the Joint Economic Committee*, December 19, 1989, p. 6.

19. William H. Miller, "The Peace Dividend Scramble," *Industry Week*, February 19, 1990, p. 75.

20. *Summary of Economic Effects*, p. 8.

21. Herbert Stein, "Remembrance of Peace Dividends Past," *The American Enterprise*, March/April 1990, p. 19.

22. Rudolph G. Penner, "The Peace Dividend," *Newsday*, January 12, 1990, p. 77.

23. David E. Rosenbaum, "2 Senators Say Peace Bonus Should Pay for Social Needs," *The New York Times*, April 14, 1990, p. 8.

24. Michael R. Gordon, "Cheney Calls 50% Military Cut a Risk to Superpower Status," *The New York Times*, March 18, 1990, p. 20.

25. Kirkpatrick, "Beyond the Cold War," p. 5.

26. Howard, "Springtime of Nations," p. 30.

27. William F. Scott, "Soviet Military Doctrine: Continuity and Change?", in Green and Karasik, *Gorbachev and His Generals*, p. 10.

28. Quoted in Jack Beatty, "A Post-Cold War Budget," *Atlantic Monthly*, February 1990, p. 75.

29. Marshall D. Shulman, "How Well Do We Know This Man?", *New York Times Book Review*, June 17, 1990, p. 5.

30. Quoted in William Flannery, "Soviet Warning Time Growing," *St. Louis Post-Dispatch*, June 14, 1990, p. B-1.

31. U.S. Central Intelligence Agency, *The World Factbook 1989* (Washington, D.C.: U.S. Government Printing Office, 1989), p. 323; William E. Odom, "Is the Guns-Butter Tradeoff Valid in the 1990s?", *Hudson Institute Briefing Paper*, April 12, 1990, p. 3; James W. Davis, "War Will Always Be With Us," *St. Louis Post-Dispatch*, June 22, 1990, p. 3D.

32. Bill Keller, "The Making of a Post-Communist Disorder," *The New York Times*, January 21, 1990, p. 3E; Davis, "War Will Be With Us."

33. Everett Carll Ladd, "In U.S., a New View of the East in '89," *Christian Science Monitor*, December 26, 1989, p. 18.

34. "Views on Spending and Peace," *The New York Times*, January 25, 1990, p. A15.

35. Based on *New York Times*/CBS News Polls; see "Few Now Expect Nuclear War," *The New York Times*, May 30, 1990, p. A6.

36. Hyland, "America's New Course," p. 12; see also William G. Hyland, *The Cold War Is Over* (New York: Random House, 1990).

37. Cited in "Indicators of Change in Soviet Security Policies," *Atlantic Council Bulletin*, April 16, 1990, p. 4.

38. Edward N. Luttwak, "The Shape of Things to Come," *Commentary*, June 1990, pp. 22–23.

39. G. A. Keyworth II, *Distributed Surveillance and Targeting*, Remarks to the New Alternatives Workshop of the Defense Nuclear Agency, Washington, D.C., May 15, 1990, pp. 1–10.

CHAPTER 3

Downsizing the Defense Companies

The weapon systems used by our armed forces in the Persian Gulf came from existing inventories. The low current levels of military production orders mean that the major defense companies are at a crossroads. Do they convert their excess capacity to civilian production? Or do they streamline and slim down from their current peaks? The conversion approach claims that it will keep in place the jobs of defense workers who face layoffs. The cutback alternative is designed to maintain the financial health of the firms as they adjust to a very different set of market opportunities.

It is fruitless to debate the conversion and cutback alternatives in the abstract. There is a substantial history of defense companies trying to weather defense cutbacks via converting—or to use the more businesslike term "diversifying"—into civilian markets.

THE DIVERSIFICATION APPROACH

Ever since World War II, defense contractors have been trying to use their special talents in other areas of the economy. Companies that specialize in defense work, or their military-oriented divisions, have been successful in diversifying into a few large but very narrowly defined markets.

The expansion from aircraft to missiles was a natural progression. Similarly, the extension of their capabilities to the design and production of space systems—both military and civilian (NASA)—was accomplished very well. Several large aerospace companies also have designed and produced substantial numbers of civilian passenger aircraft but, except for Boeing, profitability has been illusive.

By and large the numerous attempts on the part of the larger, specialized defense contractors to penetrate civilian nonaerospace markets on any major scale have produced few sustained successes. Most of these ventures (as will be discussed) have been abandoned or sold off. The remainder generally operate at marginal levels. These negative experiences have been so frequent—and many of them have been such a drain on the companies—that they now constitute a major obstacle to further diversification efforts.

Nevertheless, those negative experiences have not deterred a growing chorus of people outside the defense industry from urging the adoption of government policies requiring the major contractors to engage in extensive "conversion" planning activities. Nor has knowledge of the past prevented individual scientists and engineers in the defense companies from coming up with exotic suggestions for commercializing their work: death rays that will treat cancer, electric rail guns that will lift commercial payloads into space, and nuclear reactors that will hurl astronauts to Mars.[1]

History of Diversification Efforts

The peak-and-valley nature of military spending has motivated defense contractors to try to use their capabilities to sell new products or to enter new markets in an effort to maintain the size of their operations. In turn, the waves of diversification efforts, but hardly the volume of business activity, have reflected the actual peaks and valleys in military procurement.

After World War II, the older and more established industries—such as automobile, rubber, and steel, which had originally converted from civilian markets—experienced little difficulty in returning to their traditional lines of business. Backlogs of pent-up demand and accumulated wartime savings eased this transition. On much smaller levels, similar adjustments occurred after the Korean and Vietnam Wars.

To a substantial degree, the same outlook now faces many of the companies and employees in the defense economy. Of the more than 3 million Americans whose work at jobs in private industry is financed by defense spending, about 2 million are employed by subcontractors who sell primarily to civilian markets. A truck driver often does not even know whether his cargo is military or commercial and his job is not likely to be at risk during a general cutback in military outlays—as long as the national economy continues to expand. The U.S. Labor Department estimates that fewer than 500,000 workers are making missiles, warships, ammunition, and other weaponry in factories that cannot be converted easily to civilian use.[2]

The specialized defense companies, especially in the aerospace industry, generate the bulk of the adjustment challenge. The aerospace companies (successors to the World War II airframe and aircraft pro-

ducers) had typically grown during the war from small job-shop operations to large industrial enterprises. The virtual disappearance, at
least temporarily, of their basic market when World War II ended
brought fundamental problems of adjustment. The numerous efforts
these companies made to expand into other businesses were characterized by diversity, enthusiasm, and confusion.[3]

The efforts of the aerospace companies to penetrate civilian markets took a variety of forms. Many firms attempted to use their specialized know-how by concentrating on lines where they believed that
their manufacturing capabilities would be particularly useful; for example, using their skills in fabricating light metal products to produce
aluminum canoes and sport boats. Some of the "related" products
were a bit far afield from their customary lines, including artificial
hands, other prosthetic devices, and stainless steel (as well as aluminum) caskets.

Some of the companies became subcontractors for established firms
in civilian markets, building heater cases, parts for musical instruments, automobile components, plumbing, and cabinets for radios.
Using their war-accumulated earnings and relying on tax provisions
permitting the carryback of losses as offsets against previously paid
taxes, many defense contractors acquired going concerns in other
industries. Typical acquisitions included a producer of motion picture
equipment; a manufacturer of precision parts in the automobile field;
a designer of prefabricated houses; and a maker of motor buses,
trolley coaches, and marine and industrial engines.[4]

These early diversification efforts can be grouped into three major
categories: (1) the temporary utilization of idle capacity and manpower to maintain a going organization and to tide it over until peacetime aerospace production got under way; (2) the purchase of, or
investment in, firms that would either broaden the base of operations,
or at least earn a good profit; and (3) the manufacture of items that it
was hoped would win a permanent market, thus diversifying operations and lessening dependence on military orders.

The first category—temporary diversification to satisfy transitory
war-accumulated civilian demands—is of limited relevance today. The
second is also irrelevant, as these cases would not ordinarily involve
the utilization of the physical resources—labor, plant, and equipment—of the military producers. The third category is the most pertinent, but also the least promising. Most of the activities were ultimately abandoned as unsuccessful or marginal, or sold to firms
traditionally oriented to industrial or consumer markets.

In fact, the income from all three types of new ventures was generally disappointing, generating only a small fraction of the sales volumes attained during World War II. For example, sales by the major

aircraft companies during the postwar adjustment period 1946–1948 declined to one-tenth of their former peak, and net losses totaled over $50 million.

Sales and profits remained low even after the immediate shock of postwar adjustment wore off. While military orders continued, they were much below wartime levels. Firms that had traditionally dominated civilian markets, but had temporarily converted to military production during the war, once again asserted their supremacy in those civilian areas. Thus, the specialized defense contractors were forced back to their specialized markets.

With the tremendous expansion of military orders for aircraft beginning in the latter half of 1950, the attention of the industry was refocused on military production. Priority access to key materials during the Korean War was readily available for military orders but difficult to obtain for civilian production. More basic, however, was the overriding desire of the aerospace companies to build airplanes rather than plumbing and cabinets.

With cutbacks in military procurement at the end of the Korean War, defense firms once again gave increased attention to nonmilitary and, to some extent, nonaircraft lines of business. In making these efforts to diversify into civilian lines, defense contractors took account of some of the worst mistakes of the past, avoiding consumer markets with their onerous distribution requirements. The companies relied instead on extensions of their technology into specialized civilian governmental and industrial markets. Examples of diversification, aside from aircraft for the airline and executive markets, included industrial electronics, small gas turbine engines, nuclear reactors, wall panels for commercial building, heavy-duty land vehicles, and production for the civilian space program.

However, the volumes of diversified sales were modest. For a sample of major aerospace companies, nonmilitary sales rose from about 3 percent of total sales in 1955 to almost one-fourth by 1960, with the great bulk of the increase in sales of equipment to commercial airlines. The civilian nonaircraft work of these companies represented 0.5 percent of sales in 1955 and less than 3 percent in 1960.[5]

Nevertheless, efforts by defense contractors to enter civilian, nonaerospace markets continued through the 1980s, with similar lackluster results. Despite some substantive successes in the application of defense technology to civilian needs, the efforts as a whole were unprofitable and ultimately sold off or terminated.

In 1983, Grumman introduced the Kubvan, hoping to open a new market for aluminum truck bodies. It abandoned the effort two years later. It sold its solar energy division in 1985 and Pearson Yacht in 1986. Nevertheless, this major defense contractor keeps trying to find ways of using its military know-how profitably in commercial endeavors. In 1986, it acquired a production facility to build runabout boats.

From 1983 to 1985, the company experienced a cumulative net loss in its nonaerospace commercial production of $15 million (since then this category has been merged in its financial reports with other, more profitable items). Grumman is currently working on a contract with the U.S. Postal Service to build 18,000 special postal delivery trucks through 1992—with an option for 59,490 more. The company also has set up a division in the Far East to sell fire fighting equipment.[6]

Another major military supplier, McDonnell Douglas, has also experienced some hard knocks on the road to commercial diversification. In 1983, the company purchased Computer Sharing Services for $69 million. In 1985, it announced the objective of making its information service group a major segment of the corporation by the 1990s. The information systems sector reported annual losses from 1982 to 1989. After losing $333 million in 1989, McDonnell Douglas reduced the size of the commercial part of the information systems operation and narrowed its focus. In 1990, the company sold its computer maintenance and hardware distribution subsidiary in Santa Ana, California. Simultaneously, however, the company was working on a computerized design contract for General Motors.[7]

In 1989, General Dynamics announced that it had "decided to stick to the defense business" and pursue only those new programs for which the government need is "strong and valid."[8] That statement can be appreciated by examining the accompanying financial report, which showed a substantial cumulative loss in the company's nongovernmental programs over the previous eight years.

Likewise, Boeing—the most successful builder of commercial jet airliners—reported a cumulative deficit in its nonaerospace, nongovernment sales over the 1981–1988 time period. Boeing entered the mass transit business in the 1970s to offset the decline in its helicopter business. Its experiences were hardly unique for major defense contractors. After encountering a variety of difficulties in dealing with the Department of Transportation, several large cities, and union restrictions, it left the business. At its peak, Boeing's transit production employed about 150 engineers and 400 factory workers compared to about 9,000 employees laid off by its helicopter division.[9]

The Curtiss-Wright Corporation provides the most extreme example of the shortcomings of naïve conversion efforts by defense contractors. This pioneering aviation firm—which built more aircraft during World War II than any other U.S. company—planned on the assumption that the military market would never recover from its post–World War II lows. The company therefore diversified with a vengeance into a host of miscellaneous industrial product areas.

Curtiss-Wright never did recover to its previous highs. While its former competitors now enjoy annual sales of aircraft, missiles, and space vehicles measured in billions of dollars, the company's revenues from its assortment of parts and components totaled a modest $212 million in 1989.

Although the actual numbers on the aerospace industry's diversification look much better than would be expected from its experiences, they are deceptive. By 1975, the nonaerospace sales by the major aerospace companies rose to $4 billion, or 15 percent of their total revenues. The 1980 total of nonaerospace sales, $11 billion, came to 19 percent of the industry's aggregate volume. In 1988, the aerospace industry reported nonaerospace sales of $22 billion, or 19 percent of its total volume for the year, the same ratio as in the beginning of the decade.[10]

The figures do need more detailed analysis. For example, Rockwell International, a major defense contractor, reports that its civilian sales rose from 55 percent of its total revenues in 1987 to more than 75 percent in 1989.[11] However, the company was formed as the result of a merger between Rockwell-Standard (an established company in civilian markets) and North American Aviation, a mainstay defense supplier. The recent growth in the corporation's civilian business came about mainly from expansion in the Rockwell-Standard divisions rather than from diversification of the aviation divisions.

The Rockwell form of expansion in civilian production is surely useful. For one thing, it is helpful from the viewpoint of the shareholder interest in diversification of risk; however, it furnishes no indication of the ability to use the factories, people, and other defense industry resources in civilian markets. The company's 1985 purchase of Allen-Bradley, a leading producer of electronic and electrical controls for industrial automation, was likely a wise move for the shareholders, but it represented little conversion of defense capabilities.

Moreover, the Rockwell experience is far from unique. After several decades of trying to penetrate the electronics market through internal product diversification, Lockheed purchased Sanders Associates in 1986. Three years later, the company closed down the main plant of its older electronics division. Only about 15 percent of the employees there were moved to New Hampshire to work at Lockheed Sanders.[12]

In 1985, General Dynamics decided to enter the small airplane market, a natural extension for a major aerospace manufacturer. It did so, however, by acquiring Cessna Aircraft Company, an established producer of general aviation, rather than by using its own facilities and personnel.

In other instances, large diversified firms bought out specialized defense contractors. General Motors acquired Hughes Aircraft, General Electric picked up RCA, and Textron merged with AVCO and

Bell Helicopters. Sperry Rand and Burroughs combined to form Unisys. The formerly independent military suppliers no longer show up separately in the various reports on the military market. Their military-oriented divisions, however, face the same adjustment problems as do other defense contractors.

WHY DID DIVERSIFICATION GO SOUR?

A recent review of the literature in the field of economic adjustment and conversion in the United States failed to find even one successful civilian conversion in today's marketplace. An econometric analysis of the spillover of military research and development to civilian R&D provides little empirical evidence of that widely anticipated phenomenon.[13]

An early, comprehensive study sponsored by the U.S. Arms Control and Disarmament Agency concluded that, "There is a discouraging history of failure in commercial diversification efforts by defense firms."[14] Moreover, the profitability of nondefense, nonaerospace diversification efforts was usually—although not always—below that experienced in defense and space business.

Robert Rauner, director of the Defense Department's Office of Economic Adjustment, told a House Banking subcommittee in 1989 that several defense-related firms attempting to enter new civilian markets could not find any current examples where the economic conversion approach had successfully moved products from the defense to the nondefense market. His study showed that five years or more are typically required to convert and use nondefense plants to produce and market a new or different product.[15]

Other analysts have reported equally pessimistic conclusions on the ability of defense contractors to penetrate civilian, nonaerospace markets. Robert DeGrasse, Jr.'s, evaluation of the diversification efforts of six defense contractors in the aerospace, electronics, and shipbuilding industries was not very enthusiastic. He noted that attempts to enter the mass transit market by Boeing (trolley cars), Rohr (subway cars), and Grumman (buses) all failed in part because their products were too complex and unreliable.[16]

He also reported that Kaman Corporation successfully moved out of aerospace and into the bearings and musical instrument businesses; however, much of Kaman's new work bypassed the firm's aerospace personnel. The goals and standards familiar to those involved in defense production were not compatible with commercial success. One example is creditworthiness of customers: this is the key in selling musical instruments; the question does not even arise in sales to the federal government.[17]

Even Seymour Melman, that staunch advocate of "conversion"

planning, recently testified to a House Banking Subcommittee that there have been no substantial cases of conversion to civilian production since the immediate post–World War II period. He described the case of one firm attempting to produce a class of civilian vehicles. The chief engineer said that, since previously their people had been building vehicles with the speed of sound, designing and producing something that would move at 50 miles per hour would be like falling off a log. Melman commented, "They fell off."[18]

It has been noted frequently that today's defense contractors include many managers, engineers, scientists, and production workers who have done little but military-oriented work during their entire careers. The physical plant and machinery, and the technologies applied, in a modern military industrial firm are far different from what is standard in civilian commercial firms. The technologies embodied in the designs of the products themselves have diverged much further.

A common set of themes arises from studies of the diversification experiences of military contractors. The major defense companies are very special business organizations. They are very good at what they are set up to do—design and produce state-of-the-art weapons and comparable civilian systems—but they have, for the most part, failed at commercial diversification. They differ, in both capabilities and shortcomings, from typical commercial companies in terms of technology, organizational structure, marketing, and financing.

It is not very surprising that the Soviets, in attempting to convert a portion of their defense industry to civilian production, have encountered similar difficulties. Problems encountered in *konvertsia* include retraining the work force, redesigning production areas, and adapting technological processes. The enterprises involved have experienced lower income and the workers lower wages. Much of the high-tech equipment used for producing weapon systems is being scrapped, discarded, or greatly underutilized. Moreover, some Soviet commentators and industrialists have questioned the whole basis of the conversion effort. They consider it inefficient to apply costly defense-industry capital equipment, technology, and expertise to tasks for which they are often unsuited; making dairy equipment out of titanium can only be described as an expensive absurdity.[19]

The Soviet Union seems to be encountering experiences similar to those of U.S. defense firms following World War II. Soviet aviation factories have been ordered to design machines that make pear jelly and fur wraps. An engine plant is supposed to build pasta production lines. Another defense complex was ordered to begin packaging tons of oat flakes a day. The "conversion" record of the Soviet Union thus far has been as poor as that of its U.S. counterpart.[20]

A variety of explanations is given for the inability of the American aerospace and other large specialized government contractors to use their capabilities successfully in commercial endeavors (aside from airline equipment). The principal reasons for past failures fall into two major categories: lack of management motivation and lack of required capabilities.

The lack of management motivation is due to such basic factors as their belief that strong incentives to change have been absent most of the time. Thus, defense company personnel who are concerned with reorienting their operations to more traditional lines of industry obtain limited interest or support from management. These factors are cumulative and interacting.

The absence of incentives in the past often has resulted from the belief of the top managements that there are adequate sales opportunities in military-related government work—or that there soon will be.[21] Moreover, the profit rates are normally higher than on risky commercial ventures in which the companies have little previous experience. Also, their many prior unsuccessful diversification attempts have engendered a strong conviction that adequate commercial opportunities do not exist for companies that have become oriented primarily to government work.

The unsuccessful commercial diversification efforts of the defense companies have led to very limited management support for or interest in further attempts at diversification. This is evidenced by the far smaller magnitude of investments made in comparison with more traditional military or airline projects. Another indication is the reluctance to commit their full-time senior management or their top technical personnel to these diversification ventures.

The second set of reasons for unsuccessful commercial diversification is more objective and more compelling. It relates to the very specialized capabilities of these government contractors. These firms—compared with commercially oriented companies—have relatively low capitalization, little if any commercial marketing capabilities, and limited experience in producing at high volume and low unit cost. Moreover, their entire administrative structure is geared to the unique reporting and control requirements of the governmental customer. Those defense firms that do operate in civilian markets tend to maintain operationally separated, insulated divisions that have little contact with each other, merely reporting to the same top management.[22]

One obstacle is the difference in pay scales. Scientists, engineers, and production workers of defense firms tend to make more money than do their counterparts in commercial industry, and sometimes more than do their colleagues in the commercial operations in the same company.[23] That phenomenon is often described in terms of a "risk premium" incorporated in the wage and salary structure of defense contractor employees.

The lack of commercial marketing experience is another familiar refrain in defense industry circles. If the federal government is not the principal customer, then the defense contractor has to go through the painful process of developing a sales force that can win contracts in the civilian marketplace. For example, Grumman developed and tried to sell a minivan years before Chrysler popularized the vehicle. According to Weyman Jones, a company vice president, the project failed because of the lack of a distribution system.[24]

Because of the more specialized nature of military equipment, there is less emphasis on volume production at low unit costs. Rather, these firms are used to producing at extremely close tolerances and unusually high quality, under great pressure from the governmental customer to develop ever more advanced equipment. Meeting that last 1 percent of military specifications is very expensive. In contrast, in commercial work the company usually starts off with broader specifications and then trades off continually between improving the product and lowering the cost. Thus, firms used to the environment of weapon system design and development do not develop the cost orientation needed to perform and compete successfully in commercial markets.

A new model of refrigerator at half the price of current types may have a large market even if it will not last as long. The second best missile, in contrast, may hardly be a bargain. The comparison, of course, is oversimplified. Nevertheless, it illustrates the different nature of product innovation characteristic of commercial competition as compared to technological competition in the military field.

It is thus not hard to understand why defense company managements have become so reluctant to move from fields they have mastered into lines of business quite alien to them. Their lack of knowledge of nondefense industries is pervasive. It includes ignorance of products, production methods, advertising and distribution, financial arrangements, funding of research and development, contracting forms, and the very nature of the private customer's demands. Moreover, most of the facilities used by these companies were built for the purpose and not merely converted to defense uses, as was the frequent case during World War II. Also, a large share of these assets is owned by the military establishment and only leased by the defense contractors.

In a 1985 study for the President's Economic Adjustment Committee, the Battelle Memorial Institute stated that, in order to be cost effective, defense plants have been designed with a single product or production process in mind. "Therefore, by their very nature, [these] production facilities do not easily lend themselves to reuse."[25]

Clearly, the type of company that can successfully design and build a new multibillion dollar intercontinental ballistic missile (ICBM) network or space exploration system has a very different capability from that of the soap, steel, toy, or other typical cost-conscious but low-technology company operating in the commercial economy.

Large defense firms, however, have positive resources. Their engineering design and development capability is especially strong. Their work forces are often primarily large aggregations of scientists, engineers, and supporting technicians. Compared with the most technically oriented industry serving commercial markets, such as drugs or chemicals, the typical aerospace or electronics company has several times the number of scientists and engineers to support a given volume of end-item sales. This unique work force enables it to perform research extending the state-of-the-art and to prepare complex engineering designs.

Related to that attribute is a management that is capable, some say uniquely, of managing the development, production, and integration of large and complex systems; this ability is often termed *systems management.* That ability surpasses any comparable nondefense firm in terms of the magnitude of resources being marshalled.

Similarly, these companies possess positive but specialized production capabilities. They are experienced at producing high-value items incorporating advanced engineering and scientific design. A related manufacturing asset is the ability to work with exotic materials and to close tolerances. The hard fact, however, is that the demand for this set of valuable but costly capabilities is very limited.

Despite the numerous lamentations concerning their lack of marketing ability, these firms have been most successful in penetrating one large and rapidly growing market area—government business for new high-tech products. In fact, they have experienced unparalleled success in selling complex systems involving advanced technology to a select governmental clientele. Their knowledge of defense and space markets, customer requirements, and public contracting procedures is detailed and often authoritative. Thus, despite its well-earned reputation for outstanding marketing and management, Procter and Gamble has not considered diversifying into the government market to offset a bad year in consumer products!

Hence, a balanced appraisal does yield some positive strengths on the part of the government-oriented aerospace corporations—their striking engineering and scientific talent for developing new products and services, their systems management capability, and their knowledge of how to serve government agencies requiring state-of-the-art equipment where quality advances are more important than cost containment. These are a set of capabilities that cannot be duplicated in the commercial economy, which the government will continue to need.

THE FUTURE DIRECTION OF DEFENSE CONTRACTORS

Although the bottom is not about to fall out of the military market, a period of belt-tightening has begun. The most likely outcome is a substantial decline in the overall volume of defense business for the early 1990s, but with defense spending remaining high by any historical standard. The broad product and market base of many of the companies involved should help the defense industry handle the transition to a smaller military market. However, the painfulness of the adjustments ahead should not be underestimated.

The Primary Defense Contractors

There is great variety among the major defense contractors. Many of the large aerospace companies—such as General Dynamics, Grumman, Lockheed, Martin Marietta, McDonnell Douglas, and Northrop—rely on the Department of Defense for most of their income. Some, notably General Dynamics, are widely diversified within the military market, producing aircraft, missiles, tanks, and submarines. Others, like Martin Marietta, have gained fairly secure niches within that market. Still others, such as McDonnell Douglas, have diversified to a significant degree into commercial aircraft work (but without attaining profitability). Most of these companies should be able to weather the storm, though not necessarily at their current volumes of sales and employment.

Companies like Grumman and Northrop, which are dependent on just a few weapon system contracts, may be in for a relatively difficult time, depending on the future of those specific military products. They surely are more vulnerable than the more diversified defense contractors and are responding accordingly. Northrop reduced its research and development effort 46 percent in real terms between 1985 and 1989. Grumman's company-initiated R&D slipped by 78 percent during that time period, after adjustment for inflation.[26] Servicing their high-debt load limits the ability of these companies to invest in new undertakings, be they civilian diversification efforts or projects involving defense business.

Because of the military's great dependence on the major defense contractors for designing and building key weapon systems, their survival as a group seems quite assured. Nevertheless, a shakeout of their present numbers is likely. Substantial excess capacity coupled with weak finances characterize this key segment of the defense industrial base. Thus, mergers and consolidations are likely to reduce the number of current players. Some of the financially weaker firms may be acquired by civilian-based companies. In the view of many in the defense industry, a smaller group of stronger firms will enhance the long-run survivability of this group of companies.[27]

Major Defense Divisions of Civilian-Oriented Companies

In contrast, other major defense contractors look primarily to commercial markets for the bulk of their sales. Examples of large companies with important defense segments include Boeing, Litton, Raytheon, Rockwell, Tenneco, and United Technologies. In most of those firms, the defense divisions are quite separate from their commercial activities. Boeing represents an interesting transition since the 1950s, from a firm that was then overwhelmingly dependent on defense business.

In other cases—AT&T, Ford, General Electric, General Motors, Honeywell, and Westinghouse—defense work is a minor part of their total sales. However, each of the companies in this latter group are individually large and important defense contractors. General Electric is fairly well diversified in the military market, with products ranging from nuclear reactors for submarines to navy missiles to space systems. Yet, cutbacks in the purchases of new aircraft will hurt this major supplier of jet engines.

The transition to lower levels of defense spending should be relatively straightforward. In some cases, the firms will benefit from the expansion of civilian markets, especially if macroeconomic policy succeeds in maintaining high aggregate levels of economic activity. Because their contracts with the Pentagon generally are less profitable than their commercial sales, some of these companies will respond to shrinking military markets by phasing out defense business or trying to sell their defense segments. In one prior military cutback, AT&T's highly regarded Bell Laboratories exited from this market.[28]

Smaller Contractors and Subcontractors

Less attention is usually given to the very large array of small businesses, some of whom are prime contractors, and the far greater number that are subcontractors to the large firms. These smaller companies provide the necessary components and parts vital to every weapon system (ranging from fasteners and seals to pumps and castings). The erosion of the defense industrial base in recent years centers on the enterprises in this category. Many of them will be hurt in

the defense transition, especially as large prime contractors pull business back into the parent company.

In a recent survey of 120 of its subcontractors on the M-1 tank,
General Dynamics found that 15 percent of the firms would have to
close a plant if production of the tank was ended.[29] On the other
hand, many of the smaller firms tend to be more capable of dual
military–commercial work than the larger and often more muscle-
bound primes.[30]

FACING COMMON PROBLEMS

How should defense contractors react to the current and impending
reductions in the military market? Stanley Pace, former chief executive of General Dynamics, responds to the prospect of lower defense
budgets in a very straightforward manner, "We've all come from
smaller companies. We can all go back to being smaller companies."[31]
He concedes that the company could be 30 percent smaller, in real
terms, by the end of the decade.[32] Similar sentiments are voiced by
Malcolm Currie, chairman of Hughes Aircraft Company (a major
defense-oriented subsidiary of General Motors), "The defense industry does not have to be at its present peak size to be a very healthy,
profitable, vital industry."[33] Don Fuqua, president of the Aerospace
Industries Association, echoes this viewpoint:

> I do not minimize the impact on our industry of the defense spending
> cuts we know are coming. But we're declining from an all-time peak, and
> we believe that we'll be able to maintain a moderately healthy level of
> defense activity.[34]

Ralph Hawes, retired executive vice president of General Dynamics, goes on to point out that there will be a consolidation in the
industry. "There is going to be less business to pursue, which means it
will get more competitive."[35] A representative of McDonnell Douglas
reported in 1990 that the company had no plans to start or buy any
new or unrelated businesses. "We want to make use of our existing
capabilities and strengths."[36] Pace of General Dynamics provides a
solid justification of that general position:

> We do not as a company have to provide our shareholders with a totally
> balanced portfolio. They perfectly well have the capability of balancing
> their portfolio . . . by their own investments . . . [37]

To some degree, defense companies started in the late 1980s to
adjust to the shift from a rising to a declining military market. New
orders for military aircraft fell from $24 billion in 1985 to $17 billion
in 1988. However, an important partial offset was a substantial

amount of modernization work on older aircraft. Also helpful is the fact that the Department of Defense has a backlog of $260 billion of unexpended budget authority, up from $92 billion in 1980. These funds can support a high level of future defense spending even in the face of large reductions in new appropriations.

More important for a lucky few—especially Boeing, Rockwell, and their many subcontractors and suppliers—are the continued high level of demand for commercial jet airlines and the "second wind" enjoyed by NASA as the budget for civilian space systems rises once again. As a result, the aerospace industry as a whole set a new sales record in 1989. Moreover, the U.S. Department of Commerce forecasts a healthy 3 percent annual growth for the industry through 1994. As of late 1990, Boeing alone reported an order backlog of over $100 billion.

Some important segments of the military market are continuing to grow even during an extended period of general cutback. A prime example is command, control, communications, and intelligence systems, especially vital in monitoring compliance with arms reduction agreements.[38] Loral is an example of a defense supplier benefiting from the sharper focus on electronics gear in the prospective Pentagon budgets. To the extent that the armed forces keep flying old planes instead of buying new ones, they will need to update their communications and fire-control systems.

Individual defense companies face varying business futures. In 1990, Lockheed Corporation reported a backlog of about $7 billion (enough to cover more than a year's sales), while Martin Marietta showed a $13 billion backlog of unfilled orders (more than three times its annual sales volume). Interestingly enough, commercially dominated Boeing lost more than $470 million on its military production in 1989 and anticipated more red ink on its defense work in 1990.[39]

Even Grumman's $6 billion backlog looks healthy. Every defense contract, however, contains a standard clause that says that the entire contract can be cancelled at the convenience of the government, with the contractor only being reimbursed for the costs occurred that far.

Mergers and Acquisitions
Many defense contractors are laboring under heavy indebtedness. The ten companies making up Standard & Poor's Aerospace index more than doubled the ratio of their long-term debt to shareholder equity between 1985 and 1989. The ratio was 14 percent in 1985 and rose to 37 percent by 1989.

There is considerable diversity among major defense contractors. At the beginning of 1990, Grumman's total debt equaled a painfully high 100 percent of its net worth (or shareholder equity). The ratio for Northrop was not much less, at 92 percent; for Lockheed and McDonnell Douglas it was 91 percent. In contrast, the debt-to-equity ratio for Boeing was a very modest 5 percent; for Martin Marietta it was 34 percent.

In response to the need for funds, several defense-oriented companies have followed the practice of other firms and cashed in low-yield assets. Northrop, for example, sold its corporate headquarters in Los Angeles (and leased back the facility). This transaction reduced the company's debt by more than $200 million.

A substantial downsizing is the most sensible response to the greatly reduced market for military equipment that seems likely in the 1990s. The sooner the major contractors reduce their excess capacity— through restructuring, mergers, sales of assets, or simply closing down unneeded facilities—the stronger will be their ability to withstand the competitive rigors of the new military marketplace. The alternative to this painful but necessary course of action will be rising debt loads and continued takeover threats that will weaken their capability to survive as viable firms in this unique and important sector of the economy.[40]

This prescription is not so radical as it may seem at first. Many mergers have occurred in the defense industry over the years: McDonnell Aircraft acquired Douglas Aircraft, Electric Boat merged with Consolidated Aviation to form General Dynamics Corporation. Rockwell International is the result of consolidating North American Aviation and Rockwell Standard. Boeing acquired Vertol Aircraft. United Technologies combined United Aircraft and a variety of civilian companies such as Carrier and Otis Elevator. In the 1980s, several aerospace prime contractors acquired electronics firms and other key subcontractors.

On the other hand, the current market valuation of the shares of most of the defense firms is so low that any substantial purchase of other companies by them would dilute the holdings of existing shareholders very greatly. Moreover, few of these firms have large amounts of cash to risk on commercial diversification. The shape of things to come may be seen by looking across the Atlantic. The consolidation of defense firms is a clear trend in Western Europe. Germany's Daimler-Benz acquired Messerschmitt-Bolkow-Blohm. Britain's Plessey was taken over by a combination of West Germany's Siemens and the United Kingdom's General Electric Company.

RESPONDING TO CHANGES IN THE MILITARY MARKET

Today, a combination of continued budgetary pressures to cut defense expenditures plus the greatly reduced tensions between the two military superpowers is resulting in a downward path of orders for major weapon systems that may well turn out to be a long-term phenomenon. (During Operation Desert Storm, most of the new orders went to smaller, civilian-oriented companies providing special food and personnel protection items.) Defense Secretary Cheney has recommended curtailments or delays in three major aircraft programs— the B-2 bomber, the C-17 transport, and the advanced Tactical Fighter—and he has cancelled a fourth—the A-12 attack aircraft.

During the late 1980s, the Congress and the Department of Defense made many changes in procurement procedures that reduce the profitability of defense business. (For details, see Chapter 8.) All of these developments have been reflected in the exodus from the military market of tens of thousands of subcontractors.

Simultaneously, in the 1980s the existence of a large base of prime contractors forced all in the group to assume greater risks and bid aggressively. They were motivated by the need to utilize capacity and by the fear of missing key milestone programs and thus being left out of a whole generation of technological advancement.

This process increased the tendency of the contractors to act in effect as bankers, helping to finance the military build-up. While the defense budget was rising, this approach kept a large base of contractors afloat. Now, with the prospects of fewer defense dollars to spend, the government is changing its tune. In the view of defense analyst Jon Kutler, the military customer is currently saying to its contractors, "Sorry, I've lost my high-paying job and can no longer afford the mortgage payments on that expensive home you're building for me."[41]

Barring a large and unforeseen expansion in the military budget for procuring large weapons systems, the major U.S. defense firms will look significantly different by the mid-1990s than they do today. They will be down substantially from the peak size they attained in the 1980s and it is likely that there will be fewer of them. To the extent, however, that they avoid wasteful and fruitless "conversion" attempts and simply streamline their operations, they can achieve that new condition with few bankruptcies or hostile takeovers and with reasonable levels of profits and jobs.

Stanley Pace of General Dynamics reminded the Senate Armed Services Committee that the few unfilled commercial needs there are will probably be adequately met by commercial companies that are highly experienced in those markets. Pace concluded that "money spent on trying to convert a tank plant, or a missile plant, or a submarine plant to commercial products will be wasted."[42]

An indication of the shape of things to come was Lockheed's painful decision in early 1990 to close down all its aircraft production at Burbank, California, the city where it was founded. The company consolidated its airplane operations at its two other locations—Palmdale, California, and Marietta, Georgia. Honeywell decided to spin off its torpedo and munitions business to its shareholders after trying unsuccessfully to sell the segment to other companies. Varian Associates dropped most of its defense operations to focus on more profitable lines of electronic equipment.[43]

In the spring of 1990, more than thirty defense electronics divisions were reported to be up for sale by large multi-industry corporations. Chrysler, Eaton, Ford, Phillips, Schlumberger, and United Technologies were all trying to lower their exposure to a declining defense business or simply to get out of money-losing ventures. However, the government's regulatory regime restricts defense industry mergers and selloffs in two ways: by controlling the transfer of security clearances, and by limiting the assignment of contractual rights from an existing contract holder to a third party. In practice, this means that foreign ownership is greatly discouraged.[44]

There does seem to be an invisible floor under which the armed services are reluctant to see the heart of the defense base fall. Thus, in 1990, the army awarded a $414 million contract to Raytheon for missile ground-control equipment, in good measure to prevent disruptions or layoffs at the company's missile production operations.[45]

On the positive side, defense contractors can be expected to continue to search for new applications of their existing product lines, especially in markets close to the ones they now dominate. Grumman won an $841 million contract in 1987 to help NASA manage the development of the manned space station. It also is working on a $1.1 billion contract with the U.S. Postal Service to build more than 99,000 delivery trucks by 1993.[46] The Sikorsky Aircraft Division of United Technologies Corporation produced $206 million of helicopters for the Coast Guard to intercept drug smugglers. Lockheed sold two radar planes to the Customs Service for $58 million. Boeing has succeeded in selling some of its Vertol helicopters to oil companies to service offshore drilling platforms.

Hughes Aircraft and Hewlett-Packard have signed a joint marketing agreement to try to market a civilian version of Hughes' tamper-proof military PCs and workstations to banks, insurance agencies, and other corporate customers. Rockwell is using the huge airplane hangers in its Palmdale, California, facility that was originally built for the B-1 bomber program to repair and service commercial aircraft. One of its early customers is Federal Express. So far, Rockwell has been able to call back only a handful of the former 5,000 employees who had worked on the B-1.[47]

Martin Marietta won a $900 million contract from the Federal Aviation Administration to help overhaul the nation's air traffic control system. The list goes on, but, in the aggregate, these close civilian applications of military products represent a minor fraction of the military market. The $1 billion being spent annually for drug interdiction equipment is dwarfed by the $120 billion allocated each year to the development and acquisition of weapon systems.[48] Moreover, it is too soon to say whether these new diversification efforts will be successful financially.

FORCING DEFENSE COMPANIES TO "CONVERT"

In the face of large layoffs of defense company employees, congressional representatives from defense areas have become a chorus of supporters for government to "do something." House Majority Leader Richard Gephardt (D-MO) has formed a task force of House Democrats who have proposed defense conversion legislation. Senate Majority Leader George Mitchell (D-ME) has established a task force on the U.S. Economy in the 1990s: Productivity Growth and Defense Adjustment, chaired by Senator Don Riegle (D-MI). In 1990 Senator Tim Wirth (D-CO) and the late Senator John Heinz (R-PA) co-chaired a bipartisan Task Force on Defense Spending, the Economy, and the Nation's Security.

Many individual bills have been introduced on various aspects of defense adjustment and conversion and one or more is likely to be enacted. Senator William Roth (R-DE) has proposed the Base Conversion, Community Development, and Worker Opportunity Act—a bill designed to benefit local communities when nearby military installations are closed down. It would require the federal government to offer the property to the locality before it went to any federal agency or could be sold to the public. In turn, the community (or county or state government) would have to pay for the training of the civilian employees laid off by the base closing and reimburse the federal government for severance pay.

Congresswoman Rose Oakar (D-OH) introduced the Economic Stabilization, Adjustment, and Defense Industry Conversion Act to establish an Economic Stabilization and Adjustment Council that would set up a program of economic adjustment for workers and communities hit by defense cuts. Congressman Sam Gejdenson (D-CT) proposed the Economic Diversification and Defense Adjustment Act along similar lines.

In the fall of 1990, Congress took a few initial steps on the defense conversion issue. It authorized a $200 million adjustment effort as part of the fiscal year 1991 authorization bill for the Department of Defense based principally on existing programs of the Departments of Commerce, Defense, and Labor such as community planning and worker training. The legislation makes communities eligible for planning assistance through the Defense Department's Office of Economic Adjustment. The statute also establishes a new readjustment grant program under the existing Job Training Partnership Act. The most comprehensive conversion proposal is that of Congressman Ted Weiss (D-NY); it is the bill that has attracted the greatest support from the promoters of "conversion."[49] He has introduced legislation on economic conversion since 1977, with little initial response. Congressional interest in the subject is growing, however, as demonstrated by congressional hearings on Weiss' and similar proposals in 1988, 1989, and 1990. Major labor unions are lining up in support of the general notion of a federally sponsored conversion effort. The Machinists are leading a coalition of unions that includes the Auto Workers, the Electrical Workers, the Steelworkers, and the Oil, Chemical, and Atomic Workers.

The essence of Weiss' proposed Defense Economic Adjustment Act is to require each defense plant to set up joint business–labor "alternative use committees" to develop plans for shifting production to peacetime use when defense contracts are canceled. Benefits are also provided to unemployed defense workers and their communities. In addition, the bill establishes a public–private Defense Economic Adjustment Council to oversee the entire process and to provide support and guidance.[50] Most other conversion proposals are variations of the Weiss bill, typically on a more modest scale. Thus some special attention to Congressman Weiss' idea is appropriate.

Alternative Use Committees

Congressman Weiss' bill would require that every military facility of 100 or more employees—both bases and defense plants—set up an alternative use committee.[51] His proposal covers every business that has a defense contract or subcontract, no matter how small a share of its total activity is devoted to defense work, as long as 100 or more people are on the payroll. Tens of thousands of defense contractors, subcontractors, and suppliers would be included.

Each alternative use committee is to have at least eight members equally divided between management and labor. Localities within which the facility is located may appoint nonvoting representatives to the committee, who would participate in an advisory capacity. Each committee is directed to prepare plans for converting the facility and its resources to the manufacture of civilian products. These plans would be implemented if there was a "substantial" cutback, reduction, or elimination of the facility's defense contracts.

The alternative use committees are given a broad set of mandates. Each is to evaluate the assets of the defense facility and the resources

and requirements of the local community in terms of physical property, manpower skills and expertise, accessibility, environment, and economic needs. The thrust of Congressman Weiss' approach is to try to
maintain the status quo in each locality covered by the bill. As he
stated when introducing the 1989 version of the bill, "The Defense
Economic Adjustment Act provides a detailed plan for preserving the
jobs of those affected by decisions to eliminate unnecessary military
spending."[52]

The alternative use committees are to develop detailed plans for
converting the facility to "efficient, nondefense-related productive
activity." The plans are intended to provide the local community and
the employees of the defense facility with "a viable and workable
blueprint for the conversion of the facility." The circumstances trig-
gering such ambitious plans are unusually vague:

> [I]n the event the facility is affected by a government decision to reduce,
> modify, or close the facility, terminate any defense contracts, or disap-
> prove a license to sell or export defense materials to nongovernmental
> parties . . .

In the case of each of the larger (and many medium-size contractors), the "conversion" would be triggered almost instantaneously.
There is a constant ebb and flow of contracts, with old ones being
terminated and new ones being signed. The cancellation of the small-
est contract would supposedly trigger the conversion activity for the
entire facility even if the same firm simultaneously received a massive
multibillion dollar new defense order to be produced at the same
location. A "defense facility" would have to actuate its "conversion
plan" even if defense business represents an infinitesimal portion of
its total activity—and even if that nondefense portion was rising
rapidly. It is not apparent why disapproving a single export license
should be sufficient grounds to convert the entire facility.

The stipulated content of the required conversion plan is substantial. Each plan shall "maximize" the extent to which the personnel
required for the "efficient" operation of the converted facility can be
drawn from people with the types and levels of skills possessed by the
employees of the facility prior to its conversion. The plan must also
specify the numbers of personnel, by type and level of skill, employed
at the facility prior to conversion, whose continued employment is not
consistent with the efficient operation of the facility after "conversion."

The next required part of the plan is to specify the number of new
positions, by level and type of skill, that would be required. Here, too,
it would be hard to make more than the roughest guess, but the
planners would also have to specify "in detail" the new plant and

equipment, and modification to existing plant and equipment, required for the converted facility. The capstone would be a financial plan, including an estimate of financing requirements.

Each plan must provide for extending the labor contract, wages, and other benefits to workers until conversion to nondefense-related operations is completed. For employees displaced by the closing of a defense plant, each committee shall provide occupational retraining and reemployment counseling services—or ensure that such retraining and services are provided by some government agency. (See Chapter 4 for more on existing government services to the unemployed.)

The degree of compulsion in the planning and implementation activity is awesome. Any contractor who fails to submit an alternative use plan or refuses or fails to carry it out shall be barred from future defense contracts for three years, forfeit termination payments due it on existing or recently cancelled contracts, and lose eligibility for tax credits.

The compulsion and sanctions in the Weiss bill are surprising in view of the negative evaluation offered by the Battelle Memorial Institute:

> Based on our experience, the concept of an office of conversion in which advanced planning conducted by government-sponsored alternative use committees is used to convert industrial facilities from defense production to civilian production with a one-to-two year time frame will most likely result in very limited success and will not likely be cost-effective.[53]

The Defense Economic Adjustment Council

The Weiss bill—like most other conversion proposals—would also establish an unwieldy twenty-two-member Defense Economic Adjustment Council to oversee the entire conversion effort. The Council would consist of ten cabinet officers and other senior federal officials, six representatives of the "business-management community," and six from labor unions. Such a committee with a majority of private citizens to exercise the powers of the federal government would certainly be an innovation in governmental structure.

The Defense Economic Adjustment Council would do more than coordinate and advise. It would establish the criteria for eligibility for assistance, determine which communities are eligible, and rule on eligibility appeals. Moreover, it is expected to quickly solve the key problems that perennially face decision makers entering new lines of business. It would have to do so by preparing a Conversion Guidelines Handbook that is to contain all of the following:

- The basic requirements of programs for professional retraining of managerial personnel to reorient them from defense work to civilian enterprise.

- The basic requirements for the length and nature of occupational retraining for production workers and junior level administrative employees.
- A checklist of critical points requiring attention at each stage of the conversion process.

One year of advance notification would be required of plans to cut back or terminate a defense contract or a military base. Because the federal budget is sent up to the Congress about seven months before the start of a fiscal year, the notification requirement would mean, in practice, notice of 1.5 years before any actual cutback. The scope of the notifications would be very broad, covering "reduction, technical changes, or elimination of a program. . . . " Given the hundreds of technical changes that are normally made in the course of producing a single weapon system, the paperwork flow would be substantial.

Assistance to Workers and Communities

Many conversion proposals would extend unemployment compensation beyond the normal twenty-six weeks' duration. The Weiss bill is far more generous. All employees who lose their jobs ("in whole or in part") by a cutback in the volume of defense work would be eligible for two years to benefits equal to 90 percent of the first $20,000 of annual earnings and 50 percent of the next $5,000. Those who lose their jobs within six months prior to the "reduction of the volume of defense work" also receive the benefits. In addition, the employer would have to continue paying into the employees' pension fund in behalf of each of those laid off workers for a period of two years. No explanation is given for that windfall, or more generally why unemployed defense workers should be treated so much more generously than other people who are out of work.

Also, the employer would be required to maintain for two years any medical and life insurance coverage that was in force when the employee was working. There is no provision for recovering these large costs under defense contracts.

Federal adjustment assistance of undesignated amounts would be provided for communities and workers while a defense facility was being "converted." Communities "seriously" affected by defense cutbacks would also be eligible for federal planning assistance. According to Representative Weiss, the Defense Economic Adjustment Council would encourage regional and national planning to provide information "indicating where local people should be looking to see what they should be doing." That supposedly would serve as a guide for "what the economy really needs."[54]

Several states have undertaken some modest conversion planning on their own. In 1990, Washington State allocated $200,000 to identify areas likely to be hurt by future defense cuts and to start initial conversion planning for generating new civilian business. Massachusetts is funding a retraining effort and paying consultants to help small defense suppliers find alternative markets.

Views of some California government officials, however, may be closer to the prevailing attitude. Richard M. Allen, of the State Commerce Department, says: "What is government going to do? Tell these companies they have to make refrigerators? Ultimately, conversion will be left to the marketplace."[55]

Cost and Financing

No estimate of cost is contained in the materials accompanying the conversion proposals. When asked about the cost, Representative Weiss replied, "I think it is really almost impossible to project."[56]

He has suggested several methods of financing in his congressional testimony. One is to allocate 0.5 percent of the defense procurement budget for "economic conversion purposes." The other is to require that 1.25 percent of each defense contractor's sales to the Department of Defense be used for economic conversion purposes. On the basis of current levels of military budgeting and production, either approach would constitute a major new federal spending program, in excess of $1 billion per year.

Rationale for the Proposed Legislation

Much of the support for the current proposals to "convert" defense industries to civilian tasks arises from the fear that citizens will resist large defense cutbacks if they think the result will be losing their jobs. Hence, in order to defuse the opposition to lower military spending, leaders in the peace movement seek to convince the public that attractive civilian alternatives exist for defense contractors. Congressman Weiss is very clear on that point:

> By creating viable alternatives to military spending, economic conversion would assure the millions of workers in military dependent industries that their jobs will not be sacrificed in the effort to achieve meaningful arms control. . . . This would significantly enhance the prospects for ending the nuclear arms race.[57]

Seymour Melman of Columbia University straightforwardly described the essentially political aspect of the thrust for conversion planning: "Conversion planning is vital in order to diffuse the legitimate fear of the seven and a half million people now directly dependent for their livelihood on the military system."[58]

One fallacy of this line of thinking is the assumption that people who object to large defense cutbacks do so solely out of economic self-interest. That may be the case for quite a few directly involved in defense work, but it ignores several more basic factors.

Many people whose incomes and jobs are not affected support high levels of defense because they view the world differently than the advocates of conversion. That is, they believe that the United States exists in a dangerous international environment, with potential threats coming from such varied sources as terrorist gangs and small nations with modern military capability, as well as from conventional "super power" rivalry. Thus, they sincerely believe, a high level of defense is needed for the nation's welfare.

Some critics are too ready to impugn the motives of defense industry executives. An insight into the industry thinking was conveyed by an executive of Rockwell International explaining the changing outlook for the military budget, "No matter how big your political action committee is, you can't turn back Eastern Europe. You don't want to."[59]

Another shortcoming of the "conversion" position is the adverse experience of the past. As we have seen, by and large, past attempts by large defense contractors to use their capabilities beyond the aerospace market have been unsuccessful.

The most enthusiastic supporters of conversion planning acknowledge the sad history of previous defense industry diversification efforts. Even Professor Melman, whom Congressman Weiss acknowledges as the intellectual guru of the conversion movement, writes that "close scrutiny suggests that managements of the . . . military-industrial firm are infused with a trained incapacity for operating civilian enterprises functioning in the civilian marketplace."[60] On another occasion, Melman has been quoted as saying, "These fellows couldn't produce anything for Sears & Roebuck to save their lives."[61]

Representative Weiss makes a similar point:

> Thus, unlike most firms in a free enterprise system, their [defense firms'] focus is not on making cheaper or better products. . . . Often, these firms manufacture products which are essentially useless to the civilian population and uncompetitive in international markets.[62]

Rather than beating the defense companies over the head, perhaps the conversion enthusiasts should reflect on the broader conclusion of the Battelle Memorial Institute study cited earlier:

> . . . history has shown that specialized industries which experienced significant loss in markets often just simply disappear, as in the case of the steam locomotive . . . The ability of such companies to diversify into anything other than a similar product has met with very limited success . . . [63]

The conversion advocates also ignore the need to maintain an adequate defense research, development and production base should the current optimistic view of the international climate undergo another shift. Sadly, history provides numerous examples of the cyclical nature of superpower relations and of the abrupt shift from belligerency to *glasnost*—or *detente*—and back again. Moreover, the "conversion" strategy focuses on keeping existing jobs in place. That approach is a recipe for stagnation.

The limited ability to transfer defense technology to civilian uses has not been due to lack of trying. If the companies on their own want to continue such high-risk attempts, we should wish them well. "Conversion," however, is not an attractive use of taxpayer money and, directly or indirectly, the money for such efforts would be taken from funds voted by the Congress.

The "conversion" process would also be a step toward increased governmental control of private business. According to the World-watch Institute, "Conversion goes beyond a mere reshuffling of people and money. It involves a political institutional transformation."[64] In view of the vagueness with which the provisions are drawn, enactment of bills like Congressman Weiss' Defense Economic Adjustment Act would provide a field day for disputatious lawyers, bureaucrats anxious to expand their turf, and consultants who want to develop plans to increase the power of government.

Seen in a longer-term perspective, the conversion debate measure is a dispute about the role and power of government in our society. The answer seems clear: In a period of budget stringency, there is no compelling case for devoting public resources to force feeding "conversion" efforts. Nor is it obvious why public policy should interfere with the voluntary shift of resources to other sectors of the economy. Indeed, a large reduction in defense spending—and a concomitant reduction in federal deficit financing—would be a fine opportunity for increasing the extent to which consumers, producers, and investors make their own decisions on the use of their income and wealth.

Under the circumstances, we would expect that Congressman Weiss, Professor Melman, and their colleagues would welcome the opportunity presented by defense cutbacks to shift resources to the more productive and competitive civilian marketplace. They would, however, have to abandon their preference for government planning of economic change.

OUTLOOK

Given an international political environment warranting a continued high level of defense spending by the United States, it is important that there be significant competition among the remaining defense producers. The government should not become excessively reliant on any one of them for any major category of weaponry. In essence, that means not squeezing the contractors too hard in a vain attempt by the Pentagon to minimize the effects of budget cuts on weapon system procurement.

The status quo does not adequately meet these conditions. It is not just the view of the defense industry itself, which can be dismissed as self-serving, but of disinterested outsiders and even of some officials of the Department of Defense. Such is the conclusion of a late 1989 survey of defense industry executives, governmental officials, and private opinion leaders by Yankelovich Clancy Shulman that was commissioned by the accounting firm of Ernst and Young.[65] Describing the "uncertain" health of the defense industry, the study reports several related problem areas:

1. Lower financial returns by defense contractors than experienced by commercial manufacturers.
2. Rising foreign competition.
3. An acute shortage of acquisition and scientific personnel on the part of the Department of Defense.
4. Siphoning off of valuable industry and government management resources because of duplication of oversight and auditing.

The study concludes that a new relationship built on trust and mutual respect needs to be forged between the federal government and the defense industry. Eighty percent or more of each group surveyed (industry, Congress, Defense Department, and independent opinion leaders) share this view, noting that otherwise a continued erosion of the defense industrial base will occur. Most respondents, however, are pessimistic about the likelihood of the necessary changes being made in the next three to five years.

Moreover, when the question turns to the nitty-gritty matter of profits, a sharp cleavage develops between the views of private sector officials and those in the public sector. More than 90 percent of the industry respondents believe that government is squeezing industry profits too much. Moreover, about two-thirds of the independent opinion leaders share this belief. In contrast, only about one-fourth of the Defense Department sample agree and only 15 percent of congressional respondents.

Gregory Treverton of the Council on Foreign Relations describes the impediments to military reform as "legendary." He cynically adds that he suspects that politicians and the public like this system the way it is.[66] Nevertheless, public dissatisfaction with the status quo in military policy continues to grow, and it seems increasingly appropriate to develop the kinds of policy changes developed in Chapter 8.

Turning to the private sector, defense companies can choose between two different models of corporate behavior in responding to large cutbacks in the military budget. To simplify, we can call these the Boeing and Grumman approaches.

When faced with a very large decline in the orders for its basic aerospace product line back in 1971, Boeing took the painful actions required to reduce the size of the company accordingly. Little effort was made to diversify into new markets. More than one-half of the entire work force was laid off. One wag rented a billboard for a memorable message, "The last one out of Seattle, please turn off the lights."

Indeed, Boeing's cutbacks were painful, extending to experienced engineers and craftsmen with considerable seniority in the company. However, the downsizing left the company in a strong enough financial position to plan for—and to lead—the next upturn in commercial aircraft sales and production. The result is a world class corporation with a record high work force of approximately 160,000.

In contrast, Grumman has invested much of its resources in a wide variety of nonaerospace diversification efforts, in both commercial and governmental markets. The result has been unsuccessful, in the process weakening Grumman's basic financial condition. To add the proverbial insult to injury, it did so without achieving the job creation objective that motivates the conversion approach. In June 1990, the company offered early retirement to more than one-fifth of its entire work force.[67]

If there is any conclusion that comes out of this chapter, it is that defense contractors—no different from other for-profit businesses—are not eleemosynary institutions. To expect them to behave in that manner is futile. Of course, the Boeing approach is initially painful, especially to the people laid off, their families, and their communities, but such changes are what separate a dynamic private enterprise economy such as the United States from the static centrally planned societies that characterized Eastern Europe until very recently.

Change is an essential aspect of a modern competitive economy. In the 1980s the tremendous expansion of the aerospace and other defense companies required attracting people and capital from other parts of the economy, often to the discomfort and displeasure of those other companies and their managements, stockholders, and suppliers. Pleasant or not, we should not expect that type of movement always to be in one direction. Nor should we anticipate that the current ranking of defense contractors will prevail over the coming decade.

Some perspective will benefit both the defense companies and their employees, including those who fear they will soon lose their jobs.

They could do worse than cite the compelling words of a long-term critic of high levels of military spending:

> Even if Fidel Castro shaved off his beard and became a fellow of the American Heritage Foundation, we would still need the military–industrial complex for quite a while longer.[68]

NOTES

1. William J. Broad, "Defense Industry Goes Hustling to Make a Buck Without the Bang," *The New York Times*, April 8, 1990, p. E5.

2. Louis Uchitelle, "Economy Expected to Absorb Effects of Military Cuts," *The New York Times*, April 15, 1990, p. 14.

3. See Murray L. Weidenbaum, "Product Diversification in the Aircraft Manufacturing Industry," *Analysis Journal*, May 1959, pp. 3–7; Murray L. Weidenbaum, "Problems of Adjustment for Defense Industries," in Emile Benoit and Kenneth Boulding, eds., *Disarmament and the Economy* (New York: Harper & Row, 1963), pp. 66–86.

4. "Aircraft Firms Diversifying Products," *Automotive and Aviation Industries*, February 15, 1946, pp. 17–18 et ff; "Aircraft Makers Diversifying," *Business Week*, September 28, 1946, pp. 21–27.

5. U.S. Congress, House of Representatives, Committee on Armed Services, *Aircraft Production Costs and Profits* (Washington, D.C.: U.S. Government Printing Office, 1956), p. 2725.

6. *1988 Annual Report* (New York: Grumman Corporation, 1989), p. 4.

7. *1988 Annual Report* (St. Louis: McDonnell Douglas Corporation, 1989), p. 2, and reports for earlier years; Adam Goodman, "Sticking to Their Guns," *St. Louis Post-Dispatch*, March 5, 1990, p. 1BP.

8. *1988 Annual Report* (St. Louis: General Dynamics Corporation, 1989), p. 3.

9. Robert W. DeGrasse, Jr., "Corporate Diversification and Conversion Experience," in John E. Lynch, ed., *Economic Adjustment and Conversion of Defense Industries* (Boulder, Colo.: Westview Press, 1987), p. 98.

10. *Aerospace Facts and Figures. 1989/90* (Washington, D.C.: Aerospace Industries Association, 1989), p. 15.

11. *1989 Annual Report* (Los Angeles: Rockwell International, 1990).

12. *1988 Annual Report* (Los Angeles: Lockheed Corporation, 1989).

13. John E. Lynch, "Introduction," in Lynch, *Economic Adjustment*, p. 5; Daniel P. Maserang, *Estimating R&D Spillovers in Major Defense Contractors*, a doctoral dissertation presented to the Sever Institute of Washington University, August 1990, p. 147.

14. Denver Research Institute, *Defense Industry Diversification*, U.S. Arms Control and Disarmament Agency Publication 30 (Washington, D.C.: U.S. Government Printing Office, 1966), p. vii.

15. U.S. House of Representatives, Committee on Banking, Finance and Urban Affairs, *Economic Diversification* (Washington, D.C.: U.S. Government Printing Office, 1989), p. 19.

16. Robert W. DeGrasse, Jr., "The Military Economy," in Suzanne Gordon and Dave McFadden, eds., *Economic Conversion* (Cambridge, Mass.: Ballinger Publishing, 1984), p. 15.

17. DeGrasse, "Corporate Diversification," pp. 104–6.

18. House Committee on Banking, *Economic Diversification*, p. 40.

19. Christopher Wilkinson, "Perestroika: The Role of the Defense Sector," *NATO Review*, February 1990, pp. 24–25; "Beating Swords Into Vacuum Cleaners," *RAND Research Review*, Spring 1990, p. 5; "Converting Soviet Arms Factories," *The Economist*, December 15, 1990, p. 21.

20. "Beating Swordmakers Into Shoemakers," *Washington Post Weekly*, December 10, 1990, p. 11.

21. For an earlier study along these lines, see Murray L. Weidenbaum and A. Bruce Rozet, *Potential Industrial Adjustments to Shifts in Defense Spending* (Menlo Park, Calif.: Stanford Research Institute, 1963).

22. Lloyd G. Dumas, "Making Peace Possible," in Gordon and McFadden, *Economic Conversion*, p. 69.

23. Ibid., p. 21.

24. Louis Uchitelle, "Difficult Switch for Arms Makers," *The New York Times*, April 23, 1990, p. C2.

25. Battelle Memorial Institute, "Feasibility of Prompt Implementation of New Technologies by Civilian Industries to Offset Defense Contractor Cutbacks," in *Economic Adjustment/Conversion: Appendices* (Washington, D.C.: President's Economic Adjustment Committee, 1985), p. N-7.

26. Philip Finnegan, "Companies Sacrifice R&D to Survive Cuts," *Defense News*, July 2, 1990, p. 1.

27. Statement of Norman A. Augustine, Martin Marietta Corporation, before the House Armed Services Committee, March 21, 1990, p. 9.

28. Ibid., p. 8.

29. Richard W. Stevenson, "Suppliers Brace for Arms Cuts," *The New York Times*, June 18, 1990, p. C-1.

30. See Gordon Adams, *Economic Adjustment to Lower Defense Spending*, Testimony to the Senate Armed Services Committee, May 4, 1990, p. 10.

31. Leslie Wayne, "Arms Makers Gird for Peace," *The New York Times*, December 17, 1989, p. 1-F.

32. Andy Pasztor and Rick Wartzman, "As Defense Industry Shrinks, Suppliers Face Widely Varying Fates," *The Wall Street Journal*, May 24, 1990, p. A8.

33. Ralph Vartabedian, "Prospects for Defense Spending," *Los Angeles Times*, December 24, 1989, p. D3.

34. David C. Morrison, "Cushions for Contractors," *National Journal*, January 13, 1990, p. 65.

35. Vartabedian, "Defense Spending," p. D3.

36. Goodman, "Sticking to Their Guns," p. 4BP.

37. Ibid.

38. Bob Poos, "Cheney Says C3I Systems Growing Despite Pentagon Budget Cutbacks," *Federal Computer Week*, April 23, 1990, p. 6.

39. Rick Wartzman, "Boeing Reports Strong Results, Splits Stock 3–2," *The Wall Street Journal*, May 1, 1990, p. A8.

40. Jon B. Kutler, "Downsizing America's Defense Industry," *Los Angeles Times*, January 21, 1990, p. D3; William E. Kovacic, "Merger Policy in a Declining Defense Industry," *Antitrust Bulletin* (forthcoming).

41. Kutler, "Downsizing."

42. Statement by Stanley C. Pace before the Senate Armed Services Committee, May 4, 1990, p. 5.

43. James E. Ellis, "Who Pays for Peace," *Business Week*, July 2, 1990, p. 69.

44. Kovacic, "Merger Policy."

45. Andy Pasztor and Gary Putka, "Raytheon Wins Army Contract of $414 Million," *The Wall Street Journal*, May 22, 1990, p. A4.

46. Lee E. Koppelman and Pearl M. Kamer, *Maximizing the Potential of Long Island's Defense Sector in an Era of Change* (New York: Long Island Regional Planning Board, 1988), p. 45.

47. Ellis, "Who Pays for Peace," p. 69.

48. Eric Weiner, "New Strategies for Military Suppliers," *The New York Times*, April 12, 1990, p. C-1 et ff.

49. Lester R. Brown et al., *State of the World* (New York: W. W. Norton & Co., 1990), p. 170.

50. Committee on Banking, Finance and Urban Affairs, *Economic Conversion*, pp. 39–46, 349–78; U.S. House of Representatives, Committee on Banking, Finance, and Urban Affairs, *Economic Diversification* (Washington, D.C.: U.S. Government Printing Office, 1989), pp. 94–105.

51. The analysis of specific provisions is based on the proposed Defense Economic Adjustment Act (H.R. 101), introduced in the 101st Congress on January 3, 1989.

52. Honorable Ted Weiss, "The Defense Economic Adjustment Act," *Congressional Record*, January 3, 1989, p. E24.

53. Battelle, "Feasibility of Prompt Implementation," p. N-26.

54. Weiss, "Defense Economic Adjustment Act," p. E24.

55. Cited in Ellis, "Who Pays for Peace," p. 70.

56. Testimony of Honorable Ted Weiss in U.S. Committee on Banking, Finance and Urban Affairs, Economic Conversion, p. 8.

57. Weiss, "Defense Economic Adjustment Act," p. E24.

58. Seymour Melman, "Introduction to Conversion," in William Meyers, *Conversion From War to Peace* (New York: Gordon and Breach, 1972), p. 14.

59. Quoted in "Congress Is Lobbied for Military Projects," *The New York Times*, April 9, 1990, p. A10.

60. Seymour Melman, *Pentagon Capitalism* (New York: McGraw-Hill, 1970), p. 173.

61. Steve Berg, "Military Industries Urged to Serve Civilian Economy," *Minneapolis Star-Tribune*, May 21, 1990, p. 8A.

62. Weiss, "Defense Economic Adjustment Act," p. E24.

63. Battelle, "Feasibility of Prompt Implementation," p. N-26.

64. Brown, *State of the World*, p. 157.

65. Yankelovich Clancy Shulman, *The U.S. Defense Industry* (St. Louis: Ernst & Young, 1989).

66. Gregory Treverton, "The Defense Debate," *Foreign Affairs*, 1990 Special Issue, pp. 183–96.

67. "Grumman Plan on Retirement," *The New York Times*, June 23, 1990, p. 19.

68. George P. Brockway, "Don't Cash Your Peace Dividend," *The New Leader*, March 19, 1990, p. 15. The Heritage Foundation is a conservative public policy institute in Washington, D.C.

CHAPTER 4

Helping the People Affected

With few exceptions, each of the major defense contractors has laid off thousands of its employees since early 1990. Curtailed levels of spending for national defense in the early 1990s will likely result in substantially lower employment in both the Department of Defense and in the many private companies that hold military contracts. The question is what efforts can and should be made to help those employees during the transition to civilian life.

In 1988, the total number of jobs resulting from defense came to 6.5 million, or 5.7 percent of total national employment.[1] However, because the private sector employment is concentrated in durable goods manufacturing, where wages and output per worker are higher than in the rest of the economy, defense represents a larger share of GNP than of employment.

THOSE WHO WORK FOR DEFENSE COMPANIES

More than 3 million private jobs are generated by the purchase of military weapons and equipment from a great variety of companies and nonprofit organizations. For example, defense-related civilian employment includes workers assembling tanks, people who make the parts that are used by the tank assembler, and the employees of the firms providing business and research services to the companies building the tanks and supplying the components. Given the limited range of the likely defense cutbacks, most of these people are likely to keep their present employment.

Several hundred thousand of these men and women are vulnerable to layoffs over the course of the next several years, with the exact numbers depending on the size and composition of the defense budget cutbacks that are carried out. Some of these workers will find nondefense work with their current employers, especially in the case of the more diversified companies. Many more are likely to accept civilian jobs with other firms. Others may temporarily leave the work force or join the ranks of the unemployed for a period of time.

A U.S. Labor Department report provides a useful perspective. In 1989, 2,341 establishments reported "mass layoffs" (defined as at least thirty-one days' duration, involving fifty or more individuals who filed initial claims for unemployment insurance during a consecutive three-week period). Only about 5 percent of the 572,000 people laid off were identified as "defense-related."[2] Thus, nondefense employment shows considerable variability and terminations of defense worker employment should be seen in that context.

Moreover, defense contractor cutbacks need to be considered in light of the recent experience of the industry itself. For example, in July 1990, McDonnell Douglas announced that it would trim its work force by 17,000. As expected, this was greeted as grim news in the major centers of the company's employment, notably St. Louis. Yet, after the cutback, the company's total employment was scheduled to be one-third or more above what it was in the early 1980s. (In January 1991, however, the Defense Department cancelled the A-12 aircraft, being developed jointly by McDonnell Douglas and General Dynamics.)

From a national or macroeconomic point of view, foregone defense outlays will be spent for civilian programs (public and private) and employment will be created elsewhere in the society. In large measure, reemployment opportunities for current defense workers will depend on the general health of the national economy.[3] In many specific cases, however, the skill requirements and the locations of those new positions are likely to differ substantially from the defense jobs that are eliminated. For varying adjustment periods, the newly unemployed people will have to draw on a variety of public and private agencies.

Background Information

For many defense employees, unemployment may be a new or at least not a recent experience. As a Brookings Institution team of economists wrote, "As new companies and new industries emerge, others decline and their work forces become available for more productive tasks." These economists, however, go on to quickly acknowledge that the transition from one job to the next can impose steep costs on some workers.[4]

The very act of looking for a new job differs widely among individuals with different levels of formal education and occupational specialization. Inexperienced workers with a minimum competence in basic skills tend to find jobs rather quickly. Experienced workers with more specialized skills usually have fewer, albeit better, job openings to choose from.

On average, people with extensive formal education such as college training find jobs more quickly than other experienced workers. In contrast, well-paid workers with highly specialized training but limited formal schooling (especially those with less than a high school education) tend to fare the poorest in the labor market. Even if attractive jobs are available in another area, relocation costs are often high for experienced workers. They are likely to own their own homes, have a working spouse, and have strong ties to family, school, and community.[5]

The great majority of workers (almost nine out of ten) finds jobs without the use of formal job agencies, public or private. The most frequently used methods of locating new employment are (1) directly contacting prospective employers, (2) asking friends and relatives about job openings, and (3) answering "want ads" in newspapers. However, the shutdown of a large factory or a major reduction that results in the layoff of friends and relatives may dry up a worker's job information.[6]

In large-scale layoffs, experienced workers may find few alternative job opportunities for the specific skills they possess in the localities in which they currently reside. If they are willing to relocate, however, they do possess attractive characteristics from the viewpoint of potential employers: job commitment, discipline, and productive work habits. Most laid-off workers receive substantial retraining, but much of it is on the next job rather than via a formal training program.[7]

Private Efforts
Most discussions of defense "conversion," as noted in Chapter 3, show little awareness of the existing voluntary efforts of defense contractors to aid laid-off employees. Studies of earlier defense cutbacks show that organized information about other job possibilities significantly lowers the economic loss from unemployment.[8] In 1990, for example, General Dynamics established a $2 million fund for a transition center to help its hourly workers find new jobs, prepare resumes, and train for new careers. In the same year, McDonnell Douglas' California aircraft division developed an "inplacement" effort to assist employees hit by layoffs find other jobs in the company as well as to help with redirecting their careers.

In August 1990, about one-half of the 4,500 McDonnell Douglas employees in the St. Louis area who received notices attended the first of two job fairs with representatives of 120 firms who were gathered together by the company.

Such efforts are not unusual. A mid-1990 survey of the members of the Aerospace Industries Association reported that more than 60 percent provide severance pay and advance notice to scientific, engineering, and administrative personnel. More than one-half of the companies extend those benefits to technicians and more than one-third cover production workers hit by cutbacks.

In addition, nearly 85 percent of the companies surveyed offer outplacement services (counseling, help with resumes, job fairs, etc.) to their professional staffs, and two-thirds or more do so for all other workers. The average cost of outplacement per employee covered—for all job categories—ranges from a low of $100 to 15 percent of salary.[9]

Such forward-looking efforts are in contrast to the passive "benefits" contained in the typical conversion bill.[10] Moreover, such employer-sponsored efforts have become very widespread. For example, in the face of military cutbacks, the Grumman Corporation decided in 1990 to offer 6,000 of its 24,000 employees early retirement, including a supplement to their accrued pension benefits. Corporate officials believe that this early retirement effort will both support their redirection efforts and be the most compassionate way of reducing the company's work force.[11]

A recent survey of personnel practices in 104 large U.S. companies showed that nine out of ten offer outplacement services to workers being laid off. Two out of three firms provide early retirement incentives, alternative employment with the company, and extended health benefits. Only one-half of the firms surveyed give early notice of layoff and slightly more than one out of three provide retraining opportunities.[12]

Unions also have been active in developing transition programs for unemployed defense workers. In the case of layoffs at Lockheed, the union local of the International Association of Machinists set up a "life-line" assistance program. The Colorado AFL-CIO has established a retraining program for government employees whose jobs were eliminated by military base shutdowns. Funded with state and federal grants, the Colorado program retrained and placed all 289 workers displaced at Fort Carson.[13]

When GTE Corporation dismissed 2,000 workers in a plant closure in San Carlos, California, the company embarked on ambitious "outplacement" activities, including reaching out to other companies in the area to identify job openings and holding on-site job fairs for potential employers. It also set up employee workshops on how to prepare job resumes and how to look for a job, in addition to individual counseling.

All but 35 of the more than 2,000 workers participated, and 85 percent of the employees had found new jobs one month prior to the actual plant closing.[14] Of course, this has not been a universal experience, but the GTE case underscores the need for informational assistance to give newly laid-off workers a basis for starting their individual job searches.

Governmental Efforts

The Office of Economic Adjustment in the Defense Department offers useful assistance in a quiet, unobtrusive way. Over the past quarter of a century, this small unit has helped more than 100 communities adjust to base closings. It often serves as a catalyst for local and private efforts.

Transitional assistance is needed by many of the people directly affected by defense cutbacks and an elaborate social safety net is already in place. Three major federal government programs assist laid-off workers—job search, training, and unemployment compensation. Most of the actual contact with individual applicants occurs at federally funded state employment agencies. Specifically, the U.S. Employment Service provides job search assistance, mainly to people with limited job skills, at more than 2,000 offices operated by each of the fifty states. Most unemployed workers visit these offices in connection with applying for cash unemployment benefits.

The unemployment insurance program is operated by the states under federal guidelines, paid for by federal and state payroll taxes. Typically, these employer-financed benefits provide dislocated workers with temporary income equal to approximately 70 percent of the wages previously earned (up to some designated dollar limit), usually for a maximum of twenty-six weeks.

An extended private source of income for some involves supplemental unemployment benefits. These payments cover dislocated workers who are out of work longer than twenty-six weeks. The benefits are established through collective bargaining agreements between companies and unions and are managed by them.

Under the Job Training Partnership Act of 1982, state employment agencies use federal money to provide job search assistance, job development services, prelayoff assistance to workers who have received termination notices, and relocation assistance.

In 1988, Congress passed two laws designed to help in the case of large-scale layoffs. The Worker Adjustment and Retraining Notification Act (WARN) requires employers to give workers, unions, and local communities at least sixty days' notice before closing a plant with fifty or more employees or terminating large numbers of workers (defined as one-third or more of the work force or 500 or more

employees).[15] This new law is likely to cover most of the defense
cutbacks that are anticipated, as would the Economic Dislocation and
Workers Adjustment Assistance Act. This latter statute requires each
state affected to set up a "rapid response" dislocated worker unit,
which can react quickly to plant closings and mass layoffs.

A few states have enacted plant closing statutes that provide additional benefits. Massachusetts employers must extend group health
insurance for ninety days after designated layoffs; the requirement in
Connecticut is for 120 days. In Maine, severance pay of one week for
each year of service is mandated for employees who have been with
the company for at least three years.

With the intent of making the military's civilian work force reductions relatively painless the Pentagon, in January 1990, established a
freeze on hiring civilian workers. The aim was to reduce the military's
civilian payroll by 40,000 jobs in fiscal year 1990. To the extent that
future reductions in the Pentagon's civilian payrolls require actual
layoffs, the people involved will be eligible for many of the same types
of assistance available to employees of defense contractors who lose
their jobs. In addition, the more experienced civil servants will be
eligible to compete for a variety of jobs in other government agencies.

Extending the Social Safety Net

One aspect of the existing social safety net is inadequate, and the
shortcomings are not limited to unemployed defense workers. Because the government's employment service is run by the individual
states, the focus is invariably on job openings in specific localities. For
most occupations, that is a sensible approach.

In the case of defense adjustment, however, that method does not
suffice for two interelated reasons. First of all, the layoffs by the larger
military contractors tend to be very substantial and they are occurring
at a time of general contraction of the overall defense labor market.
Thus, engineers laid off by Northrop in the Los Angeles area are
unlikely to find local employment with Lockheed (and vice versa).
They need to search in other geographic areas, which respond primarily to nondefense business trends.

The second reason is that defense engineers and technicians have
been quite mobile over the years. They are part of a national labor
market. All this underscores the need for more detailed and more
current information on job opportunities on a nationwide basis. A
modest amount of special testing and counseling could also help
match former defense industry workers with suitable job openings in
the civilian economy.

It is ironic that, at a time when the availability of engineers and other technically trained personnel is rising due to defense cutbacks, high schools and colleges around the country continue to suffer shortages of math and science teachers. Approximately 10 percent of all U.S. engineering and science faculty positions are vacant.

This is an area of the economy where a modest amount of deregulation would be helpful. A major barrier to the use of otherwise-qualified former defense industry personnel is the array of rigid requirements for high school teachers in terms of formal courses in education. As the director of the National Center for Education Information, a Washington-based research organization, reports:

> Finding enough intelligent and eager adults to teach its children is not one of them [serious problems]. It is time to open up alternative means of entering the teacher profession.[16]

Many experienced engineers, scientists, and mathematicians would like to teach, especially those who take early retirement or are hit by plant closings or large-scale layoffs. Although they may have substantial experience in corporate training programs, few of these potential teachers have taken the required two- to three-year sequence of courses in education theory, practice, and administration. Their knowledge of mathematics and the sciences, however, is typically very strong and up-to-date.

The supply of science and math teachers could be enhanced fairly quickly by setting up a special one-year graduate program in education for people with substantial technical training and experience. This second career may be especially attractive to the former defense workers who have taken early retirement. The combination of pension income and moderate salaries from teaching might, at least in some cases, approximate their previous earnings. (As we will see in the next part of this chapter, discharged service personnel also are a good potential source of teachers.)

The urge for any special treatment for defense conversion must be tempered by the knowledge that there is little reason to treat defense contractor employees more generously than people who lose their jobs when civilian companies experience hard times. To the extent that a "risk premium" has been included in their present pay scales, that risk is now becoming a reality.

THOSE WHO SERVE IN THE MILITARY

A different, and often more difficult, set of challenges faces former members of the all-volunteer armed forces who—having chosen a career in the military—did not expect to be discharged into the civilian economy. A useful benchmark is Secretary of the Army Michael Stone's prediction that the army could cut as many as 250,000 soldiers from its ranks by the mid-1990s. An upward limit on the range of possible troop reductions is the estimate of the CBO that a 4 percent annual cut in real defense spending during 1991–1995 could result in a cumulative reduction of about 400,000 in total military personnel.[17] Such a large cutback—almost one-fifth of the total military roster—is bound to pose serious policy and personal problems. The Defense Department believes that a troop reduction of more than 50,000–75,000 per year will require large-scale involuntary separations.[18]

The absolute size of the military manpower reductions likely in the next few years will be much smaller than those that occurred at the end of the Korean and Vietnam conflicts. Following the Korean War, an average of 250,000 troops was discharged annually for three years. After the Vietnam War, the annual rate of discharges averaged 230,000 for six years. There are, however, important differences.

Today's military has a much higher proportion of career people— 53 percent of enlisted personnel have four or more years of service compared with 39 percent in 1974; the rest were draftees or short-termers. Under the voluntary military, unlike the previous cutbacks, there is no large pool of draftees anxious to return to civilian life. On the other hand, much of the expansion in active duty forces in 1990– 1991 has been met by calling up members of the reserves, who look forward to returning to civilian life.

The military establishment will be facing a very different challenge with the settlement of the Persian Gulf crisis. In the words of Brookings Institution military manpower expert Martin Binkins, "For the last forty-something years, we were worried about how do you get people into the military; now we're worried about how to get them out."[19] After all, many of those now serving in the armed forces were actively enticed with promises of exciting, rewarding careers. Thus, reducing the number of personnel already in the military could involve both involuntary separation of substantial numbers of people and damage to the morale of those remaining.

There are many directions military manpower policy can take. For example, if the Department of Defense reduces the size of its active-duty force by 115,000 a year and does so in a balanced way that includes fewer new recruits along with decreases in those already in the military, then no more than 20,000 involuntary separations of enlisted personnel might be necessary.

The challenge involves far more than numbers. It is widely believed that high-quality troops are the most enduring benefit of the military buildup of the 1980s. A badly handled reduction in force could substantially damage that capability. Thus the military must remain an attractive career option. Otherwise, the armed services will not be able to recruit and keep the smaller but still absolutely large numbers of quality people they need.

Aside from being painful to carry out, involuntary separations might entail separation payments. Such outlays would offset, at least in the short run, the budgetary savings from the overall cutback in military manpower.

Alternatively, the Pentagon could reduce active-duty personnel mainly by cutting back on the number of new recruits. The turnover in the military is approximately 300,000 a year. This means that large cuts could be accomplished just by recruiting fewer people. Over the long run, however, this approach might leave the defense establishment with an insufficient flow of recruits to support even a significantly smaller military; for now it has the advantage of avoiding much of the problem and cost involved in involuntary separations.

Moreover, relying mainly on a smaller pool of recruits can result in upgrading the quality of those taken in at most military stations. A high school diploma is now mandatory and a score in the top half of the military's entrance test is almost essential for acceptance.[20]

Emphasizing reductions in the number of new entrants into the military would also lead to an even older force. Moreover, this approach imposes the greatest disruption on individuals who depend on the military for entry-level employment. This would particularly affect minorities who make up a disproportionately large number of military recruits. For example, the army (where the force reductions are the largest) reports that 30 percent of the enlisted soldiers are black, as is a majority of the combat noncommissioned officers.[21] The sensible objective is to get accession rates balanced at a level that will support the long-range size and composition of what the military will be. According to current planning (which is always subject to change), the Department of Defense will be reducing the size of its military strength by over 250,000, from a total of 2.1 million, over the five-year period 1990–1994. This decrease is scheduled to be accomplished by culling 135,000 troops from the army's force of 770,000 and 100,000 from the air force's roster of 571,000. The remaining modest reductions would be made in the navy.[22] In addition, the number of people in the reserves is slated to drop from 1.7 million in 1989 to less than 1.2 million in 1991.[23]

Incentives for Early Discharge
Five different approaches, of varying effectiveness, have been suggested to attain planned reductions in the size of the U.S. armed

forces. The first is to control enlistments and to reduce the length of the initial enlistment period to, say, two years. The army has lowered its annual recruitment goal from 119,000 to 97,400. The air force's quota dropped from 43,450 to 36,000. This step, although helpful, means relying mainly on attrition to achieve the smaller size of the armed forces. In 1990, the army closed ROTC units at eleven colleges and scheduled fifty more terminations in order to reduce the number of graduating cadets (and prospective second lieutenants) from 7,800 to 6,000 a year.

The second approach is to deny reenlistment for a greater number of enlisted personnel. The negative effects can be eased by instituting severance pay, now limited to officers. A frequently made proposal is to provide this benefit to enlisted personnel who have completed at least five years of active duty (the payments would equal 10 percent of basic pay multiplied by years of service).[24] A more drastic variant is to break some existing enlistment contracts, a step the military is reluctant to take. This approach would be interpreted widely as breaking faith with those officers and enlisted men who made a career commitment to military service.

A third alternative is to allow military personnel to quit the military earlier than they can under current regulations. For example, junior officers on an initial five-year commitment could be permitted to leave one year early if they decide that a military career is not for them. This privilege would not be extended to those in occupations in which the military establishment is habitually shorthanded, such as physicians and pilots. The air force has been experimenting with a "voluntary early out" program for enlisted personnel who are approaching the end of their enlistment periods. In the fall of 1989, that service allowed more than 10,000 first-term airmen to return to civilian life one to eight months early.[25]

A fourth approach is to induce midlevel officers to resign by removing the limit of $30,000 on severance pay for those who have served at least seven years. Under the current formula, officers who are passed over for promotion—and are short of the twenty years required for retirement pay—receive two months' pay for every year of service after at least five years of duty. This new benefit could apply to officers volunteering to quit (again except for key occupations) as well as those passed over.

Yet another response is to increase the power of the Selective Early Retirement Boards that pass on officers in the middle ranks. This is a power that the military services are very reluctant to use. Instead of the current practice of reviewing individual candidates every five years, the Board could rule on them more frequently. Those selected could be eligible to retire after two years in their rank, instead of three years, as at present.[26] In a variation of that approach, the Pentagon has asked Congress to let it demote designated categories of officers to enlisted status if they refuse a transfer from active duty to the reserves.

Given the long-term need for ensuring the national security, it would seem most advisable to rely on reasonable variations of the approaches that focus on voluntary actions, notably attrition and more selective recruitment. This means not pushing any one method to an extreme. In contrast, resorting to the seemingly simple but harsh approach of merely forcing out excess numbers of otherwise good military people would break faith with the men and women who have honorably served in the armed services and who want to make a career out of military service.[27]

Shrinking the size of the reserve units is a less onerous task than dealing with active-duty reductions. Almost all reservists have civilian jobs, so the Department of Defense does not have to worry so much about inflicting economic hardship on those that are eliminated. The easiest way to trim the reserve forces is to limit eligibility to join, perhaps by allowing only those who have come through the active force to enter.[28] The immediate effect on the morale of the remaining reservists is bound to be negative, however.

Safety Net for Those in the Military

For those who leave the armed forces, the Department of Veterans Affairs (VA) provides a safety net that aids in their adjustment process into the civilian work force. The VA shares this responsibility with the Department of Labor through the veterans' employment services by providing direction to state employment services with respect to veterans. This instruction includes assessment, outreach, employability training, counseling, testing, job placement, and follow-up for veterans who are out of work.

Under current law, anyone who leaves the military, voluntarily or involuntarily, is eligible for thirteen weeks of unemployment compensation after a four-week waiting period. Several members of Congress have introduced bills to extend these benefits to twenty-six weeks for those ex-servicepeople who do not receive severance pay.[29]

In addition to the state employment services, the VA provides local veterans' employment representatives. These individuals assist veterans seeking employment in job development and placement. The Labor Department's Labor–Management Services Administration provides veterans, reservists, and National Guardsmen on training duty with assistance in securing reinstatement and other employment advantages with their preservice employers.

A three-day job counseling seminar, the Transition Assistance Program, is now available in ten states on a test basis. This Labor Department–sponsored program includes training in resume writing, job interviewing, and tips on conducting a job search. These minicourses are available to members of the armed forces within 180 days of separation or retirement. The Congress is considering proposals to give involuntarily separated service personnel preference for federal jobs over other veterans.[30]

The peacetime "G.I. Bill" currently provides education benefits to enlisted men and selected reserves who leave the military after fulfilling their obligation. Under this program, those entering active duty or the reserves may contribute $100 a month from their pay for the first twelve months of service. When discharged, those who serve in the military receive up to $10,800 over a period of twenty-six months to cover study at an institution of higher learning, a noncollege degree program, apprenticeship/on-job instruction, or correspondence training. Those who were in the selected reserves receive up to $5,040 spread out over thirty-six months, but do not contribute their own money to the program's fund.

As of 1988, approximately 75 percent of all eligible service personnel were enrolling in the peacetime G.I. Bill. Of those serving in the selected reserves, 35 percent were participating. The great majority was already enrolled in an institution of higher learning.[31]

Whatever the status of the civilian labor market facing those leaving the armed forces, the shortage of high school math and science teachers is chronic. As it turns out, many of those serving in the armed forces receive extensive training in mathematics, science, and related technical subjects. Moreover, the all-volunteer military has attracted many minority members—especially men—who are in especially short supply in high school teaching staffs.

Ex-service personnel with college degrees (mainly officers) might be able to move quickly into teaching under alternative certification programs already in twenty-two states. Such programs often grant temporary teaching certificates and allow people switching careers to earn permanent certificates as they teach. The army conducts pilot programs in math and science in cooperation with community colleges and universities near military bases.[32]

There is a spectrum of benefits and services available to people hurt by defense cutbacks. The specifics vary according to whether the individuals involved were in the armed forces or had worked for defense contractors. The major "benefit," in most cases, however, is an expanding economy that generates alternative employment possibilities. From the viewpoint of society as a whole, displaced defense workers are a valuable resource. These workers have above-average skills and experience, which means they could make a significant contribution toward American productivity in the private sector.[33]

NOTES

1. Joseph V. Cartwright, *Potential Defense Work Force Dislocations and U.S. Defense Budget Cuts* (Washington, D.C.: U.S. Department of Defense Office of Economic Adjustment, 1990), p. 2.

2. *BLS Reports on Mass Layoffs in 1989* (Washington, D.C.: U.S. Department of Labor, 1990), p. 1.

3. Cartwright, *Defense Dislocations*.

4. Alice M. Rivlin, et al., *Economic Choices 1984* (Washington, D.C.: Brookings Institution, 1984), pp. 128–29.

5. Ibid., p. 141.

6. Ibid., pp. 142–43.

7. Ibid., p. 147.

8. Leslie Fishman, et al., *Reemployment Experiences of Defense Workers*, Prepared for U.S. Arms Control and Disarmament Agency (Washington, D.C.: U.S. Government Printing Office, 1968).

9. Virginia Lopez, "The Economics of 1990 and the Aerospace Worker," *AIA Newsletter*, August/September 1990, p. 5.

10. Michael Kelly, "Sticking to Its Guns," *Business Month*, June 1990, pp. 58–61; Tracy E. Benson, "Outplacement Does an About-Face," *Industry Week*, June 4, 1990, pp. 15–18.

11. "Grumman Plan on Retirement," *The New York Times*, June 6, 1990, p. 19.

12. *Rethinking Employment Security* (New York: Conference Board, 1990), p. 9.

13. John R. Oravec, "Unions Cope With Defense Layoffs," *AFL-CIO News*, June 25, 1990, pp. 1, 4.

14. Ruth H. Federau, "Responses to Plant Closures and Major Reductions in Force," *Annals of the American Academy of Political and Social Science*, September 1984, pp. 80–95.

15. *A Guide to Advance Notice of Closings and Layoffs* (Washington, D.C.: U.S. Department of Labor, 1989), p. 2.

16. C. Emily Feistritzer, "Break the Teaching Monopoly," *The Wall Street Journal*, June 29, 1990, p. A10.

17. *Summary of the Economic Effects of Reduced Defense Spending* (Washington, D.C.: U.S. Congressional Budget Office, 1990), pp. 14–15.

18. Molly Moore, "A Little Slow Getting Off the Starting Block," *Washington Post Weekly*, June 25, 1990, p. 31.

19. Quoted in David C. Morrison, "Painful Separation," *National Journal*, March 1990, p. 768.

20. Peter Applebome, "As Armed Forces Cut Back, Some Lose a Way Up in Life," *The New York Times*, May 7, 1990, p. C10.

21. David K. Carlisle, "As the Army Cuts Back . . . ," *The New York Times*, July 4, 1990, p. 26.

22. Rowan Scarborough, "GIs Might Get a Bonus to Quit," *Insight*, March 12, 1990, p. 20.

23. Peter Grier, "Shaving the Force," *Government Executive*, April 1990, p. 37.

24. "Severance Benefit Plans Compared," *Army Times*, July 9, 1990, p. 8.

25. Morrison, "Painful Separation," p. 770.

26. Scarborough, "GIs Might Get Bonus," p. 30.

27. *Meeting New National Security Needs* (Washington, D.C.: Congressional Budget Office, 1990).

28. Grier, "Shaving the Force," p. 30.

29. "Severance Benefit Plans," *Army Times*, p. 8.

30. Ibid., p. 9.

31. U.S. Congress, House of Representatives Subcommittee on Military Personnel and Compensation, *The G.I. Bill* (Washington, D.C.: Government Printing Office, 1989), p. 40.

32. Susan Chira, "As Army Cuts Back, Schools May Recruit Soldiers as Teachers," *The New York Times*, July 27, 1990, p. 1 et ff.

33. Yolanda K. Henderson, "Defense Cutbacks and the New England Economy," *New England Economic Review*, July/August 1990, pp. 3–24.

CHAPTER 5

Refocusing Military Research and Development

Military research and development (R&D) is being buffeted by several conflicting forces. The effort to reduce the federal budget deficit means downward pressure on the funds available for military R&D. The concern with promoting American competitiveness results in proposals to shift the focus of the Pentagon's R&D to civilian needs. The cost overruns in many weapon systems lead to more government red tape for the companies developing new military equipment. The success of the new, high-tech weapons in the Persian Gulf conflict, however, points up the importance of military R&D to the U.S. military arsenal and seems to vindicate the major R&D contractors.

How should public policy respond to this multiplicity of issues? Should the massive ($40 billion a year) military R&D effort be cut back along with the rest of the federal budget? Should the funds previously devoted to military R&D be shifted to a civilian agency? Should military decision makers factor in the simultaneous slowdown in outlays for civilian R&D in the United States? In short, setting R&D policy means assessing the proper role of the government in the economy.[1]

In this context, it is important to have some perspective on developments in military R&D and its relation to the civilian sector. For much of the period since the end of World War II, the scientific and technological efforts of the U.S. military establishment have set the pace for the American economy. The Department of Defense has been a major financier of R&D as well as the largest purchaser and developer of new scientific applications. In the absence of an explicit federal technology policy, the practices of the Pentagon became, to a very large extent, the de facto U.S. technology policy.[2]

Past spin-offs from military technology include computers, jet airliners, composite materials, communications equipment, and scientific instruments. For decades, many companies primarily oriented to

89

civilian markets benefited from commercial use of "spin-offs" of high-powered defense research and development.

Indeed, for much of the period since the end of World War II, a major attraction of defense contracts for commercial firms was to get abreast of the latest developments in military science and technology. The Raytheon Company adapted radar technology to develop the microwave oven (first called the "Radarange"). Boeing drew on its military aircraft design work on the B-47 and KC-135 in developing the 707 commercial airliner, although the 707 and the KC-135 were both descended from a common company-sponsored prototype (the "dash 80").

SPIN OFF OR SPIN ON?

Over the past decade, the relationship between military and civilian R&D has changed very substantially. In every year since 1981, private sponsorship and funding of R&D has exceeded the total of the federal government, both civilian and military.[3] In fact, the roles of the public and private sectors often have been reversed in the military sphere itself. If a technology has both civilian and military use, its cutting edge today is more likely to be seen in Radio Shack products than in military systems.

Dr. William Perry, former undersecretary of defense, cites the example of semiconductors, where the differences between defense and commercial technologies are not very great. Extremely detailed military specifications have isolated defense production, dividing the U.S. industrial base between defense and commercial uses. Perry believes that, due to the rigidity of military specifications and requirements, chips made for the Defense Department are ten times more expensive and nearly two generations behind their commercial counterparts.[4]

Many currently deployed systems use technologies dating to the 1970s or earlier. An acquisition process requiring as much as twenty years to move a major weapon system from R&D to deployment—such as characterizes U.S. military procurement—increases costs and limits technological innovation. The drawn-out development process also reduces the return on contractor-financed investments in defense R&D and thus curbs the incentives for such undertakings.[5]

The ability of the armed services to develop advanced weaponry now increasingly depends on how well they and their contractors can "spin-on" civilian advances to military products. Current military research in electronics, for example, is so esoteric and slow that it offers little commercial use. The tables have turned. The Department of Defense has become a net user of civilian research.[6]

The B-2 Stealth bomber and the Seawolf submarine both have computer chips in key components that are merely run-of-the-mill, rather than the latest state-of-the-art. The design of electronic parts in these weapons had to be frozen years ago in order to meet the requirements of the lengthy military production cycle. Since then, however, the civilian computer industry has continued to innovate at a rapid pace.

Many barriers impede the transfer of advanced technology from the civilian economy to the military establishment. The military acquisition process has become increasingly cumbersome, costly, and onerous (see Chapter 8). To prevent their civilian-oriented divisions from becoming "contaminated" by the military's bureaucratic approach, many companies selling to the armed services go out of their way to make sure the military's special accounting, auditing, and personnel requirements do not apply to the rest of the company. In the case of computer software, the Department of Defense has set up a standard for weapons, committing to use of software written in its Ada computer language whenever possible. As a consequence, the software industry is increasingly being divided into separate civilian and military sectors, and innovations in one sector are not quickly transferred to the other.

CIVILIAN VERSUS MILITARY R&D

There is a school of thought that maintains that the Pentagon has hogged the nation's R&D resources, luring scientists and engineers away from civilian work (see Chapter 6). Suffice it here to note that the civilian appetite for R&D seems to be quite satiable. Why else would so many conversion advocates have to argue vehemently that new federal funding forcefeed the shift of defense scientists and engineers to civilian pursuits?

It is useful to note that federal decision makers rarely make conscious decisions to finance R&D activities, aside from comparatively modest support of basic research. Most R&D outlays result from spending money on specific program areas.

Thus, the really large governmental outlays for science and technology flow from decisions to strengthen the national defense, promote energy independence, seek cures for diseases, and explore outer space. The entire budget of the National Science Foundation—the one agency devoted to promoting R&D per se—is less than 3 percent of total federal outlays for R&D.

As can be seen in Table 5-1, the R&D intensity of individual federal activities varies greatly. NASA devotes more than 52 percent of its budget to research and development, while less than 1 percent of the outlays of the Department of Veterans Affairs goes to science and

Table 5-1   Federal Agency R&D and Total Outlays in 1988

Department or Agency	R&D Outlays (in $billions)	Total Outlays (in $billions)	R&D Percentage of Total
Above-average R&D Ratios			
National Science Foundation	1.5	1.9	78.9
NASA	4.8	9.1	52.7
Energy Department	5.1	10.5	48.6
Commerce Department	0.4	2.5	16.0
Defense Department	36.5	299.6	12.2
Interior Department	0.4	5.4	7.4
Environmental Protection Agency	0.4	4.9	8.2
Below-average R&D Ratios			
Agriculture Department	1.0	50.7	2.0
Health and Human Services Department	7.1	375.1	1.9
Transportation Department	0.3	26.3	1.1
Veterans Affairs Department	0.2	27.6	0.7
Agency for International Development	0.1	5.2	0.2
All other	0.7	237.1	0.3
Total, Federal Government	58.5	1,055.9	5.5

Source: Compiled from data prepared by the U.S. National Science Foundation and the Office of Management and Budget.

technology. Similarly, more than 48 percent of the Energy Department's budget is allocated to R&D and 2 percent in the case of the Department of Agriculture.

The implications of these differences can be profound. A shift in budgetary priorities from Defense or NASA to Agriculture or from Energy to Veterans represents a de facto (though most likely unintended) decision for the federal government to spend less on R&D and more on other activities. Unfortunately, the policy implications of such changes in priorities have not received the attention they deserve. For example, a decision to increase the share of the federal budget devoted to entitlements is in effect a vote to downgrade the role of R&D.

The United States is increasingly reliant on the fruits of scientific and technological activity for its basic strength, both military and economic. We maintain our military posture not by having the largest army or navy or air force, but by having the most technically sophisticated up-to-date arsenal of weapons.

Similarly, high-tech companies tend to generate a favorable balance of trade, while the low-tech companies have suffered most severely from foreign competition. The R&D-intensive industries also experience greater increases in productivity than do the less-R&D-intensive

areas. Clearly, outlays for science and technology are a key to the continuation of both the military and the economic power of the United States.[7] This is not a justification for increasing federal spending, but for shifting its composition away from the current dominance of transfer payments (entitlements) and other consumption-oriented outlays—and toward R&D and other investment-oriented categories that can help to spur the rate of American economic progress.

TRANSFERRING CIVILIAN R&D

At the margin, some regulatory changes can help. Because American technology is increasingly oriented to civilian needs, federal acquisition regulations should be modified to encourage, or at least permit, the defense establishment to economize on its spending by drawing more on commercial product developments. Of course, that is much easier said than done.

The people in the Pentagon who make a career out of writing military specifications can be expected to object to any attempt to buy more off-the-shelf commercial products, whether they provide the Defense Department with superior technology or not. Such a shift in government purchasing on a large scale would put many regulation writers and acquisition reviewers out of work.

Also, "Buy American" provisions of the federal procurement laws inhibit purchasing from the open market, as will be discussed in Chapter 8. Officials responsible for acquisition must carefully check whether any one of the numerous components of a product contains a single forbidden foreign element. Other obstacles to buying more off-the-shelf commercial products include the rules on steering a certain percentage of procurement to small, handicapped, and minority firms and the onerous "do-it-by-the-numbers" provisions of the Competition in Contracting Act.[8]

DARPA's "Spin On" Civilian Technology

Some suggestions for utilizing the results of civilian R&D for military applications would have the Department of Defense directly subsidize civilian technology, both to generate more opportunity for "spin on" to military needs and to foster a higher rate of civilian R&D per se. Proponents of such subsidies focus on the Defense Advanced Research Projects Agency (DARPA), which they look to for support of research in semiconductors, high-density television, and similar high-tech areas.

Little-known and small in size by Washington, D.C., standards, DARPA awards contracts totalling over $1 billion each year to more than 300 corporations and universities to conduct high-risk research. Over the past thirty years, DARPA-funded projects have led to the development and commercialization of computer time-sharing, advanced aeronautics, new types of software, and new telecommunications procedures.

Created in 1958 in response to the Soviet launch of its pioneering *Sputnik* space satellite, DARPA tries to focus on generating radically new approaches to weapon system technology. While its primary goal is to lower the cost and raise the effectiveness of weapon systems, the agency is also concerned with the long-term health of domestic suppliers to the military, particularly firms in the electronics industry. DARPA projects include x-ray lithography, a sophisticated manufacturing technology that will be needed to make semiconductors later this decade, and a manufacturing technology program. The latter is intended to develop robots and other computer-assisted equipment.

DARPA is already financing private sector R&D in a variety of areas—superconductivity, advanced semiconductors, high-definition television, and very sophisticated types of integrated circuits. While DARPA justifies its sponsorship of these projects because of their expected relevance to military missions, many of the technologies being developed are expected to help American industries compete in commercial markets. About half of DARPA's budget is currently allocated to dual-use technologies that have both civilian and military applications.[9]

One of the most dramatic examples of DARPA's role is the financial backing it offered several Stanford University computer scientists to set up private companies. Three of the resulting firms—Sun Microsystems, MIPS Computer Systems, and Silicon Graphics—currently employ about 12,000 people and have combined annual sales of over $2 billion. DARPA, however, has also had its share of flops. After spending $200 million, it closed the books on an experimental helicopter-airplane. Another project that fell short was a scheme to use artificial intelligence to guide a combat vehicle over rough terrain.[10]

Some compare DARPA with the Japanese Ministry of International Trade and Industry (MITI), but MITI is a cabinet-level agency officially charged with the broader mission of enhancing the nation's international competitiveness. While DARPA operates with a much more narrow mandate, its 150 research projects still support nearly half of all U.S. graduate students in computer science and a large percentage of those in other key technical disciplines.[11]

DARPA provides $100 million a year for Sematech, the industry–government consortium for design and fabrication of new semiconductor chips. Until recent budget cuts, the agency also planned to award at least $30 million a year to develop technologies related to high-definition television (HDTV), which provides sharper pictures, thus finer detail that could be used in information displays on military aircraft and ships and in intelligence and training systems. DARPA claims that the military has a need for HDTV screens, but its support would also make U.S. electronics companies more competitive.

It is difficult to truly separate the military from the civilian justifications for this federal support of what is fundamentally an industrial undertaking. One argument for military subsidy of HDTV is that a successful commercial industry in the United States would generate high volumes of production and thus lower unit costs for both military and civilian customers. Of course, this argument would enable the Pentagon to get involved in virtually every new industry—and in many old ones as well.

Moreover, it is natural for corporate executives to be interested in federal undertakings that transfer much of the cost and risk of new commercial technology ventures to the U.S. Treasury, while they retain all of the profit potential. In contrast, private investors in new technology expect to share both the risk and the financial rewards. Thus, the prospect that federal "venture capital" (via R&D support) might become available reduces the likelihood of private investors risking their own funds.[12] Many people like to play variations of the "heads I win, tails you lose" game.

Given DARPA's record of success in cutting through the normal bureaucratic obstacles, some government and industry officials would like to give it greater responsibility in the development of high-tech industry generally. The agency is opposed, noting that there would be the danger of having to build the customary administrative bureaucracy, thereby losing its effectiveness.[13] Nevertheless, in late 1989 Congress granted DARPA the authority it requested to make outright investments—in addition to awarding specific R&D contracts—in companies doing defense-related research. In 1990, the agency used that authority to make a controversial $4 million venture capital investment in Gazelle Microcircuits, Inc., a young Silicon Valley company. Under its agreement with Gazelle, DARPA has a choice of taking royalties on products developed over a fifteen-year period, or owning 9 percent of the company's stock.

This unusual outlay by the Department of Defense enables Gazelle to avoid selling its advanced technology to a foreign company to raise money. DARPA specifically has a say in preventing Gazelle from selling itself or its technology to a foreign company. If either is likely, DARPA can arrange for a domestic buyer or get its investment back, which would pose a deterrent to any prospective purchaser.[14] DARPA can subsequently use any profits from this venture for similar investments in other companies without additional congressional approval. One by-product of the Gazelle investment was the ouster of the head of DARPA, presumably to underscore the Bush administration's opposition to such an extraordinary departure into "industrial policy."[15]

Table 5-2 International Cooperative Projects Involving U.S. Defense Contractors

Companies and Country	Product
McDonnell Douglas, U.S. Daicel, Japan	F-15 aircraft assemblies co-production
Bendix, U.S. IHH Industries, Japan	Parts for T-56 engine, P-3C aircraft
Teledyne Ryan, U.S. Mitsubishi, Japan	AN/APN-217 doppler navigation set co-production
Honeywell, U.S. Japan Aviation Electronics, Inc.	HDC-301 computers co-production
LTV, U.S. Various European partners	Co-development and marketing of multiple launch rocket system
General Dynamics, U.S. Turkish Aircraft Industries	Co-production of F-16
Raytheon, U.S. MBB, Germany Siemens, AEG Telefunken, Germany Fokker, Netherlands	Co-production of Patriot surface-to-air missile system
Rockwell International, U.S. Garrett, U.S. Promavia, Belgium	Joint venture to offer jet squalus basic trainer to USAF
Honeywell, U.S. NEC, Japan	DPS 90 computer co-production
Seven multinational contractor teams headed by: LTV, U.S.; MBB, Germany; RCA Corp., U.S.; CoSyDe, France; Hughes Aircraft, U.S.; Lockheed, U.S.; and SNIA BPD, Italy	Architecture studies for Phase I theater ballistic missile defense, Strategic Defense Initiative
Rockwell International, U.S. General Electric, U.K.	Joint venture to bid on naval communications system for U.S. warships
United Technologies, U.S. Rolls-Royce, U.K. Turbomeca, France	Co-development of RTM 322 engines for helicopters
Loral, U.S. Elbit Computers, Israel	Joint venture to manufacture and market advanced defense electronic systems
McDonnell Douglas, U.S. British Aerospace, U.K.	Co-production of British-designed Harrier II (AV-8B)
GTE, U.S. Thompson-CSF, France	Partnership on French-designed U.S. Army communications system
Westinghouse, U.S. Plessey, U.K.	Joint R&D of dual band airborne early warning system and partnership on design of radar for E-3A AWACS for Royal Air Force

Table 5-2 (*Continued*)

Companies and Country	Product
Hughes Aircraft, U.S. Renault Vehicles Industriels, France	Hughes technical assistance in adapting U.S. TOW antitank missile to French VAB armored vehicles
Teledyne, U.S. Microturbo, France	Joint venture to bid on propulsion system for NATO modular standoff weapon
Hughes Aircraft, U.S. MBB, Germany SMI Aerospatiale, France	Joint venture to propose derivatives of Roland missile system for U.S. Army's forward area air defense, line-of-sight program

Source: Author's analysis.

Lewis Branscomb, director of the Science Technology and Public Policy Program at Harvard, warns against using the military budget to support private sector technology. Defense R&D, he says, tends to be too slow, too centralized, and too micromanaged to be transferred successfully to the private sector. Defense researchers tend to be too far removed from commercial markets to have much impact.[16]

A more fundamental objection to giving the Department of Defense—rather than the marketplace—the power to choose which technologies and which firms will receive funds is that it will politicize the process. Claude Barfield of the American Enterprise Institute believes that such has been the case with DARPA:

> DOD has increasingly supported industrial policy and technology commercialization proposals that it has little competence to evaluate and that often merely advance the goal of special interests to raid the public treasury.[17]

As for the argument that the United States is becoming too dependent on foreign technology, the fact is that American firms—civilian and military—exist in an increasingly global marketplace. Many defense contractors have entered into cooperative projects with companies overseas. LTV is co-developing and marketing with European partners a multiple launch rocket system. Rockwell International and Garrett are teaming up with Promavia of Belgium to offer a basic trainer to the U.S. Air Force. Three major aircraft engine producers (United Technologies in the United States, Turbomeca in France, and Rolls-Royce in the United Kingdom) are jointly developing a new engine for helicopters (see Table 5-2 for these and other examples).

Other developments in the global economy muddy the water further still. Are IBM Japan and Fuji Xerox American firms? What about

Sony America and Honda USA? The very notion of a national company is undergoing a fundamental transformation.

The National Advisory Committee on Semiconductors laments the fact that the Japanese semiconductor industry is far outpacing the U.S. industry in capital investments in the future—and therefore urges the federal government to come to the industry's assistance. The committee admits, however, that the Japanese companies got their lead by investing more heavily than did their American counterparts at a time when U.S. firms were outselling their Japanese counterparts—and therefore could have afforded to stay ahead of the foreign competition.[18] The shortsightedness of the American companies directly led to the current situation.

Subsidizing R&D

Past experience in government-subsidized R&D includes such ventures as the billions of dollars wasted in the abortive attempt to develop a commercial synthetic fuels industry to reduce U.S. dependence on imported energy.[19] The basic failure of "industrial policy" efforts extends back to the days of the Reconstruction Finance Corporation scandals in the 1950s. Our national experience demonstrates that the older companies by dint of their years of support of political candidates, have greater clout in government than do the newer growth industries. The "sickies" also have more incentive to devote time and effort in the political arena than do healthy companies.

We need go no further than the Corps of Army Engineers for an illustration of this. The Corps' military functions are first rate. In contrast, its civilian dam building is embroiled in politics and generates numerous projects with little economic justification. The Corps' sorry record of generating "pork" for powerful legislators is hardly a precedent to justify expanding the promotional role of the Department of Defense in the civilian economy.

Rather than having the Defense Department serve as an agency of industrial policy, some analysts have urged a strengthened Department of Commerce that would invest more heavily in developing the nation's technology base.[20] Indeed, in late 1988, the Congress expanded the staid old National Bureau of Standards into the National Institute of Standards and Technology (NIST). The expanded agency is gearing up to hand out to the private sector $10 million in seed money to develop high-tech proposals in areas ranging from fire prevention to HDTV. Current proposals being considered in Congress would raise NIST's subsidy kitty to $250 million a year by 1992.[21] That approach—where a federal agency determines which new areas of technology private companies can pursue—is only marginally better than giving the role to the Pentagon.

Congress' Office of Technology Assessment (OTA) has suggested creating a new civilian technology agency that could either be lodged in the Department of Commerce or kept independent. Reacting to the argument that the government should not try to steer technological development too directly, OTA says that the proposed civilian agency should consider entire technological systems rather than particular technology.[22] Nevertheless, in light of past experience, we should be concerned that R&D funding might be used as a subterfuge to enact an "industrial policy" for the United States.

To some extent the response of the supporters of more federal funding is to resort to verbiage. According to former Commerce Department counselor Wayne Berman, business executives do not want an industrial policy—"they want the government involved in high-risk, long-term, expensive, high-technology research projects."[23] Or, in the words of one academic supporter, "The government should not give handouts, but it should help strategically placed industries at strategic times."[24] Inevitably the political process, however, would decide which "high-risk, long-term," "strategic" industries and projects are to be selected. The lucky few chosen would, by definition, meet those subjective requirements; politically weak companies by default would not be "strategic" or "high-risk" or "long-term." The results would be indistinguishable from a federal spending program formally labeled "industrial policy."

The lessons of history yield a more positive approach, in particular the Japanese response in 1987–1988 to the rapidly rising yen in the world currency markets. On their own, Japanese companies took quick and tough actions to restore their global competitiveness. Within weeks or months of the change in the external financial environment, many of them adopted vigorous campaigns to improve productivity. Executives reduced their own salaries. Efforts were made to upgrade quality. Some manufacturing operations were quickly moved to lower-cost locations. MITI was not in the forefront of these necessary business adjustments to change.

There is an American counterpart to these actions. Since the mid-1980s, many U.S. companies have taken the painful actions necessary to reduce costs, raise productivity, and improve their competitiveness. Quality has become a key focal point. Moreover, counter to the general impression about the short-range orientation of American business, private sector outlays for R&D in the 1980s exceeded public sector expenditures for R&D.

INDEPENDENT RESEARCH AND DEVELOPMENT

While Congress debates the desirability of new subsidies to technology, another factor inhibiting the pace of technology in the defense sector is the increasing restriction on how much of the cost of contractor-initiated but defense-related R&D (usually referred to as IR&D—independent R&D) can be charged off on defense contracts. This is significant, since the major defense industries are truly the high-tech industries of America—electronics, aerospace, computers, motor vehicles, and chemicals, in that order. Companies in the first two categories are the major designers and producers of aircraft, missiles, and space vehicles, and the firms in the next two groupings provide components or other important weapons, such as tanks.

The regulation of IR&D started with the Vinson-Trammell Act of 1934, which limited the profits on naval vessels and aircraft to 10 percent of the total contract price.[25] This restriction, defined in practice as a percentage of costs, demanded a definition of acceptable costs. The pertinent Treasury regulation (Decision 5000) identified the indirect R&D cost items that would be recognized by the government, including a reasonable portion of "general experimental and development expenses," indirect engineering expenses, and "bidding and general selling expenses."

The positive aspect of Vinson-Trammell was that defense-related R&D and proposal preparation costs were recognized as legitimate expenses chargeable to defense contracts. The negative aspect was that the government would decide which specific items would qualify.

The requirement to define acceptable costs was extended by the World War II "excess profits" tax and the pricing of military contracts. That general requirement continues, but after World War II the Armed Services Procurement Regulation was rewritten to restrict allowable R&D to those costs specifically related to the items covered by the contract. General research expenses not provided for in the contract were disallowed, even if they were motivated by the desire to design new or improved products for the military market.

Many defense contractors responded by insisting on including IR&D costs as a condition of doing business with the government.[26] A basic compromise was reached that, with major modifications, is still operative. The military continues to fund a major portion of IR&D costs, but only after considerable review and regulation. The Department of Defense now reimburses contractors, on average, for only about 40 percent of the independent R&D that they do.[27] The sums involved are hardly trivial. In 1983, major defense contractors spent approximately $4 billion on IR&D, almost one-tenth of total company-funded R&D reported by the National Science Foundation that year.[28] One disturbing aspect is that the Department of Defense is reimbursing a larger portion of contractor bid and proposal costs than of independently sponsored R&D. Rather than encouraging high-risk innovation, the current reimbursement policy fosters more sophisticated marketing.[29]

The incentive effects of the government's R&D policy should not be ignored. On the basis of a detailed analysis of defense company practices, a team of RAND Corporation researchers concluded that, over a period of several years, the typical firm spends an additional dollar of its own funds for IR&D in response to a dollar of increased government support. They found evidence that a firm's IR&D projects are more diverse, less conservative, and further from a company's main lines of business than they would be if the companies had to pay the full cost of their R&D. The IR&D process also promotes the movement of technologies into new defense capabilities.[30]

Most studies of the social returns of industrial R&D conclude that they far outweigh the private returns and the returns to other uses of capital. Table 5-3 contains a representative listing of IR&D programs of major contractors. They constitute an impressive array of advances

Table 5-3 Independent Research and Development by Defense Contractors

Company	Project	Benefit to Military
Boeing	Reduce vibration in helicopters	Reduces helicopter damage and increases crew productivity
General Dynamics	Develop fly-by-wire control system	Incorporated into F-16 aircraft
General Electric	Do research on jet engines	Used in propulsion systems for F-14, F-16 and FA-18 aircraft
General Motors	Digital electronic control for small turboshaft engines	Creates operational reliability and reduces unscheduled maintenance
Honeywell	Advances in radar altimeter	Reduces size, weight and power requirements
McDonnell Douglas	Advance technology for using engine exhaust to provide extra lift	Incorporated in C-17 transport to minimize takeoff and landing distances
Rockwell International	Reduce observability of B-1B to enemy radars	Creates ability of B-1B to penetrate enemy defenses
Textron	Stronger and lighter composite materials	Improves aircraft performance
TRW	Improve rocket engine performance	Increases range of Tomahawk missile by 10–20 percent
Westinghouse	Improve high performance radar	Lowers cost and increases maintainability and reliability of radar

Source: National Benefits of IR&D (Washington, D.C.: Aerospace Industries Association, 1988).

in defense-related technology, ranging from reducing helicopter damage to enhancing the reliability of radar.

According to RAND researchers, however, IR&D should not be viewed as a private entitlement program exempt from normal public-sector decision-making practices. Given the nature of budget restraints, the basic question is how much reduction of present procurement are we willing to trade for future capabilities and a broader technology decision base. It really means creating a balance between today and tomorrow.[31] A study for the National Bureau of Economic Research estimates that the subsidy value of IR&D exceeds that of the R&D tax credit, so the funds provided are quite substantial.[32]

At a time when a peace dividend is envisioned by many civilian beneficiaries of government spending, military IR&D is an inviting target for budget cutters. Budget decision makers, however, need to take into account the likelihood that policies that decrease government support for IR&D also will reduce industry R&D expenditures—and also induce firms to leave the defense market.

More technical policy changes (which are urged for other purposes) could reinforce the downward pressures on military R&D. For example, eliminating contractors' proprietary rights to data, as some have urged, would reduce the amount and quality of work performed under IR&D; if contractors are denied the opportunity to profit from the results, they will likely do less of it. Department of Defense negotiators perceive that this is already happening. In many ways, IR&D cost recovery does resemble the tax credit for R&D, which is another government effort to promote industrial R&D. The tax credit does not involve any government ownership of the results.[33] The companies receiving the R&D tax credit keep all proprietary rights to the research that they perform—and nobody has questioned that practice.

SOME POLICY CONCLUSIONS

There are many important tasks that only government can perform, ranging from ensuring the national security to providing a system of justice. The one thing, however, that the American political system cannot do well at all is to make critical choices between particular firms and competing technologies. Yet, whatever the military threat, technology will continue to be an important element in U.S. national security policy.

A far more satisfying response than massive subsidies to high-tech firms is to reduce existing obstacles. Some of those barriers involve outmoded thinking. The vice president for R&D in a large manufacturing company described the problem clearly: "Probably what is more important [than the amount of funding] is the quality of the research, the attitudes of the people that do it, and the direction in which it is aimed."[34]

American scientists also contend that, despite superior American achievements in science per se, Japanese firms are tough competitors because they assign more talent to such engineering activities as detailed product design and quality control. Scientist Lewis Branscomb reports that Japanese firms place their most talented engineers in production, unlike the U.S. practice.[35] The director of the computer science laboratory at M.I.T. adds, "We value creativity and innovativeness, and we don't value production . . . the money is not in invention, it's in production."[36]

In contrast, much of the Japanese product development is done in the factory where the product is produced rather than in a remote laboratory. Thus, Japanese firms often enjoy quicker responsiveness to market opportunities, lower costs, and equal or better quality than American manufacturers.

Many of the obstacles to commercializing technology have been erected by governmental policies in the tax and regulatory areas. Yet to offset that by using taxpayers' money to promote the well-being of any company or industry in the marketplace is fundamentally unfair to the companies that pay those taxes. Worse yet, such an approach is destined to turn any effort to promote competitiveness into another political pork barrel.

Those who are seriously concerned about developing public policy to encourage technological advancement would do well to focus on generating a policy environment that does more to foster innovation and competitiveness.

A good place to start is by cutting away the growing thicket of permits, restrictions, and other regulatory obstacles that delay any new undertaking, be it the sale of a new product or the building of a factory.[37]

The adverse impact of delay is greater than generally realized. McKinsey and Co. shows that high-tech products that come to market six months late but on budget earn 33 percent less profit over five years. In contrast, coming out on time and 50 percent over budget cuts profits only 4 percent.[38] The longer it takes for an innovation to be approved by a government agency—or the more costly the approval procedures—the less likely it is that the new product or process will be introduced. In any event, innovation will be delayed.

Reducing the regulatory burdens facing American companies would do far more to accelerate the pace of innovation in the United States than the customary array of subsidies to business (whatever their guise, be it "industrial policy," "competitiveness," or a new label).

There is one key area of science and technology support where government traditionally has been the major source of support. The federal government provides two-thirds of the funds for basic research. Virtually all economists agree that, because of "market failure" (the inability of the sponsoring firm to capture all of the benefits of the basic research it pays for), the private sector underinvests in this key segment of R&D.

The policy implication is clear. As military outlays for R&D decline, federal civilian support of basic research should rise. That should not be accomplished by giving the Pentagon new R&D responsibilities, even for such desirable areas as environmental research. The National Science Foundation, which is not tied to any single potential user, is the best available agency for the sponsorship and support of basic research. In contrast, applied R&D should continue primarily to be the province of the private sector. Some innovation in private R&D spending patterns would be helpful, especially in emphasizing the importance of technological improvements in the process of production.

Public policy has an important role to play, but as I have shown here (and elsewhere), that role is to eliminate or at least reduce the many obstacles that over the years government itself has unwittingly placed in the way of the advance of technology and its utilization.

NOTES

1. B. R. Inman and Daniel F. Burton, "Technology and Competitiveness: The New Policy Frontier," *Foreign Affairs*, Spring 1990, p. 117.

2. *Technology and Competitiveness* (New York: Japan Society, 1990), p. 17.

3. National Science Foundation, *Science Resources Studies Highlights*, April 27, 1990, p. 3.

4. *May 22, 1990 Task Force Minutes*, Task Force on Defense Spending, the Economy and the Nation's Security, Washington, D.C., p. 2.

5. Joseph F. Pilat and Paul C. White, "Technology and Strategy in a Changing World," *Washington Quarterly*, Spring 1990, p. 87; see also Peter Grier, "Pentagon Arms Suffer From High-Tech Gap," *Christian Science Monitor*, June 8, 1989, p. 7.

6. Jacques S. Gansler, *Affording Defense* (Cambridge: MIT Press, 1989), p. 91.

7. Murray Weidenbaum, "A Note on R&D Changing National Priorities," *Technology in Society*, Vol. II, 1989, pp. 331–34.

8. James Kitfield, "Buy More Off the Shelf," *Military Forum*, September 1989, p. 15.

9. Inman and Burton, "Technology and Competitiveness," p. 131.

10. Evelyn Richards, "Should Uncle Sam Be Technology's Godfather?" *Washington Post Weekly*, May 7, 1990, p. 71.

11. Ted Agres, "DARPA Bets on High-Risk R&D," *Research & Development*, November 1989, p. 42.

12. David G. Soergel, "Why Executives Loved DARPA's Craig Fields," *Insight*, June 18, 1990, pp. 5–6.

13. Ibid. For a less enthusiastic appraisal of the military use of DARPA research, see *Submarine Technology: Transition Plans Needed to Realize Gains From DOD Advanced Research* (Washington, D.C.: U.S. General Accounting Office, 1990).

14. Andrew Pollack, "Technology Company Gets $4 Million U.S. Investment," *The New York Times*, April 10, 1990, p. C15; Richard Danca, "DARPA Invests in GaAs Firm, Can Keep Profit," *Federal Computer Week*, April 16, 1990, p. 28 et ff.

15. Bob Davis, "Ouster of Defense Aid Craig Fields Sparks Discord, Congressional Criticism," *The Wall Street Journal*, April 23, 1990, p. A16.

16. Quoted in *Technology and Competitiveness*, p. 19.

17. Claude E. Barfield, "Should the Pentagon Play a Major Role in Supporting U.S. Industrial Competitiveness: CON?" *Challenges*, May 1989, p. 5.

18. *A Strategic Industry at Risk* (Washington, D.C.: U.S. National Advisory Committee on Semiconductors, 1989), p. 9.

19. *Synthetic Fuels: An Overview of DOE's Ownership and Divestiture of the Great Plains Project* (Washington, D.C.: U.S. General Accounting Office, 1989).

20. "Rethinking the Military's Role in the Economy," *Technology Review*, August/September 1989, p. 63.

21. Mark A. Kellner, "NIST to Fund Private High-Tech Projects," *Federal Computer Week*, April 23, 1990, p. 1.

22. Eduardo Lachica, "Panel Urges Civilian Technology Agency to Help U.S. Manufacturers Regain Edge," *The Wall Street Journal*, March 1, 1990, p. B4.

23. Quoted in Fred Barnes, "Bushwhacking," *Business Month*, January 1990, p. 71.

24. Gary H. Anthes, "Economist Supports Fed High-Tech Involvement," *Federal Computer Week*, February 19, 1990, p. 28.

25. 48 Stat. 505; 34 USC 496.

26. Arthur Alexander, Paul Hill, and Susan Bodilly, *The Defense Department's Support of Industry's Independent Research and Development* (Santa Monica, Calif.: RAND Corporation, 1989), p. 7.

27. Frank Lichtenberg, "The Private R&D Investment Response to Federal Design and Technical Competition," *American Economic Review*, June 1988, p. 551.

28. Ibid., p. 553.

29. C. D. Vollmer, "The Future Defense Industrial Environment," *Washington Quarterly*, Spring 1990, p. 95

30. Alexander, et al., *Defense Department Support*, p. vii.

31. Ibid., p. 41.

32. Frank Lichtenberg, *Government Subsidies to Private Military R and D In-*

vestment, Working Paper No. 2745 (Cambridge, Mass.: National Bureau of Economic Research, 1988).

33. Ibid., p. 93.

34. Quoted in Catherine Morrison, et al., *Keys to Competitiveness* (New York: Conference Board, 1988), p. 9.

35. Lewis M. Branscomb, *Toward a National Policy on Research and Development*, a paper presented to the Conference Board, New York City, October 8, 1987, p. 5.

36. Alan Murray and Urban C. Lehner, "What U.S. Scientists Discover, the Japanese Convert—Into Profit," *The Wall Street Journal*, June 25, 1990, p. A1.

37. Murray L. Weidenbaum, *Business, Government, and the Public*, Fourth Edition (Englewood Cliffs, N.J.: Prentice Hall, 1990), pp. 19–165.

38. Ashok Guptu and David Wilemen, "Accelerating the Development of Technology-Based New Products," *California Management Review*, Winter 1990, p. 25.

PART II

RUNNING
THE MILITARY
AT LOWER COST

CHAPTER 6

Reconciling Economics and the National Security

Fads and fashions are not limited to the retail sector of the economy. For years, many analysts bemoaned the heavy burden of military expenditures borne by the American economy. More recent events generated a wave of optimism in anticipation of a generous peace dividend that could be directed from military to "unmet" social needs. The pendulum seems to be swinging again. Some perspective is needed to temper any impending shift from gloom to euphoria—and perhaps back.

In 1987, Paul Kennedy of Yale warned that too large a proportion of a nation's resources allocated to military purposes likely would lead to "a weakening of national power over the longer run."[1] Former Senator J. William Fulbright seemed to believe that the United States had already attained that sad state. In early 1989, he wrote that the United States had "become a militarized economy."[2] By December 1989, Seymour Melman of Columbia University was renewing his perennial plea to convert a military establishment that was the reason the United States is "no longer a first-class industrial economy . . . "[3]

The doom peddlers always seem to have a field day, especially in competing for public attention. Yet, as James Schlesinger has noted, perhaps the United States should have done better in the period since World War II, "but we have not done all that badly."[4] The United States remains the leading economic, political, and military power in the world. In this spirit, a recent survey of Japanese views reported that "the United States is still a vital nation with unchallenged military power, the world's largest economy, an affluent lifestyle, and natural abundance that leaves resource-poor Japan in awe."[5]

The notion that the United States is in decline is at best (or at worst) only a relative concept. The United States is not becoming poorer, and its economy is not weak or feeble.[6] In 1989, U.S. farms, mines, factories, and offices produced over $5 trillion of goods and services—a record high and more than double that of second-place Japan with a bit more than $2 trillion.

This upbeat conclusion is not just the result of Americans patting themselves on their backs. Similar—and more strongly worded—sentiments were voiced by Fernand Rau, managing director of Credit Européen:

> Since the early eighties, after a decade of relative decline, the United States has clearly regained its rank as the leading economic and political superpower in the free world. Neither the erratic movements in the dollar exchange rate, nor the huge U.S. balance of payments deficit and foreign debt can reverse that judgment which is shared by a great majority of Europeans.[7]

If, to use Senator Fulbright's dramatic term, the United States has become a militarized economy, then it appears that the worst is behind us. The civilian influences are not only greater, but they are rising more rapidly. If we refer to Paul Kennedy's truism that allocating "too large" a proportion of our resources to defense weakens national power, then perhaps that allocation has not been too large after all. The outlook today is for that allocation to continue to shrink.

The changing role of defense in the American economy may shed some light on the debate over "peace dividends," "conversion," and so on. On the basis of a variety of economic and statistical analyses, I arrive at a more modest and very different set of conclusions than do authors such as Kennedy, Fulbright, and Melman. First of all, the military burden, although significant, has been far from overwhelming. In fact, the trend has been downward for decades. Second, the reductions now taking place are merely an acceleration of that downward trend. For the United States as a whole, economic adjustments to the contemplated changes in defense spending will be modest—both in terms of dislocation to be suffered and opportunity to redirect the nation's resources.

It is useful to begin by measuring changes in the size of the defense sector and its use of key national resources. It is also instructive to address several related points: What is the opportunity cost of defense spending? How much defense can we afford? How much do we need to assure national prosperity? How much to assure national security? Can we afford to cut more?

MEASURING THE DEFENSE SECTOR[8]

There is no generally agreed upon method of measuring the burden of military spending on the economy. In part that is so because many of the items purchased by the military establishment are so different from the typical civilian marketbasket. Supersonic fighter aircraft, nuclear powered submarines, aircraft carriers, and ICBMs have few commercial counterparts. We do know that today's large defense arsenal has consumed many times the resources of the U.S. military effort in World War II, although at a much slower pace.

In absolute terms, the outlays of the Defense Department are huge, totaling $290 billion in the fiscal year 1990. That sum exceeds the combined sales of General Motors, Exxon, and IBM. The Defense Department's budget is greater than the GNP of Australia, India, or the Netherlands. The defense sector of the GNP is of generally comparable magnitude to the military budget and fluctuates along a very similar trend line. Aside from some timing adjustments (such as measuring the delivery of equipment rather than the payment for it), the entry in the national income accounts is a bit smaller because it excludes transfer payments to military retirees and purchases of land and other existing assets.

The most widely used measure of the military role in the economy is the ratio of defense spending to GNP. For the United States, that relationship is now less than 6 percent. Depending on the analyst's policy preference, it can be shown that the ratio is up or down from some earlier base. Defense spending is now a larger fraction of GNP than it was during the Carter administration, when it reached a low of 4.8 percent; it is much lower than during the Kennedy period, when it attained a peak of more than 9 percent.

U.S. defense spending, however, has expanded in absolute size over the past century. From about $1 billion in 1938, defense outlays rose to $290 billion in fiscal year 1990, or at a compound annual growth rate of 12 percent. That was a far more rapid increase than occurred in the population of the country (1 percent) and the rate of inflation (5 percent for the GNP deflator). Because the overall economy was also expanding during that period, however, it is more helpful to focus on the changing relative position of military outlays—especially for the postwar period.

The most revealing fact is that the relative importance of defense to the American economy has followed a declining trend line since the end of World War II, when defense spending reached a record peak of 41 percent of GNP. The pattern since then certainly has been uneven, but each subsequent peak has been progressively lower—the Korean War, 14 percent; the Vietnam War, 10 percent; the Reagan buildup, 6.5 percent (see Figure 6-1).

The same generally downward trend is visible when comparing each successive interwar period. Thus, in the years following World War II and before the Korean conflict, defense spending peaked at 10 percent of GNP. Following the Korean War and before the Vietnam War, the ratio reached a high of 9 percent. After the Vietnam conflict

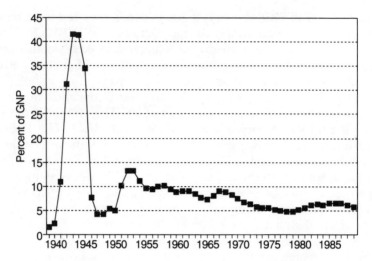

Figure 6-1. Defense Outlays as a Percentage of GNP. (*Source:* Computed from data in *Economic Report of the President,* February 1990.)

and before the Reagan buildup, the ratio of defense to GNP peaked at 7 percent. Likewise, each successive valley was lower than the previous one.

Very recently, a combination of domestic fiscal pressures and international political developments has accentuated this downward pattern. The point is that the current budget-cutting mood is not an abrupt change but merely an intensification of an ongoing trend.

A generally downward trend is also evident when we compare the military's use of key resources. The Department of Defense's share of the nation's labor force (1.7 percent) in the fiscal year 1990 is down from a peak of 4.3 percent in 1955, but also down from 2.2 percent in 1975. The 1990 ratio was lower than for any other year since World War II.

The military share of R&D also sloped downward over this period, and dramatically so despite a modest upturn in the 1980s. The current ratio of 30 percent is less than half of the 1960 figure of 62 percent. As noted in Chapter 5, a strategic but overlooked development occurred in the 1980s. The private sector replaced the public sector as the primary source of sponsorship and funding of the nation's R&D.

The military share of the federal budget is down very substantially—from almost 70 percent in the early 1950s to 23 percent in 1990. This contradicts the notion that "half of all federal tax dollars go to the Pentagon."[9] The absolute size of defense purchases of goods and services surely looms large for all the available statistical measures. The Department of Defense is a major "customer" of

American business. Nevertheless, the overall pattern is clear: the economic impact of defense activities in the United States peaked decades ago and has been declining, albeit irregularly, ever since.

Examining Some Broader Relationships

There is no shortage of studies that purport to show an inverse relationship between the concentration of a nation's economy on defense and its poor economic performance.[10] Thus, the argument goes, the United States spends both absolutely and proportionately more on defense than does Japan and, therefore, has a consistently lower rate of economic growth. Yet South Korea, which devotes a larger share of its GNP to defense than does Japan, generally records an even more rapid growth rate. To jump to a heroic conclusion from either comparison is surely simple-minded. Other factors—such as the national saving rate and the volume of private investment—are more critical influences on a nation's growth. Still, it has become fashionable to equate the slippage in the U.S. share of world trade and global economic activity with the comparatively large percentage of U.S. GNP devoted to defense. Let us pursue that point.

It is easy to show that the United States has lost its "supremacy" in the global economy in the four decades since the end of World War II. In 1950, the GNP of the United States represented approximately 45 percent of the world's gross product. In the past few years, in striking contrast, the U.S. share has dropped to about one-fourth of the global total[11] (see Figure 6-2).

Some historical perspective is useful. In 1950, the economies of Western Europe and Japan were still recovering from the devastation

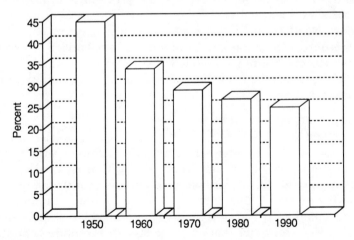

Figure 6-2. U.S. Share of World GNP. (*Source:* Computed from Central Intelligence Agency data.)

of World War II. Under those circumstances, the American economic giant had little difficulty dominating many world markets. Such a powerful position was bound to be transitory, however, as the foreign competitors regained their traditional strength, with very substantial help from both the U.S. government and its citizens.

It is intriguing to note that the Soviet Union did not take such a benign attitude. It shackled the economies of defeated nations within the sphere of its control, but the poor economic performance of the Soviet bloc economies in the decades following World War II is hardly a tribute to that approach.

Statistical comparisons, whether favorable or unfavorable, have their limitations. Thus, in the 1950s and 1960s—when the economic power of the United States was rarely questioned—a rapid spread of collectivist and antimarket policies took hold in many parts of Western Europe and Asia. In the 1980s, however, during the period of supposed U.S. decline, this trend was reversed. In many parts of the world, a dramatic expansion occurred in the role of market forces, economic incentives, price competition, and the privatization of economic activity. The relative decline of the U.S. economy can, therefore, hardly be attributed solely, or even primarily, to defense expenditures.

THE OPPORTUNITY COST OF DEFENSE

Whatever resources are allocated to national defense are obviously not available for other purposes. In an economy close to full employment, it is reasonable to assume that, in the absence of the military's demand, many of those resources would go to meet civilian needs. The question is which areas of the civilian economy have in the past decades yielded resources to defense—and which sectors might claim those resources following a reduction in military budgets. Viewed in terms of the opportunity foregone to use the people, machinery, and materials in some other ways, what has been the "opportunity cost" of defense spending?

Consumption Versus Saving

Economists argue over whether increases in defense spending come primarily out of resources that otherwise would be devoted to investment and would thus contribute to economic growth far more directly. To the extent that such is the case, the opportunity cost of defense spending is higher than if the money would go for current consumption—for items that generate little or no future benefit.

The likelihood that defense demands substantially crowd out private investment rests in good measure on the notion that a large and growing federal deficit forces the Treasury to expand its presence in capital markets. This puts upward pressure on interest rates. In turn, rising interest rates inhibit private capital formation. It would seem intuitively that the expanding deficits that so often accompany a military buildup are a factor in rising interest rates. However, the empirical evidence on the causal relationship between budget deficits and interest rates is not very impressive.[12]

As would be expected, during World War II, when the U.S. economy was pushing very hard against the limits of productive capacity, the rapid expansion of military demand had a strong negative effect on investment. Studies of broader and more recent time periods, however, come up with very different results. They all tend to show that defense has not drained investment funds from the civilian economy. Specifically, the investment share of GNP has not varied inversely to the defense share; rather, it is primarily consumption that moves inversely with defense spending.[13] Bruce Russett of Yale University has come up with the most succinct conclusion, "Private consumption has indeed been the largest alternative use of defense money. Guns do come partly at the expense of butter."[14]

There is, of course, a two-way effect between defense spending and economic activity. Whether military spending stimulates economic growth or inflation depends in part on the availability of unused productive capacity. If capacity is already fully utilized, then the expansion in military demand will compete with the civilian economy and thus push up prices. If additional capacity is available, however, then the result is likely to be a higher total rate of output in the economy. Indeed, books have been written on the impacts of defense spending on the structure of an economy.[15]

The way in which defense spending is financed is an important factor in evaluating its economic impact. Paying for an increase in defense outlays by government borrowing generates repercussions in financial markets very different from those resulting from tax increases. The type of tax increase is also significant. Raising corporate tax rates has more direct and depressing effects on private investment than do enacting sales taxes or even increasing personal income tax rates. Although much attention is placed on personal saving, the great bulk of saving in the United States—a basic source of financing new investment—occurs in the business sector of the economy.

Research and Development

A related aspect of the opportunity cost debate is the widespread belief that military spending on research and development "crowds out" civilian R&D. Amitai Etzioni has written:

Barriers have sprung up between the defense and space R&D and the civilian economy, and as these are not surmounted, there is but little spillover and an actual drag on the economy as space-defense R&D drains creative manpower from civilian use.[16]

The recent tendency for military technology to lag behind its civilian counterpart makes more worrisome the perennial charge that increases in military R&D activities come at the expense of civilian R&D. The Pentagon supposedly has drawn professional and technical personnel away from commercial work and has channeled R&D funds into corporate and university projects geared to short-run payoffs.[17]

Extending the analysis in Chapter 5, an important way of examining the question is to compare the trend of military R&D with total R&D performed in the U.S. economy, including both the public and private sectors. Such analyses show that military and civilian R&D are almost as likely to move in the same direction as in opposite directions.[18] One criticism that can be leveled at this approach, however, is that some of the civilian R&D has been induced by military demand, especially in the form of the independent R&D sponsored by defense contractors, a portion of which is reimbursed as part of overhead expenses allocable to defense contracts.

Let us consider, therefore, another way of examining the question as to whether defense R&D "depletes" civilian R&D. By focusing entirely on federal R&D (both military and civilian), the analysis is not influenced by any tendency of military procurement to induce R&D on the part of defense contractors in the private sector. The period 1949–1988 (the years for which data are available) can be divided into two categories: years in which military R&D was a rising share of the GNP and years in which military R&D was a declining share.

Figure 6-3 presents the results for the first category (years of buildup). It can be seen that civilian federal R&D, also computed as a percentage of GNP, moved in the same direction nine times out of nineteen, in the opposite direction seven times, and showed no change in three years.

Figure 6-4 contains the results of a similar analysis of the second category (years of cutback). It can be seen that civilian R&D moved in the same direction eight times out of nineteen, in the opposite direction nine times, and registered no change twice. To sum up, the military and civil R&D shares of GNP moved in the same direction in seventeen years, in the opposite direction in sixteen years, and registered no change in five years. Using this statistical approach, it can be seen that military and civilian R&D trends are just as likely to move in tandem as not.

It is pertinent to note that the current cutback in military R&D is

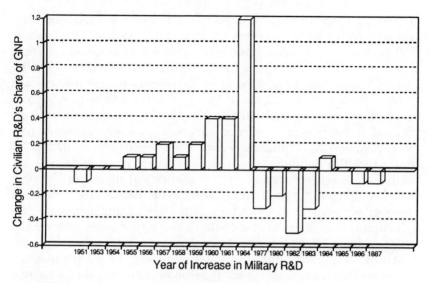

Figure 6-3. Movement of Civilian R&D when Military R&D Rises. (*Source:* Computed from *Budget of the United States Government, Fiscal Year 1990.*)

being accompanied by widespread concern over a similar downturn in civilian R&D. In 1989, for the first time since 1975, the National Science Foundation reported that spending on corporate R&D in the United States did not even keep pace with inflation—declining about

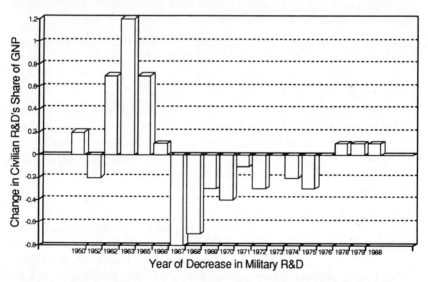

Figure 6-4. Movement of Civilian R&D when Military R&D Falls. (*Source:* Computed from *Budget of the United States Government, Fiscal Year 1990.*)

1 percent from 1988 (in real terms).[19] If military R&D ever "depleted" civilian R&D, then that effect is surely not now taking place.

There are many reasons for arriving at a conclusion so different from that of the conventional wisdom that military R&D comes at the expense of civilian R&D. First of all, the trends in both military and civilian R&D may be influenced by a common set of factors, such as changes in society's general desire to promote science and technology. Second, nondefense and defense engineers and scientists are not perfect substitutes. Specialization is great and interdisciplinary mobility is low. At least in the short term, therefore, fluctuations in defense demand will leave large segments of the science and engineering professions unaffected.[20] I recall in my own days in the defense industry a number of occasions in which large firms were simultaneously laying off engineers in their defense divisions and hiring other engineers in their commercial divisions (and vice versa).

Third, despite low interdisciplinary mobility, the supply of engineers and scientists is not fixed. It responds to demographic factors, changing occupational preferences, or any variations in job opportunities. Supply can also be augmented by in-migration from other countries (and reduced by out-migration) and by pulling in people from related fields such as physics and mathematics. Also, technicians can be promoted and scientists and engineers deterred from moving into management positions.

The economic effect of defense R&D is more complicated—and perhaps more positive—than is generally appreciated. In the words of economist Richard R. Nelson:

> To the extent that the net defense impact on R & D . . . has been positive, our defense effort has raised the demand for scientists and engineers, and has thereby stimulated an increase in the output of these people by our educational institutions.[21]

Finally, a little statistical perspective is useful. About 18 percent of the nation's engineers are employed in defense-related industries.[22] Thus a change of one-third in defense spending, according to the Office of Technology Assessment, would generate only a 6 percent overall shift in the use of the U.S. engineering work force.[23]

Defense and the Budget

It is also instructive to evaluate the changing role of defense in national priorities. The most widely used measure of that relationship is the share of federal government outlays directed to defense (see Figure 6-5). The trend here is basically similar to that shown in Figure 6-1 for the GNP. The large portion of the federal budget directed to defense spending during World War II—around 90 percent—has not been

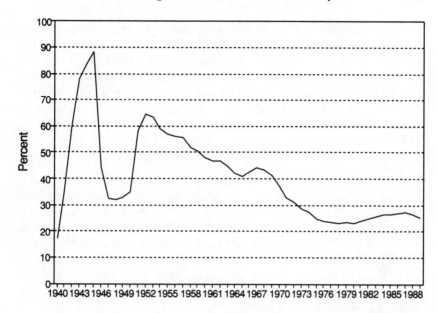

Figure 6-5. Defense Portion of Federal Spending. (*Source:* Compiled from U.S. Office of Management and Budget data.)

equaled since then. A secondary peak occurred during the Korean War, when defense spending accounted for almost 70 percent of the budget.

Since then, the defense share of the federal budget has dropped to a low of 23 percent in 1980. It reversed to a high of 28 percent in 1987, after which it continued its decline. To a large extent, the downward trend in the military share of the federal budget resulted from the fact that civilian program outlays were growing at a much more rapid rate during the 1960s, especially in the "entitlement" programs, notably Social Security and other benefits primarily going to the middle class.

Paradoxically, the ability of the Reagan administration to withstand pressures for cutting defense spending in the early 1980s made it difficult to make deep reductions in civilian expenditures, especially entitlements and farm subsidies. With some success, proponents of the latter raised the issue of "fairness" as a justification for limiting reductions in nondefense programs. During the rapid military buildup of the early 1980s, federal civilian expenditures continued to rise in real terms, although not as rapidly as the economy as a whole.

By the mid-1980s, the pressures of general budgetary trends began to influence military outlays. A combination of expansions in both military and civilian spending programs in the early 1980s, coupled with substantial reductions in income tax rates, led to unparalleled budget deficits. The persistence of these triple-digit deficits beyond the 1981–1982 recession led to the adoption of institutional restraints on federal spending, in the form of the Gramm–Rudman–Hollings legislation. The military budget was a major target of Gramm–Rudman–Hollings, and annual appropriations for the Department of Defense since the mid-1980s have been less than the amounts necessary to keep up with inflation.

Defense Spending and Voter Sentiment

Americans often have an ambivalent attitude toward the value of defense expenditures. We simultaneously view the military use of resources as a burden to the nation, and as a prop to whole industries and regions. I can cite from personal experience the frustration of dealing with members of Congress who, in public, advocate large reductions in military spending and the next day come to the White House in a frantic but private effort to "save" the weapon systems being produced in their districts.

Part of the problem is that what passes for benefit/cost analysis in the political sphere is usually done from a local rather than a national perspective, and there is little likelihood of fundamental change. Try closing any unneeded defense base—or reducing the numbers of aircraft or missiles being purchased. The overwhelmingly negative public reaction will quickly demonstrate the point that the political process gives the benefits to the locality far greater weight than the costs borne by the rest of the nation. This helps to explain why, at least in modern times, Congress has not cancelled the production of a single weapon system, despite the volume of debate on military waste in committee hearings and in the *Congressional Record*.

For example, when in 1989 the Department of Defense wanted to close down the production of a fighter aircraft, the business leadership of the community in which it was produced rose up in fierce opposition. In a widely circulated statement, they contended that shutting down the production line "would damage the U.S. economy . . . " It is intriguing to note that the major supporting data were more political than economic, " . . . eliminating jobs in 232 congressional districts."[24]

With the shift to a more rapid curtailment of defense spending, congressional lobbying has become more organized and blatant. Over two dozen members of the House of Representatives, covering both parties, have created an official Stealth Caucus, whose sole function is to lobby for the continuation of the Stealth Bomber (the B-2). One member of the caucus, in upbraiding California Senator Alan

Cranston for supporting termination of the program, made it clear
that this was a pork barrel rather than a national security issue:

> [O]ur senior Senator has essentially abandoned 17,000 people in South-
> ern California who depend upon the B-2 program for their liveli-
> hood . . . [25]

The cost to the nation of maintaining an obsolete military base or a
marginal defense production program may far exceed the benefit to
the nation. To the powers that be in the locality in which the expenditure is made, however, such an esoteric analysis is irrelevant. Invariably, the local people see the military outlay as essential to their continued prosperity and consider it sufficient to justify their vehement
support. Similarly, secretaries of defense in administration after administration use claims of positive economic impact as a means of
justifying higher military budgets.

HOW MUCH DEFENSE CAN WE AFFORD?

Can we afford to spend more on defense if we need to? "Yes." Do we
need to continue the current level of defense spending in order to
maintain economic prosperity? "No."

These conclusions are a result of studies begun in the 1950s and
1960s on the economics of disarmament, when military spending was
a much larger share of the U.S. GNP. In 1958, the Committee for
Economic Development concluded that the risk that defense spending of 15 percent or more of the GNP "will ruin the American way of
life is slight indeed."[26] In 1963, Edward Mason of Harvard University
noted that the effective limit to maintaining a high level of defense
spending was political. He concluded that " . . . there is not much
doubt that in the face of deepening emergency even higher expenditures would be accepted."[27]

As a practical matter, it seems that Mason is right. The pertinent
question in current debates on defense spending is not the ability of
the U.S. economy to produce defense goods and services, but the
willingness of society to devote a substantial share of its resources to
that purpose. As Herbert Stein of the American Enterprise Institute
recently wrote, rather than talking about being unable to afford a
larger defense program, people should be saying that they prefer
some other use of the national output, such as private consumption or
investment.[28]

A recurring concern is that a military buildup may be inflationary. I
am in the seemingly awkward position of having been on both sides of

that debate. In early 1966, I sounded the alarm on the inflationary potential of the Vietnam buildup. Yet in 1981, I maintained that the Reagan buildup would not be inflationary.[29]

What did happen? Recent history shows that a rapid expansion in military demand can indeed generate strong inflationary pressures. The U.S. participation in the Vietnam War provides an example of a rapid rise in military procurement simultaneous with an upsurge in inflation. On the other hand, rapid expansion of defense spending in the early 1980s was accompanied by a very substantial reduction in the rate of inflation.

The key difference between the two periods was in monetary policy. Responding to strong pressure from President Lyndon Johnson (the chairman of the Fed was summoned to "the ranch"), the Federal Reserve in 1965 began to accommodate the expansion of federal deficit spending with an easy money policy. In contrast, in 1981 the Reagan administration supported the Federal Reserve's efforts to slow down the growth in the money supply simultaneous with the military buildup taking place. The contrasting results of these two periods demonstrate once again that inflation is primarily a monetary phenomonen and that any link to a military buildup is indirect at best.

The same studies that show that the American economy can handle a much higher level of military spending also conclude that the growth and prosperity of the United States do not require the current high level of national security expenditure. The President's Committee on Economic Impact of Defense and Disarmament, chaired by Gardner Ackley, reported in 1965 that, "Experience testifies to the ability of the American economy to adjust successfully to major reductions in defense expenditures."[30] The Ackley Committee drew on the adjustment experiences following World War II and the Korean War. The post-Vietnam adjustment furnished another case in point.

In a variety of econometric simulations, Lawrence Klein and Kei Mori estimated that a short transition would occur after a large cutback in defense spending. Temporarily, unemployment rises as the economy's growth rate slows down. Subsequently, however, the peacetime economy follows a more rapid long-run growth path.[31] More recent analyses by the economic consulting firm DRI have yielded basically similar conclusions concerning Secretary of Defense Dick Cheney's potential reduction of $180 billion in the defense budget over the next five years—" . . . the national economy can cope with this transition without major problems."[32]

Indeed, that has been the experience in the recent past. Following an initial adjustment period—with its attendant pain and uncertainty— many localities wind up with a stronger economy after the defense cut. A study of 100 former military bases reported that, during the period 1981–1986, 128,000 new civilian jobs replaced the 93,000 military jobs that were lost. This 7 percent average annual increase in employment at these sites during the period surveyed compares favorably to the average annual increase of 2 percent in employment nationally. Three-fourths of the closed bases became industrial and office parks; most of the remainder was used by colleges and vocational technical schools.[33]

These positive results are not surprising when we consider the valuable assets that the military often leaves behind—land, buildings, airstrips, deepwater harbors, rail liners, and infrastructure such as water, sewer, gas, and electricity lines. Kinross Township in the Upper Peninsula of Michigan experienced one of those success stories. When Kincheloe Air Force Base was closed in 1976, the region lost a total payroll of $28 million. Currently, twelve industrial companies and fifteen retail businesses use the former base. The local tax base has doubled. The civilian payroll created by the new ventures is $110 million.[34]

Looking ahead, surplus military airfields can provide the necessary relief for airport and airway congestion that has accompanied the doubling of air travel since the advent of airline deregulation. No sooner did the Air Force announce that it was considering closing Pease air base in New Hampshire than the Boston Airport authority stated that the military facility would make a fine second airport for that busy metropolitan area. Westchester County's Stewart Airport, formerly Stewart Air Force Base, underwent just such a successful conversion. In 1990, the announcement that George Air Force Base in California would be closed led the nearby city of Adelanto to urge its use as a new regional airport to alleviate the congestion in Los Angeles.[35]

However, the poor environmental practices of many military installations will make it difficult to transfer them readily to civilian use in the near future. The three military bases in the Oakland–Alameda area near San Francisco are on valuable waterfront property suitable for hotels, conference centers, and shopping malls, but hazardous waste stored at the bases has polluted the underground water. Meeting the required environmental impact statement process is likely to be both expensive and time consuming.[36]

On balance, the generally accepted belief among economists—a belief not as universally accepted by policymakers—is that, given a reasonable period of adjustment and following policies familiar to most students of Economics 101, the American economy can attain prosperity with a greatly reduced defense establishment.

At a more microeconomic level, the occupations, industries, and regions benefiting from the changes in sectoral demands will likely be different from those that participated most actively in the military buildup. On the basis of past experience, a geographic shift in income and employment can be expected, from the aerospace and electronics companies on the West Coast and New England to the more conventional industries in the Midwest.

SOME BROADER RELATIONSHIPS

My favorite candidate for Washington's oddest couple is an economist talking to a military leader. The mutual suspicion is awesome. Almost every admiral or general looks at an economist as someone with little knowledge of national security needs, but someone anxious to put a dollar sign on everything. In turn, the economist sees the military officer as oblivious to the realities of limited resources and often offended by the mere mention of cost.

This chapter has tried to shed some light on the important but uneasy relationship between economics and the national security. The Medicis may have provided one of the earliest and most incisive analyses of that relationship in their durable motto, "Money to get the power. Power to keep the money." Surely, for the foreseeable future, the Department of Defense will be a major claimant on the resources of the United States even if substantial reductions are made from current levels of defense spending. Therefore, considerations of efficiency will continue to be relevant even as the United States enters a period of lower world tensions.[37]

Moreover, a strong and growing economy is important to the national security. Consider for a moment the possibility of the United States going into a deep and prolonged depression. That would substantially, albeit temporarily, reduce this nation's economic strength, thereby perhaps also its willingness to maintain a large military establishment. Then again, the pump-priming argument would arise to justify higher levels of defense spending in order to provide jobs for the unemployed. In any event, such a major deterioration of the U.S. economic position would discourage our allies and perhaps weaken their ability and willingness to continue current international security arrangements.

There surely is no continuing correct share of GNP that should be allocated to defense. The ratio that exists at any time is the accidental result of the federal government responding to a variety of internal and external pressures. A high or even rapidly rising level of defense spending does not necessarily mean that a nation is becoming more secure. Likewise, attaining a share of GNP achieved during an earlier period is no measure of the adequacy of defense. The base period used for comparison may have been lower or higher than that required for sustaining a given level of military strength.

As we have been reminded so recently, an interdependence exists with the defense outlays of other countries, both antagonists and allies. A carefully constructed program of mutual arms reduction could well result in enhancing the sense of security of both the United States and the Soviet Union. Nor does increasing the efficiency with which we use military resources (getting more bang per buck) necessarily mean that the Pentagon's budget can be cut if a potential enemy is simultaneously increasing its military efficiency.

However, higher levels of defense expenditure may not necessarily equal expansion in military strength; some spending literally goes down the drain. Highly publicized cases of $600 toilet seats are exercises in cheap (but effective) politics rather than examples of costly procurement. After all, airlines pay as much for similar pieces of equipment, which are far more expensive than the household toilet seat.

Far more important are the billions of dollars that are spent for programs that subsequently are cancelled. Between 1957 and 1970, the Department of Defense terminated eighty-one military projects after spending a total of $12 billion on them. More recently, $4 billion was expended on the development of the Sergeant York anti-aircraft gun before the Pentagon terminated the project.

Moreover, the very concept of national power is illusive. The factors that contribute to a nation's security include formal military strength in a fundamental way; however, a large military establishment does not suffice. Conflicts among nations are at times resolved through means that are primarily nonmilitary, such as competition in terms of natural resources, technology, economic strength, or ideology.

A confrontation of societies is more than a confrontation of formal military power. Opportunities arise to use nonmilitary strength for national security purposes, especially in peacetime. As Charles Hitch (the highly regarded former head of the RAND Corporation's Economics Division) noted, "the nation with the largest economic potential can best afford a bold foreign policy."[38]

To return to the point made at the outset of this chapter: the defense program is a relatively minor player in the American economy—accounting for one-fifteenth of the GNP and an even smaller proportion of the nation's work force (see Figure 6-6). Moreover, the ongoing debate on the proper future levels of defense spending should start off with the knowledge that the economic importance of defense in the United States has been declining for many years. Economic activity in the United States marches essentially to the

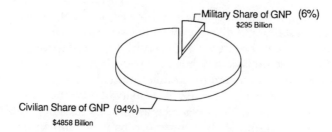

Figure 6-6. Military Share of GNP, 1989. (*Source:* Department of Commerce, Bureau of Economic Analysis.)

beat of civilian drummers. The massive economy of the United States is neither propelled nor redirected by modest shifts in the relatively small share of GNP devoted to military purposes. Furthermore, its powers of adjustment are substantial.

Any consideration of the economic policy responses to further reductions in defense spending should take account of the fact that the ability of an economy to adjust to shifts in economic forces is greater in the long run than in the short run. The reaction of the American economy to the sharp run up in oil prices in the 1970s furnishes a good example. The initial responses—both in the public and private sectors—often bordered on panic. Fifteen years after the initial shock, the United States has adjusted fairly well to much higher levels of energy prices, and in the process has become a less energy-intensive society.

Similarly, the initial responses to cancellations of military programs can be painful to individual companies, their employees, and the surrounding communities. With the protection of the social safety net described in Chapter 4, however, resources will shift to civilian uses, although not necessarily in the same location. In the longer run, decisions by business firms, consumers, and investors can be expected to accommodate to the revised pattern of demand—unless the government has stepped in with a misguided effort to prevent change.

The adjustments required by defense cutbacks are surely not basically different from the responses that occur regularly from shifts in consumer demand or from technological changes that yield new products that eliminate markets for older products, or from changes in the pattern of foreign trade. As the Ackley Committee noted, " . . . major readjustments in the use of resources do continually occur in a free economy and, on the whole, fairly successfully."[39]

In any event, for the range of likely disagreements about the future size and composition of the military budget, economic constraints are not likely to be particularly binding. It would be unfortunate if political pressures instituted such constraints, especially on the basis of misreading economic analysis. This is not a plea for adopting any particular level of military outlays. Rather, the amount of resources that the United States devotes to the defense establishment should be determined fundamentally on national security grounds—with due regard to the pressures of competition from other demands on the public purse and the dictates of efficiency in the use of public resources.

NOTES

1. Paul Kennedy, *The Rise and Fall of the Great Powers* (New York: Random House, 1987), p. xvi.

2. J. William Fulbright, *The Price of Empire* (New York: Pantheon Books, 1989), p. 136.

3. Seymour Melman, "What to Do With the Cold War Money," *The New York Times*, December 17, 1989, p. F-3.

4. James R. Schlesinger, "We Sometimes Forget . . . How Powerful This Nation Is," *New York Times Magazine*, June 18, 1988, p. 27.

5. Susan Chira, "With Mixed Emotions, Japan Sees U.S. in Decline," *International Herald Tribune*, July 1, 1988, p. 4.

6. C. Michael Aho and Marc Levinson, *After Reagan: Confronting the Changed World Economy* (New York: Council on Foreign Relations, 1988), p. 9.

7. Fernand Roll, "An Economist's Perspective on the Future of Europe," address given at Miami University, Oxford, Ohio, September 30, 1988, p. 2.

8. This section draws on the author's *Military Spending and the Myth of Global Overstretch* (Washington, D.C.: Center for Strategic and International Studies, 1989) and "Defense Spending and the American Economy," *Defence Economics*, April 1990, pp. 233–42.

9. Melman, "Cold War Money," p. F-3.

10. See, for example, R. P. Smith, "Military Expenditure and Capitalism," *Cambridge Journal of Economics*, Vol. 1, 1977, pp. 61–76.

11. *Economic Report of the President* (Washington, D.C.: U.S. Government Printing Office, 1990); *Handbook of Economic Statistics* (Washington, D.C.: Central Intelligence Agency, 1988); "World Output in the 1980s," *Economic Insights*, July/August 1990, p. 19.

12. William Niskanen, "Uneasy Relations Between Budget and Trade Deficits," *Cato Journal*, Fall 1988, pp. 507–20.

13. See Jerry Hollenhorst and Gary Ault, "An Alternative Answer to: Who Pays for Defense?" *American Political Science Review*, Vol. 65, No. 3, 1971, p. 761; Bruce Russett, *What Price Vigilance?* (New Haven: Yale University Press, 1970), p. 141; Kenneth Boulding, "The Impact of the Defense Industry on the Structure of the American Economy," in Bernard Udis, ed., *The Economic Consequences of Reduced Military Spending* (Lexington, Mass.: Lexington Books, 1973), p. 228; David Aschauer, "Fiscal Policy and Aggregate Demand,"

American Economic Review, March 1985, pp. 117–27; Kenneth Boulding, ed., *Peace and the War Industry* (New Brunswick: Transaction Books, 1973), p. 5; David Gold, *The Impact of Defense Spending on Investment, Productivity and Economic Growth* (Washington, D.C.: Defense Budget Project, 1990), p. 3; Mark A. Wynne, "The Long Run Effects of a Permanent Change in Defense Purchases," *Federal Reserve Bank of Dallas Economic Review*, January 1991, pp. 1–16.

14. Russett, *What Price Vigilance?* p. 141.

15. For a fascinating analyis of how military production affects a local economy, for good and bad, see David Thomas, *War, Industry and Society: The Midlands, 1939–45* (London: Routledge, 1989).

16. Amitai Etzioni, "Federal Science an Economic Drag, Not Propellant," in Seymour Melman, ed., *The War Economy of the United States* (New York: St. Martin's Press, 1971), p. 132.

17. Richard DuBoff, "What Military Spending Really Costs," *Challenge*, September–October 1989, p. 4; Seymour Melman, *Pentagon Capitalism* (New York: McGraw-Hill, 1970).

18. Murray L. Weidenbaum, "Defense Spending and the American Economy," *Defence Economics*, May 1990, p. 237; Gold reached a conclusion that is a variation of this theme: there is no long-term trade-off between defense R&D and civilian R&D. See Gold, *Impact of Defense Spending*, p. 3.

19. One R&D specialist questions the NSF data base and comes up with a more optimistic evaluation for earlier years. See Claude E. Barfield, "The Truth About Research," *The New York Times*, March 4, 1990, p. 25.

20. Lynn E. Browne, "Defense Spending and High Technology Development," *New England Economic Review*, September/October 1988, p. 5.

21. Richard R. Nelson, "Impact of Disarmament on Research and Development," in Emile Benoit and Kenneth Boulding, eds., *Disarmament and the Economy* (New York: Harper & Row, 1963), p. 115.

22. *The 1982 Post Censal Survey of Scientists and Engineers* (Washington, D.C.: National Science Foundation, 1984), p. 60.

23. *Science and Technology Resources in U.S. Industry* (Washington, D.C.: U.S. National Science Foundation, 1989), p. 24.

24. St. Louis Regional Commerce and Growth Association, Military Affairs Committee, *A Cutback in F-15E Production Would Increase the Risk of War* (St. Louis: RCGA, 1989). The author provides a St. Louis example simply because he lives there and not because the special interest pleading is any greater than in other areas of the country. Indeed, it often has been less.

25. David C. Morrison, "Defense Contractors Trying to Hold on," *National Journal*, April 14, 1990, p. 887.

26. *The Problem of National Security* (New York: Committee for Economic Development, 1958), p. 27.

27. Edward S. Mason, "Economic Growth and United States Strategy," in David Abshire and Richard Allen, eds., *National Security* (New York: Frederick Praeger, 1963), pp. 880–81.

28. Herbert Stein, "America's Second Fiscal Revolution," Challenge, July–August 1989, p. 6; see also Herbert Stein, *Governing the $5 Trillion Economy* (New York: Oxford University Press, 1989).

29. Michael R. Gordon, "If Defense Spending Is on the Rise, Can Inflation Be Very Far Behind?" *National Journal*, June 20, 1981, pp. 1101–5; Murray L. Weidenbaum, *Economic Impact of the Vietnam War* (Washington, D.C.: Georgetown University, Center for Strategic Studies, 1967).

30. *Report of the Committee on the Economic Impact of Defense and Disarmament* (Washington, D.C.: U.S. Government Printing Office, 1965), p. 8.

31. Lawrence R. Klein and Kei Mori, "The Impact of Disarmament on Aggregate Economic Activity," in Udis, *Economic Consequences*, pp. 76–77.

32. "The Retreat of Defense Spending," *DRI U.S. Forecast Summary*, December 1989, p. 3.

33. The data do not include military personnel stationed at the bases. Office of the Assistant Secretary of Defense, Force Management and Personnel, *Summary of Complete Military Base Economic Adjustment Projects* (Washington, D.C.: U.S. Department of Defense, 1986), pp. 3–12.

34. Federal Reserve Bank of Minneapolis, "Defense Cuts Inevitable," *Fedgazette*, June 1990, p. 5.

35. *Southern California's International Business and Transportation of the Future* (Adelanto: City of Adelanto Government, 1990).

36. Jerome Chandler, "Instant Airports," *Frequent Flyer*, April 1990, pp. 20–21; Louis Uchitelle, "Economy Expected to Absorb Effects of Military Cuts," *The New York Times*, April 15, 1990, p. 14.

37. Thomas G. Pownall, "Defense Procurement Can Improve," *Financier*, November 1986, pp. 44–46; Murray Weidenbaum, *Rendezvous With Reality* (New York: Basic Books, 1990), Chapter 4, "A Strategy for Controlling Defense Spending."

38. Charles J. Hitch, "Domestic Economic Policies for National Security," Background Paper (New York: Committee for Economic Development, 1955), pp. 7–8.

39. *Committee on the Economic Impact of Defense*, p. 18.

CHAPTER 7

Understanding
the Defense Industry

A necessary prelude to reforming the military–industry relationship is to understand it. The Pentagon was once described as the place where Franz Kafka meets Alice in Wonderland.[1] Truly, military and civilian decision making differ so substantially that they are almost worlds apart.

The way the military establishment makes its purchases from the private sector differs in many important regards from standard commercial practice. There are also special business–government relationships with companies that produce weapon systems and other specialized equipment for the Department of Defense. These firms are subject to more detailed government control than any other branch of the American economy, but most studies of government regulation of business ignore this sector. Those who have worked on defense studies, however, have no doubt about the degree of government involvement. In a specialized volume on managing defense acquisition, General George Sammet, Jr., formerly commanding general of the army material command, and Colonel David Green, former army program manager, described the nature of military procurement:

> Although defense is not called a regulated industry, it is controlled by the government as though it were. All effort is controlled through congressional legislation and regulations such as the Federal Acquisition Regulation . . . The defense buyer is in fact a regulator.[2]

THE NATURE OF THE MILITARY CUSTOMER

The military market is dominated by a monopsonistic purchaser (one buyer) of products that are not yet designed or for which production experience is lacking and at prices for which there is little precedent.

As a consequence, we have seen the rise of government-oriented corporations—or the specialized defense-oriented divisions of primarily civilian-oriented firms—that are locked into defense work. A two-way symbiotic relationship develops, since the government becomes almost totally dependent on these firms. Although 70 percent of the number of procurement awards go to firms classified as small business, more than 80 percent of the dollar value of the contracts is received by the larger firms.[3]

Over the years, about one-half of the value of prime contracts has been subcontracted; however, subcontracting does not necessarily spread the work. Much of it stays within members of the "club" of large defense contractors. General Dynamics builds fuselage sections for the KC-10 tanker (and for its commercial sister the DC-10) for McDonnell Douglas and parts of the Space Shuttle fuselage for Rockwell. Conversely, General Dynamics subcontracts components of the Stinger missile to Raytheon. Each of these firms competes with each other to be the prime contractor on other weapon systems.

The Monopsonistic Military Market

The Department of Defense is the one customer for aircraft carriers, supersonic bombers, ICBMs, nuclear submarines, and other weapons that are the major component of military procurement (see Figure 7-1). Because the market is so completely subject to the changing needs of this one customer, relationships between buyer and seller differ fundamentally from those in civilian sectors of the economy. By its selection of contractors, the government controls who enters into and who leaves this market. It also determines the potential growth of these firms and is in a position to impose its ways of doing business on them.

Classic market forces are largely absent in major weapons acquisition. Conventional business arrangements, involving multiple buyers and multiple sellers who enter into fixed contracts for production and acceptance of rigorously defined goods, simply do not apply to most weapons acquisition projects.

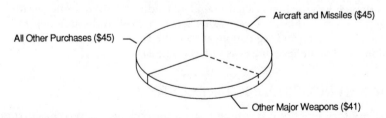

Figure 7-1. Military Purchases in 1988 (in billions of dollars). (*Source:* Department of Defense.)

This single-customer market makes for an extremely keen and novel type of "either/or" competition. For a specific product, a company generally is not competing for a share of the market, but for all of it. Boeing and General Dynamics were rivals for the F-111 aircraft contract; General Dynamics won. Similarly, McDonnell Douglas produces all F-15 aircraft, as a result of a design competition it won against two other aerospace firms.

One study described the current state of competition for large defense contracts as "desperate" because it is now characterized by a single customer who buys new weapon systems very infrequently. For example, if an aerospace company did not bid on the advanced tactical fighter, it may not have an opportunity to bid on another new tactical airplane for a decade or more.[4]

The sharply fluctuating demands for a given type of weapon system (such as the rapid rise in demand for air-breathing missiles, subsonic jet fighters, and liquid-propellant boosters, followed by an even faster decline) are rarely seen in commercial markets. The less efficient, commercially oriented firm may lose its market position, but at least for a time it can count on making some sales of its product line, albeit at reduced prices. It rarely encounters the extreme peak-and-valley nature of military procurement characterized by intense initial government demand followed by the virtual disappearance of the market for the items.

Defense contractors commit their key scientists and engineers (who are their most strategic resource) as well as major physical facilities to programs subject to unpredictable change or even cancellation—and to products where the ultimate profitability will not be known for a decade or more. This aspect of the business, particularly when coupled with its research-intensive nature, is much more similar to the risks of the pharmaceutical industry or of pesticide producers subject to intense regulation, than to the larger and more traditional category of durable goods manufacturers with which the defense industry is often compared.[5]

Under these conditions of uncertainty, it is generally impossible to predict the cost, schedule, performance, or quantity of the final product with enough precision to permit the buyer and seller to write a firm contract covering the entire process. Instead, the two parties establish what has been called an "uneasy alliance" sharing risks and management responsibilities, under the aegis of a contract that at times is little more than a baseline for negotiations over numerous changes over the course of the program.[6]

Thus, it is not surprising that the government buyer assumes many of the risks that in more normal business activities are borne as a matter of course by the seller. Despite all of the attention focused on defense profits (and on "profiteering," "gouging," and worse), the data show that for the years 1971–1988, profits as a percentage of net worth for the largest portion of the defense sector—the aerospace industry—averaged 12.7 percent, exactly the same as for all manufacturing corporations. To be sure, the yearly fluctuations were rarely similar.[7] The annual variation in aerospace profitability (from a high of 16 percent to a low of 5 percent) was greater than for total manufacturing (with a range of 17 to 9 percent). On balance, however, an equilibrating mechanism does seem to be at work between the two sectors of the economy.

Along with the assumption of risk, however, there is a corresponding involvement by the governmental customer in the internal operations of its suppliers. The officials of the Department of Defense make many decisions that are normally part of the responsibility of business management.

Contrary to the standard Marxist cliché, then, the firms doing business with the Department of Defense are not rapacious warmongers, but companies anxious to do well in an important market. According to one analyst,

> The U.S. defense industry is peopled neither by the warmongering arms merchants some cynics suggest nor by the high-minded businessmen some industry apologists would have the public believe. It is a competitive, profit-hungry industry that employs ingenious engineers, skillful marketers, shrewd cost analysts, savvy lobbyists, and highly paid attorneys.[8]

Importance of Noncost Factors

Because of the nature of military requirements, the offer price frequently is a far less important factor than it is in commercial markets. The primary concern is obtaining a product of superior quality—the second fastest fighter aircraft is no bargain. Since the significant competition occurs before the final product is completely designed, initial estimates of total cost and ultimate performance are in any case tentative. The seller's previous cost experiences and managerial capabilities are often better indicators of the company's ability to meet the government's needs than its price estimates, but recent congressional statutes have downgraded the weight given to such factors.

Similarly, the potential contractor's past record of technical achievement and the attractiveness of the design proposal have frequently been dominant factors in the evaluation of proposals. Nevertheless, elaborate procedures are used in determining or rather estimating price, including a variety of contract types designed to provide some of the incentives of a normal competitive market that otherwise would be absent. (The actual award of the contract, however, can be affected by more subjective political pressures.)

Major suppliers of weapon systems are quality maximizers rather than cost minimizers. Their basic competence is invention and organization of huge teams of scientists and engineers. Budget overruns frequently occur because of the uncertainty in estimating the cost of designing and manufacturing items that have never been made before—and from the numerous changes in specifications that occur as technology advances, and as the customer changes its needs. Managerial shortcomings are also often a major contributor to poor cost performance.

Because of the emphasis on technology, more professional and technical workers, including engineers, scientists, and technicians, are required in military work than in general manufacturing. Relatively more administrative support staff is needed as well, including clerical and computer personnel. In contrast, substantially fewer machine setters, operators and handworkers are hired.[9]

Whether a particular program will reach the production stage depends in large part on the technical capability displayed during the research and development stage. It also depends, however, on external developments, ranging from a shift in domestic political alignments to a changed foreign policy environment.

Technical Change and Rapid Obsolescence

Abrupt changes are also a fact of life in defense contracting. Product technology may shift from liquid-fueled to solid-fueled rockets. National security planners may decide that all land-based strategic systems (such as long-range bombers) be located in the continental United States, increasing the required range for strategic aircraft. International tensions may increase or lessen. The demands of the military customer fluctuate more widely than do those of any comparable area in the private economy. Because the international situation and national goals change so rapidly, the government frequently reevaluates overall military policy and the equipment required. For example, because a potential enemy is believed to have developed missile and aircraft of great range and accuracy, the United States responds with an accelerated effort to develop secure defense systems to meet that threat (and that cycle may be repeated more than once).

The environment of constant technological change often dictates short product life cycles. New products just emerging from the production lines are made obsolete by even newer products on the design boards; thus, subsonic jet aircraft programs were cancelled when supersonic jets were developed. On the other hand, the supersonic (but range-limited) B-58 was replaced by the older, subsonic B-52 when the basing plans were changed.

Production Not for Inventory

The market for weapon systems—including aircraft, missiles, space vehicles, ships, and tanks—is characterized by production in response to an order; production for inventory is rare. This differs from most areas of the private economy. Moreover, the government buyer frequently takes the initiative in developing these new products by financing most of the research and development costs (see Chapter 5).

Rudimentary Channels of Distribution

The military market has deceptively simple channels of distribution. Basically, the manufacturer sells and delivers directly to the consumer. No middlemen are involved since the military itself maintains an extensive internal distribution system. The flow of material from the private sector producer to a central military warehouse to the base and to the final using command is analogous to the flow from manufacturer to wholesaler to retailer and to the final customer in the private sector. Because the government customer handles most of the distribution, however, defense contractors have developed very limited and specialized marketing capabilities. Over the years, this has been a substantial barrier to their attempts to sell their technological capabilities in civilian areas.

The barriers to entry into the military market are also often obstacles to market diversification. Defense contractors have to develop a special operating environment, make capital investments in very specialized equipment, utilize unusually high levels of engineering and scientific capability, follow unique accounting and reporting systems, and possess a detailed knowledge of federal regulations, security clearances, and political considerations—such as legislators trying to keep work in their districts. Once in the market, the large overhead (fixed costs) of defense production, the very thin marketing and distribution capabilities, and the very specialized labor force prove barriers to diversification (see Chapter 3).[10]

THE INDUSTRIAL DISTRIBUTION OF DEFENSE WORK

Strictly speaking, there is no specific "defense" industry. The characteristics that define this sector of the economy have more to do with how business is conducted than with what product is being produced. A great many companies in a variety of traditional industries such as

Table 7-1 Importance of Military Orders to Top Defense Contractors
Ranked by Asset Size, 1988

Asset Size	Defense Contacts as a Percentage of Sales				
	75–100%	50–74%	25–49%	Under 25%	Total
$50 billion and over	0	0	0	5	5
$10–50 billion	0	0	1	16	17
$5–10 billion	0	3	1	10	14
$1–5 billion	1	2	4	19	26
$500 million–1 billion	0	0	2	5	7
Under $500 million	2	3	2	0	7
Total number of companies	3	8	10	55	76

Source: Statistical Appendix.

automobiles serve as prime contractors or subcontractors to the military services. Most of them devote the greater portion of their resources to civilian markets (Table 7-1). The military work is often performed by a specialized division of the company.

Although a major weapon system is usually budgeted as a single entity, it is rarely built entirely by one firm. The government typically enters into contracts with different firms for various parts of the complete system, such as the engines, guidance system, and controls. Each of these contractors will ship its portion of the weapon to the company charged with final assembly (the "prime" contractor). In addition, the prime contractor will typically subcontract about one-half of the value of its order from the government. A large part of defense production thus takes place in factories that produce a wide variety of goods for both civilian and military markets.

The Composition of the Military-Industrial Complex

The composition of the major firms and industries supplying goods and services to the Department of Defense varies according to defense needs. For example, during the Korean War, when military requirements were dominated by army ordnance equipment, General Motors (at the time a major producer of tanks and trucks) was the leading military contractor. The shift to aircraft and missiles since then has brought aerospace and electronics companies such as General Dynamics, General Electric, McDonnell Douglas, and Lockheed into the forefront (Table 7-2).

A relatively few hard-goods-producing industries account for the great bulk of the dollar volume of military prime contracts: aerospace, electronics, motor vehicles, petroleum refining, chemicals, rubber,

Table 7-2 Major Defense Contractors in 1988

Rank Company	Military Awards (in $billions)	Key Products
1. McDonnell Douglas	8.0	F-18, F-15, Apache, and Harrier aircraft, R&D for missile/space systems.
2. General Dynamics	6.5	F-16 fighter aircraft, Nuclear submarines, M-1 tank, Tomahawk, Stinger, Sparrow missiles.
3. General Electric	5.7	Jet engines, nuclear reactors for submarines, communication equipment.
4. Tenneco	5.1	Nuclear aircraft carriers, submarines.
5. Raytheon	4.1	Patriot, Aegis, and Phoenix missiles, underwater sound equipment.
6. Martin Marietta	3.7	Titan missile, Apache aircraft, ammunition.
7. General Motors	3.6	Amraam, Maverick, Phoenix, and Tow missiles.
8. Lockheed	3.5	Trident missile, C-130 and P-3 aircraft, R&D for missile/space systems.
9. United Technologies	3.5	Aircraft engines, helicopters, R&D for aircraft.
10. Boeing	3.0	C-135 and E-3A aircraft, Chinook helicopters, R&D for aircraft and missiles.

Source: U.S. Department of Defense.

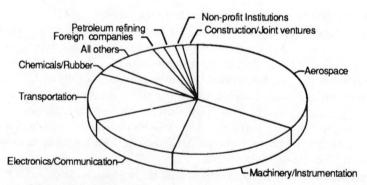

Figure 7-2.   Major Defense Contractor, by Industry, 1988. (*Source:* U.S. Department of Defense and author's estimates.)

and construction (Figure 7-2). Most American industries, such as lumber, food, textiles, primary metals, metal fabricators, services, and trade, do not loom large as prime defense contractors. Many firms in those industries, however, participate in the military market as suppliers or subcontractors to the major producer (see Statistical Appendix).

Many of the smaller second- and third-tier suppliers for the military report one or more of the following kinds of difficulties:

1. Inadequate funds for plant and equipment and insufficient working capital.
2. Inadequate technical expertise.
3. Poor fit vis-á-vis the required product mix of local prime contractors.
4. Lack of appropriate contacts on the part of subcontractors plus failure to pursue timely follow-up actions.
5. Inadequate knowledge about how to do business with the Department of Defense.[11]

Clearly, the larger the firm and the greater its defense business, the more likely it is to possess knowledge of military business procedures. In turn, such knowledge helps to maintain or increase market share.

Insight into the nature of the market can be gained by examining the companies that dominate this sector of the economy. Year in and year out, the top 100 defense companies receive approximately two-thirds of the prime contracts, by value (Figure 7-3). Contractor rankings hold fairly steady. Nine of the top ten firms in 1980 were also in the top ten in 1988. In 1988, the twenty-five firms with the largest

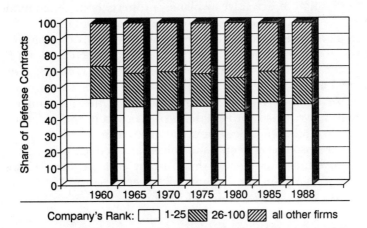

Figure 7-3. Concentration Trends in Procurement. (*Source:* U.S. Department of Defense.)

amount of contract awards received about one-half of the total, under-scoring the concentrated nature of the market.

PRICE FORMATION AND COMPETITION

There are fundamental differences between the way military depart-ments and civilian government agencies make their purchases. The typical procurement of armaments involves the government contract-ing with a private firm for an engineering effort to design and man-ufacture a product for which there is no private market. In contrast, the great bulk of procurement by civilian government agencies is accomplished by a large number of firms presenting sealed bids offer-ing to sell standard products at fixed prices.

A weapon system contract is awarded to a company after a lengthy series of negotiations and is the beginning of an extended contractual relationship with the military. The final cost of a good or service is dependent on the type of contract that has been negotiated. The Department of Defense uses two basic types of contracts—cost reim-bursement and fixed price—with many variations of each.

Fixed Price Versus Cost-Plus Contracts

Cost reimbursement contracts seem simple enough, with the govern-ment paying the costs and the producer having little incentive to cut expenses, but the actual amount the government pays depends on which costs are allowed. Many customary business expenses are ex-cluded: technical displays, unapproved overtime, business con-ferences, many of the bid and proposal expenses, employee moving costs, operation of executive airplanes, property taxes on equipment, interest payments, patents expense, and public relations.

The basic type of cost reimbursement contract is cost-plus-fixed-fee: the government bears the actual cost of production plus a fixed fee for the work. This type of contract is generally utilized for devel-opmental and initial production phases. The major incentive to the contractor is indirect—to perform so well that the government will decide to move ahead with full-scale production of the program.

Some cost-reimbursable contracts contain a direct incentive provi-sion, where producers keep a portion of any reduction in cost from the initial estimate as well as share in any cost overruns. However, there is a ceiling on the amount of "incentive profit" that can be earned as well as a floor under which the contractor's profit may not fall.

The second general category of governmental contracts are those where the price is determined or fixed at the outset. Here, incentive provisions are frequent, but with no floor protecting profits in case of major cost overruns. In view of the greater amount of risk assumed by the contractor in a fixed-price incentive contract, the target fee is normally higher than in the case of cost-reimbursement contracts, and the government's portion of the sharing formula is lower.

The firm-fixed-price contract provides the maximum incentive to control costs because all of the overrun or underrun is absorbed by the contractor. There is no provision for price adjustments. This approach is more comparable to civilian procedures than the other types of military contracts. The result is that price is unresponsive and profits are directly responsive to changes in the actual cost—the reverse of cost-plus-fixed-fee contracts.

There has been a clear tendency on the Pentagon's part to favor the fixed-price over the cost-reimbursement contracts. For 1988, fixed-price contracts were used in 79 percent of the purchase agreements, with the remaining 21 percent utilizing the cost-reimbursement approach. The Department of Defense now seems to be backing off from the heavy reliance on fixed-price contracts in response to the erosion in contractor earnings.[12] There is a widespread belief among defense industry professionals that it is impractical to use fixed-price contracts for the acquisition of weapon systems that do not exist at the time the order is placed. Almost by definition, invention of new products is frought with too much uncertainty for the costs to be estimated in advance with any precision.

Competitive Versus Negotiated Procurement

In 1984, Congress passed the Competition in Contracting Act, which decreed that whenever possible the Pentagon should seek out at least two bidders on a project. Before that time, most defense contracts were awarded with no competitive bidding. A considerable change has occurred since then.

By 1988, approximately one-half of the military contracts awarded (for which data are available) were made by means of competitive bidding;[13] however, only a small percentage of that was in response to formal advertising. Most "competitive" awards rely on negotiation between the government and its suppliers, but the Department of Defense maintains that such procurement does not signify lack of competition. In fact, there may be as many or more companies competing for a negotiated award as respond with sealed bids under formal advertising.

Effective competition, however, rarely occurs in follow-on or repeat orders for the same product. The rationale is that the company receiving the initial contract has been reimbursed for substantial start-up and learning costs as well as for the new technology that it has developed. A potential competitor for follow-on orders for that product is at a disadvantage because it would have to incur much of the expensive preparatory work already performed by the initial contractor.

Nevertheless, on occasion the armed services have found that they could achieve significant cost reductions in "follow-on" production by introducing an element of competition. The price of the Tomahawk cruise missile declined from slightly more than $1 million each in 1985 to $653,000 per unit in 1988 when McDonnell Douglas was allowed to compete with General Dynamics, the original contractor. The price of the Hellfire missile fell from $43,000 each in 1983 to $28,000 in 1988, largely because of competition between Rockwell International and Martin Marietta.

The deputy assistant secretary of defense for procurement was quoted at the time as saying, "Nothing has driven down prices as much as competition."[14] To some degree, however, the cost reductions may be illusory. Even in sole-source weapons production programs, unit costs decline over time as "learning" occurs on the part of the assembly workers, who become more experienced and thus more efficient on a project. Nevertheless, the prestigious Institute for Defense Analysis reported very positive results in its study of thirty-one defense products that had been switched from sole-source to competitive procurement. The findings showed an average savings of 35 percent when competition was introduced.[15]

In the 1980s, however, intense competition within the defense industry led to more "teaming," a process whereby two or more defense firms team up with each other to compete for a given weapon system. In theory, this approach spreads the risk and allows the companies to pool their technical expertise as to maximize opportunities for technological breakthroughs. In reality, however, team participants are potential competitors and they may be reluctant to reveal their more sophisticated innovations to each other. Also, to the extent that teaming is effective, it tends to reduce competition in the military market.[16]

Measuring the Degree of Competition
A useful method of analyzing the degree of competition in the military market is to examine the changing market positions of the dominant firms (see Table 7-3). Twenty of the top twenty-five contractors in 1971 were also in the top twenty-five in 1988. This stability results in good measure from the substantial barriers to entry discussed earlier.

In contrast, considerable mobility is evidenced by the changes in

Table 7-3 Turnover Among the 100 Major Defense Contractors, 1971 to 1988

Top 100 Contractors in 1988	Ranking in 1971					Total
	1 to 25	26 to 50	51 to 75	76 to 100	Below 100	
1 to 25	20	5	0	0	0	25
26 to 50	2	7	3	3	10	25
51 to 75	0	5	2	4	14	25
76 to 100	0	1	2	1	21	25
Total	22	18	7	8	45	100

Source: U.S. Department of Defense.

rankings of the firms that have large but not dominant shares of defense business. Of the next largest seventy-five defense contractors in 1988, only thirty were on the list of the top 100 companies in 1971. This mobility among second tier defense firms largely reflects the changing product mix of government procurement as well as the influence of technology.

LONG-TERM IMPACTS OF THE MILITARY– INDUSTRY RELATIONSHIP

In its long-term dealings with those companies or divisions of companies that cater primarily to the military market, the Department of Defense has assumed many of the management decisions about policy and procedures that are made by the companies themselves in commercial markets. In the words of one analyst, "private firms in the American defense industry are subject to public controls of unequalled scope and complexity."[17]

This government assumption of, and active participation in, private business decision making takes three major forms: (1) determining the choice of products the defense firms produce, (2) influencing the source of capital funds that they use, (3) and supervising their internal operations. This degree of government involvement arises almost exclusively in the case of weapon systems. It does not characterize the procurement of desks, chairs, and other conventional items purchased through fixed-price contracts awarded via sealed-bid competition.

The Department of Defense uses its vast financial resources to supply much of the plant and equipment used by its major contractors for defense work. In addition, the working capital of military contractors is augmented by billions of dollars of "progress" payments, paid while the work is still in progress.

Military procurement regulations provide overwhelming incentives for using government working capital. Progress payments equal to as much as 80 percent of the costs incurred on government contracts are provided without interest charge to the contractors; however, should these companies decide to rely on private sources for working capital, they will not be able to charge their interest payments to government contracts. By increasing the extent to which public rather than private capital finances the operations of defense contractors, the procurement regulations attenuate the exposure of these firms to the discipline of financial markets.

The most pervasive way in which the military establishment assumes the management decision-making functions of its contractors is through procurement legislation and rules governing the awarding of contracts. Regulations require private suppliers to "take it or leave it" when it comes to standard clauses in their contracts, which give the government contracting and surveillance power over the internal operations of these companies.

The authority assumed by the government customer includes power to review and veto a host of company decisions: which activities to perform in-house and which to subcontract, which firms to use as subcontractors, which products to buy domestically and which to im-

Table 7-4 Comparison of Civilian and Defense-Oriented Firms

Characteristic	Typical Civilian-Oriented Firm	Typical Defense-Oriented Firm
Products	Low technology	High technology
Market structure		
Demand	Competitive	Monopsonistic
Supply	Competitive	Oligopolistic
Prices	Constrained by market competition	Determined or influenced by government
Outputs	Constrained by market competition	Determined by government
Financing	Security markets	Federal government
Burden of risk	Borne by the firm	Divided between government and the firm
Managerial discretion	Relatively wide	Severely constrained
Profits	Constrained by market competition	Regulated via contract

Source: Adapted from Neil H. Jacoby, "The Corporation in Military Service," in George A. Steiner, editor, *Contemporary Challenges in the Business-Society Relationship* (Los Angeles: UCLA Graduate School of Management, 1972).

port, what internal financial system to utilize, what minimum as well as average wage rates to pay, and how much overtime work to authorize. Thus, when a business firm enters into a contract to produce a weapon system for the military, it takes on a quasi-public character. This is given implicit recognition by requirements for the firm to conduct itself in many ways as a government agency—to abide by buy-American, equal employment, depressed area, prevailing wage, environmental, and similar statutes. (Table 7-4 sets forth the key differences between defense-oriented and civilian-oriented firms; the variations in basic characteristics are pervasive, covering prices, profits, technology, and risk-bearing.)

PAST ATTEMPTS AT REFORM

A series of widely publicized shortcomings in specific military procurements arose during the rapid buildup of the 1980s. Items such as hammers, toilet seats, and coffeemakers were alleged to have been purchased for prices far exceeding their commercial market price (in most cases, the taxpayer was not "overcharged," as shown in Chapter 8). Nevertheless, significant changes were made in federal procurement policy, mainly in the direction of tightening controls over contractors. Simultaneously, the passage of the Gramm–Rudman–Hollings deficit reduction law intensified the downward pressures on the entire military budget. These new influences and requirements have increased the cost of doing business with the Pentagon and discouraged many firms from staying in the military market:

- Contractors must fund a greater share of initial research and development costs. They now share development costs with the Pentagon, which means that they often incur a loss on development contracts. Moreover, they no longer have a virtual assurance that, if the program goes into production, they will be awarded the follow-on production contracts.
- Contractors must now pay for at least 50 percent of their expenses for tooling and test equipment. In the past, these expenses were reimbursable as they occurred. Contractors must also bear the costs of marketing their weapons abroad.
- The Tax Reform Act of 1986 repealed the completed contract method of accounting for taxes and eliminated the investment tax credit. Defense contractors are now required to pay taxes annually on a portion of their completed contracts, regardless of whether they actually realize a profit on those contracts in a given year. The tax deferral permitted by the completed contract method had been a significant source of cash to major contractors.
- The Pentagon has imposed higher administrative costs on defense

contractors by virtue of more stringent government record-keeping requirements.

- Recent changes in the *Federal Acquisition Regulation* shift the burden of proof of the reasonableness of contractor costs from the government to the contractor and abolish the presumption of reasonableness previously attached to incurred costs.
- Defense contractors are now required to provide warranties for aircraft engines and for all new systems generally.
- Delays occur in awarding new contracts because of new procedures that give losing firms more opportunities to protest the awards.
- Progress payments have been reduced from 90 percent to 80 percent of costs and greater delays are being reported in receiving the money—while interest expense remains unallowable on defense contracts.
- The Defense Department's profit policy has been revised to attain a reduction in contractor earnings.
- The classification of "allowable" costs on defense contracts has been tightened.
- By statute, Congress has emphasized competitive and dual or multiple sourcing.
- Delays of three to four years occur in auditing and receiving payments on completed work.[18]

In the aggregate, the impact of these policy changes has been to decrease substantially the profitability of defense business and to reduce the attractiveness of the military market.[19] Some firms have been forced to make large zero-profit bids, while others felt obliged to invest hundreds of millions of dollars in competitive programs when there was a reasonable chance not only of losing the competition, but also of having the entire project cancelled.

Under the circumstances, it is not surprising that the major defense contractors have been reluctant to make substantial new investment in their factories and production equipment. For U.S. manufacturing as a whole, the ratio of capital spending to value of goods shipped rose from 3.8 percent in 1980 to 4.3 percent in 1985. For defense supply firms, the ratio fell from 3.9 percent to 3.6 percent.

A dramatic example is furnished by the Grumman Corporation, which developed and produced the highly complex F-14 jet fighter on equipment whose average age was thirty-four years. Most of the equipment had been provided by the government during World War II. Grumman was producing these planes basically as it had been doing for thirty years—almost entirely by hand. After tracing a pattern onto aluminum sheets, workers would guide the sheets through thirty-year-old band saws, and any required holes would be drilled manually. The rejection rate resulting from such manual operation is extremely high—as much as 70–80 percent. Not only are such operations expensive, but they also take a great deal of time, which compounds the cost.[20]

It is difficult to overemphasize the tremendous extent of government involvement in the internal operations of defense contractors. For a large defense company, an entire suite of offices is typically assigned to the military's full-time resident inspectors and compliance officers. It is hard to imagine any commercially oriented company that is permanently host to customer representatives who regularly participate in the day-to-day running of the organization.

One defense company chief executive lamented the administrative costs of dealing with the more than 600 people in the Pentagon's program office assigned to one of his company's projects. Another indicated that, in all of his manufacturing areas except defense work, he was cutting back on inspectors and pushing responsibility back to the line in order to improve efficiency and clarify the responsibility for quality and productivity. In contrast, the number of inspectors on his defense program was increasing in response to military requirements. A third CEO described production delays resulting from bottlenecks arising because military representatives had to approve all purchase orders over $5,000.[21]

Perhaps the most intrusive type of government intervention in the defense industry comes at an earlier stage of the expenditure process—when Congress authorizes new programs and appropriates new funds. It is the rare defense bill that is not saddled with all sorts of expensive "extras" before it passes both houses of the legislature. Because most of the entitlements—notably Social Security and medicare—are permanently authorized, they do not require annual appropriations. Thus, defense is the largest single budget item requiring congressional approval each year.

It is not surprising, therefore, that the defense authorization and appropriation bills become the occasion for individual members adding all sorts of riders and making a host of special requests before the bills are enacted. Many of these congressional add-ons are minor and merely silly, such as the requirement for a Marriage and Family Therapy Report Demonstration Project. Some riders, however, are major and costly, such as the additional aircraft, missiles, and ships that Congress inserts into the military budget, usually with the prodding of the senators and representatives from the area in which the item is to be produced.

You do not have to be an old Pentagon hand to reach the conclusion of humorist Russell Baker, "The Pentagon budget has replaced the old rivers-and-harbors bill as Congress' main pork course."[22] Former

Senator Thomas Eagleton provides an equally trenchant view of the congressional attitude toward the military: "a pork barrel pursuit like building dams, bridges, highways, or post offices . . . Military bases mean jobs. Weapons mean jobs."[23]

NOTES

1. Philip Gold, "Tank Production and a Catch-22," *Insight*, May 14, 1990, p. 22.

2. George Sammet, Jr., and David Green, *Defense Acquisition Management* (Boca Raton: Florida Atlantic University Press, 1990), p. 87.

3. *Prime Contract Awards, Fiscal Year 1988* (Washington, D.C.: U.S. Department of Defense, 1988), pp. 9, 13.

4. The MAC Group, *The Impact on Defense Industrial Capability of Changes in Procurement and Tax Policy* (Cambridge, Mass.: MAC Group, 1988), p. 21.

5. Ibid., p. 22.

6. G. K. Smith et al. *A Preliminary Perspective on Regulatory Activities and Effects in Weapons Acquisition* (Santa Monica, Calif.: RAND Corporation, 1988), p. 2.

7. Computed from data contained in *1988 Year-End Review and Forecast* (Washington, D.C.: Aerospace Industries Association, 1988), Table XI.

8. Jacob Goodwin, *Brotherhood of Arms* (New York: Times Books, 1985), p. xi.

9. David K. Henry and Richard P. Oliver, "The Defense Buildup, 1977–85: Effects on Production and Employment," *Monthly Labor Review*, August 1987, p. 10.

10. See Murray L. Weidenbaum, *Business, Government, and the Public*, Fourth edition (Englewood Cliffs, N.J.: Prentice Hall, 1990), Chapter 14; Jacques S. Gansler, *Affording Defense* (Cambridge: MIT Press, 1989), p. 246.

11. Lee E. Koppelman and Pearl M. Kamer, *Maximizing the Potential of Long Island's Defense Sector in an Era of Change* (New York: Long Island Regional Planning Board, 1988), pp. 19–20.

12. "Are U.S. Defense Contractors an Endangered Species?" *Aerospace Industries Association Newsletter*, June 1988, p. 2.

13. *Prime Contract Awards*, p. 45.

14. Quoted in Richard W. Stevenson, "Competition for Contracts Trims Costs for Pentagon," *The New York Times*, March 31, 1988, p. 1.

15. Richard A. Stubbing, *The Defense Game* (New York: Harper & Row, 1986), p. 225.

16. Koppelman and Kamer, *Long Island's Defense Sector*, pp. 21–22.

17. William E. Kovacic, "The Sorcerer's Apprentice: Public Regulation of the Weapons Acquisition Process," in Robert Higgs, ed., *Arms, Politics, and the Economy* (New York: Holmes & Meier, 1990), p. 105.

18. MAC Group, *Impact on Defense Industrial Capability*.

19. *The Impact of Government Policy on Defense Contractors* (Washington, D.C.: Financial Executives Institute, 1987); Gansler, *Affording Defense*, p. 243.

20. Gansler, *Affording Defense*, p. 251.

21. MAC Group, *Impact on Defense Industrial Capability*, p. 33.

22. Russell Baker, "Chops and Bacon Away," *The New York Times*, August 19, 1989, p. 13.

23. Thomas Eagleton, "Eisenhower Would Put Generals Out of Work," *St. Louis Post-Dispatch*, December 10, 1989, p. 3B.

CHAPTER 8

Reforming Military Procurement

According to every serious examination of the military procurement system, the Defense Department buys tens of billions of dollars of weapons and equipment each year in a way that is excessively bureaucratic and needlessly costly.

David Packard, former deputy secretary of defense and chairman of the highly regarded President's Commission on Defense Management, noted that the results of the current procedures for bidding on defense contracts would be just as good if "you put the names of the qualified bidders on the wall and threw darts . . . we've got a lot of complexity in this process that is counterproductive."[1]

One of the key reforms urged by the Packard Commission was the appointment of a new undersecretary of defense for procurement. Robert Costello, who held that post, lamented that the Department of Defense wastes 20 to 30 cents of every dollar it spends on procurement.[2]

A panel of senior government and business officials convened by the Center for Strategic and International Studies in 1989 echoed Costello's sentiments:

About 25 percent of the cost of research, development, and procurement of military products is wasted as a result of unnecessary oversight, auditing and regulation; program instability and poor estimates; excessive performance requirements; and overspecification of product and process in defense acquisition.[3]

Another defense industry analyst concluded that "Overmanagement has grossly stretched out the time necessary to develop weapons and has, in the process, driven up their costs . . . "[4] A 1989 study of the Japanese aerospace industry concluded that its companies consistently experience shorter development times and more flexible product designs than do their American counterparts.[5] Clearly, the very substantial cutbacks in American military spending described in earlier chapters underscore the need to focus on getting "more bang per buck." Reforms, however, need to be based on an understanding of the current military procurement process.

IMMERSING OURSELVES IN THE PROCESS

To begin, we must realize that the government's economic deregulation over the past fifteen years ignored the military procurement process. In striking contrast to the dramatic efforts to streamline civilian regulation, such as elimination of the Civil Aeronautics Board, the complexity of military regulation has continued to grow and often to accelerate. This expansion has occurred despite—or perhaps in part because of—a number of attempts at reform.

For example, in an attempt to improve the way the federal government purchases goods and services, the three major procurement agencies—the General Services Administration (for civilian agencies generally), NASA, and the Department of Defense—jointly issued a *Federal Acquisition Regulation (FAR)*. This one "regulation" is a massive two-volume handbook.

The *Federal Acquisition Regulation*

FAR supposedly replaced the cumbersome *Armed Services Procurement Regulation* and its counterparts in the other two agencies. The foreword to *FAR* clearly states, "It precludes agency acquisition regulations that unnecessarily repeat, paraphrase, or otherwise restate the *FAR* and it limits agency acquisition regulations to those necessary to implement *FAR* policies and procedure within an agency."[6]

What, then, about the bureaucrats whose turf is threatened? Inevitably, the Department of Defense issued a few supplementary instructions to deal with special situations not covered by *FAR*. The resulting Department of Defense publication, *Federal Acquisition Regulation Supplement* (affectionately known as *DAR* in the trade) is even larger than the *FAR*. In addition, defense acquisition circulars are issued periodically to modify the *DAR* and the individual services and purchasing commands write special and voluminous amplifying instructions.

The scope of the federal procurement regulation is very broad and its level of detail is very fine. Some of the topics covered include:

- Specifications for contract files (one to be kept by the office awarding the contract—with forty-one different categories of documents, a second by the office administering it, a third by the office paying it).
- Regulations for purchasing from domestic producers ("Buy Amer-

ican" laws extend to all tiers of subcontractors regardless of how remote from the prime contractors).[7]
- Encouragement to use "small disadvantaged business concerns" (each contractor must pay liquidated damages equal to the full dollar amount by which it fails to meet its small business goals).[8]
- Requirements for written affirmative action programs.
- Demonstrated compliance with clean air and clean water statutes.

In total, federal procurement generates about 290 million hours of paperwork a year. The Defense Department more than holds its own. Accounting for almost 77 percent of federal procurement, the Pentagon is responsible for about 90 percent of the procurement paperwork.[9]

The *Defense Acquisition Regulation*

The *DAR* is the Defense Department's instructions to its own procurement personnel. This "supplement" to the *FAR* is larger than Webster's unabridged dictionary.

The coverage is awesome, extending from acquisition planning to methods of awarding contracts to types of contracts awarded to cost accounting standards to patents and copyrights. The patient reader must begin with Part 1, describing the federal acquisition regulation system and continue through Part 70, covering the acquisition of computer resources.

All this is followed by twelve appendices, such as Notice and Hearing Under Gratuities Clause (Appendix D) and Department of Defense Foreign Tax Relief Program (Appendix Q). Appendix N is especially noteworthy since it is devoted to the Uniform Procurement Instrument Identification Numbering System. All it does is provide, for each military activity, a six-digit Procurement Instrument Identification Number, followed by a two-digit call/order serial number. The fact that it takes 137 pages merely to list each of those military activities suggests the vastness of the United States military establishment.

DAR also incorporates two manuals. These are reprinted in their entirety, one covering pricing and the other small purchases. Finally, six supplements are included (technically, the entire *DAR* is just a supplement—to *FAR*). Daunting in their own right, *FAR* and *DAR* are amplified in a massive body of auxiliary regulatory commands that includes court decisions and directives on the part of each of the military services. According to former Navy Secretary John Lehman, Jr., existing legislation and case law governing Navy procurement alone occupies 1,152 linear feet of library shelf space.[10]

A 1987 report issued by the Defense Department's inspector general concluded that 45 percent of the regulations on military procurement violated established criteria for writing these regulations. That is, they were either not unique to the agency or duplicated or paraphrased higher-level directives, or they were unclear or inconsistent.

In response to that report in 1989, the Office of Federal Procurement Policy reported that 881 pages of regulations had been eliminated and 816 more were either changed or simplified. That glacial pace means that there are still about 30,000 pages of federal procurement regulations that need to be changed or simplified or eliminated.[11]

THE CAUSES OF COMPLEXITY

The Department of Defense's procurement regulations are far more than a gigantic exercise in bureaucracy. They arise from four interacting factors:

- The vastness of the military enterprise.
- The congressional desire to "micromanage."
- The imposition of socioeconomic objectives.
- Human shortcomings.

In considering these four influences, it is useful to note the conclusion of a team of RAND Corporation researchers. They reported that, unlike the traditional regulatory process, regulation of defense procurement does not pursue a coherent strategy, such as trading off higher prices for higher quality. Because the defense regulatory process is so fragmented, regulations can be contradictory. They are often imposed without consideration of how they will interact with other regulations. Also, there are no provisions for evaluation or "sunset" rules.[12]

In traditional economic regulation, different products and services (trucking, electric power, and banking) are regulated separately. Each regulatory agency takes into account the distinctive features of the industry over which it has jurisdiction. In contrast, most military regulations are uniform, regardless of the product being acquired or the industry producing it.

The Vastness of the Military Enterprise
It is impossible, of course, to buy tens of thousands of items from thousands of different suppliers to be used by hundreds of different operating units without going into detail. Also, the details in the *DAR* are so overwhelming that at times they border on the ludicrous.

With more than 2 million people to feed, the military buys lots of milk and milk products. Those who think that milk is a fairly standard product underestimate the ingenuity of those assigned the task of writing procurement regulations. The Department of Defense regulations on "bakery and dairy products contracts" cover chemical and microbiological requirements and containers and equipment for dispensing milk. They also incorporate by specific reference fifteen clauses contained in other sections of the regulation:

Contract Clause	Subject
52.217-7300	Delivery vehicles
52.217-7301	Time of delivery
52.217-7302	Change in plant location
52.217-7303	Sanitary conditions
52.217-7304	Remedies under delivery orders
52.217-7305	Examination and testing
52.217-7306	Deficiency adjustment
52.217-7307	Warning
52.217-7308	Suspension
52.217-7309	Default
52.217-7310	Reinstatement
52.217-7311	Code dating
52.217-7312	Marking
52.217-7313	Responsibility for containers and equipment
52.217-7314	Containers and equipment

In a subsequent section of *DAR*, the milk tester is given very specific instructions. "When samples are selected from containers of half-gallon size or smaller, the entire content of the container shall constitute the sample; when samples are selected from containers larger than half-gallon, a half-pint sample shall be withdrawn for laboratory analysis."

In ensuring the adequacy of the quality being purchased, the procurement officers encounter the term "milk solids nonfat value." This is defined in the regulation as "the average Chicago top price for Commercial Sales, Extra, Grade, Nonfat Dry Milk, Spray . . . as reported in the aforementioned Weekly Dairy Comments, multiplied by 1.45."

The defense establishment also must enter into contracts for laundry service. It does so on the basis of either weight or number of articles. With the weight approach, a choice must be made between a presorted (bag type) or unsorted (simple bulk weight) basis. A "bundle" of clothing must contain exactly thirteen pieces, and in all cases colors must be separated from whites. The *DAR* takes the matter of laundry very seriously.

These are two simple and hardly secret activities. While details about the purchase of weapon systems are "classified," procurement is orders of magnitude more complicated.

In their book on military purchasing, General Sammet and Colonel Green give the example of a military contractor inspecting the casting of a component it purchased and was forced to reject because of pin holes. They note that pin holes do not affect either the utility of the casting or its strength. Nevertheless, small holes are not on the approved drawing and a special waiver would be necessary to get the casting accepted. The result, as any good bureaucrat would expect, is that good castings were scrapped.[13]

The military establishment has tried—in its own way—to be responsive to criticisms about the complexity of its procurement system. For example, the Defense Department permits the contracting officer to use simplified basic ordering agreements, but needs a complicated paragraph to explain when the basic ordering agreement can be used:

> A basic ordering agreement may be used to expedite contracting if after a competitive solicitation of quotations or proposals from the maximum number of qualified sources, other than a solicitation accomplished by use of Standard Form 33, it is determined that the successful responsive offeror holds a basic ordering agreement, the terms of which are either identical to those of the solicitation or different in a way that could have no impact on price, quality or delivery, and if it is determined further that issuance of an order against the basic order agreement rather than preparation of a separate contract would not be prejudicial to the other offerors.

Not surprisingly, many contracting officers prefer to bypass the "simplified" alternative.

The Congressional Desire to Micromanage

A second major influence on procurement complexity is the tendency of Congress to get involved in operational details (often referred to as "micromanagement"). In 1970, the Blue Ribbon Defense Panel reported the existence of forty separate statutes governing defense procurement in addition to the basic armed services procurement legislation. The statutes cover such diverse matters as assignment and adjudication of claims, judicial review of agency contract decisions, performance bonds, use of small business, labor standards, anti-kickback provisions, conflicts of interest, Buy American, use of convict labor, and procurement of supplies made by prisoners and the blind.[14]

Table 8-1   Legislative Micromanagement of Military Procurement, 1983–1988

Public Law 98-72 (1983) is designed to improve small business access to federal procurement information. It revises "synopsizing" requirements.

Public Law 98-94 (1983) calls for the use of independent cost estimates for major defense programs. The statute establishes a Director for Operational Test and Evaluation. It also requires a report to Congress on spare parts management.

Public Law 98-212 (1983) requires the Department of Defense to obtain weapon systems guarantees (warranties) from contractors. It prohibits the purchase of commercial products if a small business would be rejected due to lack of commercial acceptance of the item.

Public Law 98-369 (1984) sets strict standards for obtaining competition. The law establishes revised protest procedures and also revises synopsizing requirements.

Public Law 98-473 (1984) prohibits initiation of full-scale engineering development of a major system prior to notifying Congress of a competitive procurement plan or the reasons why not. The law requires notification of Congress of multiyear contracts with an economic order quantity in excess of $20 million.

Public Law 98-525 (1984) establishes requirements for the use of prequalification procedures. It also provides controls and requirements for technical data and sets rank and grade for competition advocates. It establishes tours of duty for program managers and sets rules for allocating overhead to spare parts. The law sets rules governing the commercial pricing of spare parts (lowest commercial price) and revises and codifies requirements for weapon system guarantees. It also requires identifying suppliers and sources of items provided under contracts.

Public Law 98-577 (1984) requires mandatory publication of procurement regulations in the Federal Register for a public comment period. It revises synopsizing requirements. The law also provides for the placement of SBA spare parts breakout representatives in major defense acquisition centers.

Public Law 99-145 (1985) codifies the description of allowable costs under defense contracts. It requires dual sourcing of major defense programs and codifies requirements for Should Cost analyses. It also sets revolving door rules and penalties for overcharging by contractors. The law also directs the use of work measurement standards in certain contracts.

Public Law 99-190 (1986) requires employment of Alaskan and Hawaiian residents in military construction contracts in those states. It revises description of allowable costs.

Public Law 99-433 (1986) mandates the organization of procurement policy staffs of military departments at the secretarial level.

Public Law 99-500 (1986) establishes the duties of the undersecretary of defense for acquisition. It restricts undefinitized contractual actions and revises the law pertaining to commercial pricing for spare parts. It revises the Truth in Negotiations Act as well as progress payment rates. The law establishes competition requirements for the acquisition of prototypes in major systems and revises technical data requirements. It also expands protest procedures for defense contracts.

Public Law 99-661 (1986) establishes a goal of 5 percent of procurement, R&D, and construction dollars authorized for the award of contracts to minorities and authorizes payment of a 10 percent premium for the purposes of achieving the goal.

Public Law 99-634 (1986) prohibits subcontractor kickbacks to government prime contractors.

Public Law 100-180 (1987) provides for congressional oversight of cost-of-schedule variances in certain programs. It authorizes Congress to consider programs as milestone authorization despite not having been so identified by the secretary of defense. It revises definitions in the Truth in Negotiations Act. It directs that contracting

---

(continued)

Table 8-1   (*Continued*)

officers' performance evaluations include their ability to increase awards to minority firms. It substantially revises the law pertaining to rights in technical data. The law establishes rules governing contracts costs for special tooling and special test equipment and places restrictions on purchase of foreign-made administrative motor vehicles.

Public Law 102-202 (1987) restricts purchases from Toshiba and Konigsberg Vsafenfabrikk to punish them for providing sensitive information to the Soviet Union. The law also requires notifying Congress ten days in advance before terminating multiyear contracts. It requires the undersecretary of defense for acquisition to approve all fixed price R&D contracts with a value of $10 million or more. It prohibits imports of certain types of machine tools, mooring and anchor chains, super computers, and equipment items that use textiles.

The Conference Report on HR 4264 (1988) requires establishing a long-term plan to ensure that Department of Defense profit policies are kept current. It also requires a yearly report to Congress on efforts to prevent excess profits and establishes a Public/Government Advisory Committee to consider the profit issue and report to Congress on its findings. This law establishes an Industry/Government Advisory Committee to consider ways to enhance Department of Defense and industry cooperation on such matters as self-governing oversight programs, debarment procedures, and alternative dispute procedures. It requires a report to Congress on internal Department of Defense efforts to streamline acquisition procedures. It prohibits Department of Defense from requiring prime contractors to submit proposals that will enable the United States to acquire competitive items that were developed at private expense. Finally, it requires the Department of Defense to establish a policy governing inventory accounting systems and requires contractor certification of the system.

Source: U.S. Senate, Committee on Armed Services, *Defense Acquisition Process*, 1989.

The tendency for Congress to pass such legislation has accelerated since 1970, and each legislative enactment generates a wave of implementing regulations.[15] Between 1983 and 1988, Congress enacted sixteen "micromanagement" types of provisions that complicate the military procurement process (see Table 8-1). They reflect the loss of congressional confidence in the candor and cooperation of the Pentagon, especially in responding to legislative mandates with which the Department of Defense does not agree.

Why else would Congress have to insist that the Defense Department notify it of a competitive procurement plan before beginning full-scale development of a major weapon system? Why else would Congress have to require the Department of Defense to establish a long-term plan to ensure that its profit policies are kept current? Why else would Congress have to pass a law to get the Department of Defense to establish a policy on inventory accounting systems?

Most of the new statutory requirements, at least on the surface, seem to be useful. Requiring defense contractors to provide warranties for the weapon systems they sell to the military seemed such a "natural" idea that a few years ago Congress enacted this brainstorm into law, but the results have fallen far short of expectations. When the General Accounting Office looked into the matter, they found that many of the warranties are not used, so that the Department of Defense does not get sufficient value from the added cost of requiring them.

For example, when the navy bought 80 Phalanx close-in weapon systems to help protect its ships from missile attacks, it also bought a $546,261 service warranty to protect the navy against excessive repair costs. During the twelve-month warranty period, the navy reported 251 failures on the antimissile systems; however, the contractor paid none of the repair costs. That happened because, under the warranty, the company was responsible for repairs only if the navy experienced more than 5,238 failures. The experience of the other services was just as bad.

In 1984 and 1985, the army's tank-automotive command claimed only $38,987 in reimbursements on $23.6 million worth of warranties bought on six major weapon systems. The army paid $9.9 million in warranties on its M-1 tanks, but was reimbursed for only $10,453 worth of claims by the end of the warranty period in 1987. The contractor refused to pay many of the claims because they were not filed within the stipulated ninety days.[16] The members of Congress who proposed the warranty requirement clearly did not anticipate the new and additional cost on the weapon systems.

Congress has also restricted the amount that can be spent on individual weapon systems. For example, the Department of Defense Appropriations Act for 1986 stated, "None of the funds in this act may be obligated for procurement of 120-mm mortars or 120-mm mortar ammmunition manufactured outside of the United States." Some of the restrictions get very detailed.

The tendency for congressional micromanagement of military operations shows no sign of lessening. In its report on the Department of Defense Authorization for the fiscal year 1990, the House Armed Services Committee made 215 requests on all sorts of topics. An additional twenty such studies were imposed during the debate on the House floor.[17] In large part, the congressional response represents reaction—nay, overreaction—to "scandals" or other highly publicized shortcomings, but as William Gregory has noted in his study of military procurement:

> Often . . . scandals are simply reasonable arguments over who owes what to whom under the ambiguous terms of today's capricious regulations and complex contracts, or they concern judgment calls as to how much infallibility should be expected of engineers and manufacturers in producing defense equipment.[18]

The tension between Congress and the procurement managers arises from an even more fundamental shortcoming. Legislative policy is often developed by people with little or no industrial experience. They are, therefore, more likely to concentrate on controlling profits than on improving efficiency (and thereby reducing cost—which represents about 95 percent of the price of most government contracts).

Tensions could also be reduced if members of Congress did not take such cheap shots at government officials as publicizing the case of the $110 diode (normally a 4-cent item), without also mentioning the government's accounting system for allocating costs. In this case, the Department of Defense purchased a high-value electronic amplifier in the same contract, and the prevailing military accounting method called for distributing overhead costs equally between the two items. Clearly, this procedure "unfairly" increases the cost of the low-value item and decreases the cost of the high-value item. The *total* cost that the government paid for the two items was correct; the government was *not* overcharged. This basic point was ignored in the press.

Were each defense contractor to set up a number of elaborate overhead pools, the proper charges could be allocated to each item and price disparities could be avoided. This time-consuming process would ensure that the final price paid for any one item would be more "realistic," but the government's total procurement costs would also be more expensive. For the moment, the most cost-effective solution would be for members of Congress (and the press) to forgo the luxury of taking those cheap shots.

The Imposition of Socioeconomic Objectives

The standard congressional response to a policy problem with military procurement can be caricatured as follows: Don't try to solve it. Just set up another layer of bureaucracy and tell them to worry about it.

Concerned about the inadequate competition for government contracts? Just require each federal procurement agency to designate a "competition advocate" to worry about it. Also give him/her authority to review the procurement operations of the agency and to send reports to the agency's senior procurement executive (*FAR* 6.501–6.502).

Concerned that small business does not get enough government contracts? Just require each federal procurement agency to set up an office of Small and Disadvantaged Business Utilization. Also have that office assign a "small business technical adviser" to each procurement activity of the agency and have him/her review every acquisition to determine whether a recommendation should be made to establish a set-aside program for small business. In addition, require each contracting officer to "make every reasonable effort" to find additional

small business concerns before issuing solicitations to bid. Also tell
him/her to allow the "maximum amount of time" for firms to submit
those bids.

In addition, authorize the Small Business Administration to review
(within five working days) any proposed solicitation for subcontracts
above a designated dollar threshold, then evaluate on a case-by-case
or aggregate basis the compliance of each contractor with its approved
subcontract plan (FAR 19.201–19.207). Concerned that we import too
much? Set up a reporting system that goes into exhaustive detail.

Unfortunately, this pattern of congressional response generates a
twofold benefit for legislators. Initially, the Congress can claim credit
for taking action. Subsequently, legislators can criticize the resulting
inefficiency of government.

In 1988, the House Committee on Armed Services listed thirty-
three different "social and economic programs" that generate requirements affecting military procurement. The requirements range
from government-wide provisions (such as labor standards and equal
employment opportunity) to restrictions on purchases for the military
assistance program,[19] but none is related to enhancing national security. Many of the congressional "add-ons" are designed to shelter an
industry from foreign competition, and many are advantageous to
specific groups or interests (small businesses, the blind, labor surplus
areas, Vietnam veterans, and residents of Alaska and Hawaii). Public
Law 99–661 authorizes the Department of Defense to pay a 10 percent premium in order to achieve the goal of awarding 5 percent of
procurement, R&D, and construction awards to minorities.

None of these special provisions is generated by the desire to improve the military acquisition system. Each represents another burden
placed on the system to achieve nonmilitary objectives.

A simple—but surely not easy—way of getting more "bang per
buck" would be for Congress to vote down attempts by members to
insert pure pork in military authorization and appropriation bills.
One example among a great many is the $13.5 million that Senator
Edward Kennedy (D-MA) put in for a noncompetitive contract for
military research to build what he called a "high technology resource
center" at Northeastern University in Boston. The senator's testimony
suggests that the main purpose of building this college library was to
provide construction jobs and thus help the economy of a poor community where the building is to be located.[20]

Members of Congress acting as shills for local interests is surely a
nonpartisan phenomenon. When Secretary of Defense Dick Cheney
wanted to reduce the number of F-14D fighter aircraft being ordered
from the largest Long Island defense contractor, the Grumman Corporation, the local congressional delegation lobbied aggressively and

successfully to restore the cut. Republican Representative Norman Lent (N.Y.) was quoted as saying, "If the Cheney budget were enacted, Grumman would have suffered a very hard landing."[21] Not all congressional lobbying efforts are successful. Two years later, in 1991, the Defense Department succeeded in terminating the F-14 fighter aircraft program and Grumman did announce that it was laying off 7 percent of its work force.

Nevertheless, few members of Congress ever consider the long-term effects of using defense procurement to dispense patronage and redistribute income and wealth, but the consequence is that each weapon system costs far more than it would if the overriding purpose of defense spending were simply the efficient realization of military capability.

Much of the problem results from the way in which Congress operates. Defense is so large and important that almost every member wants to get into "the act." This means that no single congressional committee sets military policy or even votes on the annual military budget.

First the budget committees (one for the Senate and the other for the House of Representatives), then the armed services committees, and then the appropriations committees hold detailed hearings at which key military personnel testify on the same issues over and over again. Subsequently, each committee reports out detailed legislation covering much of the same ground. In the aggregate, the results are the universally criticized "micromanagement" by the legislature.

On average, every working day the Department of Defense receives 450 written inquiries and over 2,500 telephone inquiries from members of Congress and their staffs *plus* three requirements for separate reports to Congress each necessitating on the average over 1,100 man-hours to prepare *plus* fourteen hours of testimony by senior Department of Defense officials *plus* almost three new audits of the Department of Defense by the General Accounting Office.[22] Fundamental change will not occur until there is more trust of the executive branch and more of a concensus on basic priorities between Congress and the administration in office.

Human Shortcomings

Much of the verbosity of military procurement regulations is an attempt to deal with the lack of training, technical skills, and experience of procurement officers.[23] The lack of quality is thus overwhelmed by sheer quantity. Over one-half million military and civilian personnel spend all or a substantial part of their workday on acquisition activities.

The turnover rate in the case of key procurement managers is awesome. One General Accounting Office survey found that the average tenure of a military program manager (including experience as a deputy program manager) was slightly over two years. During the eight to twelve years of its development, a weapon system may have four or five different military officers in charge.[24]

Secretary Cheney acknowledges the conclusion of the Packard Commission that, compared to its industry counterparts, the Defense Department's procurement staff is "undertrained, underpaid, and inexperienced."[25] Identifying these shortcomings is much easier than rectifying them. It would take an act of Congress to permit the military establishment to do something that is standard for private business—to reimburse its civilian personnel for coursework to enhance their job skills.

To deal with the qualitative shortcomings of its procurement people, the Department of Defense has inserted pages and pages of naïve and elementary language into the *DAR* such as "Profit, generally, is the basic motive of business enterprise . . . " [Section 16.101(a)] or "In certain instances, a sound decision may be possible after a simple review. . . . Under other circumstances, a more comprehensive review and analysis will be required" [Section 9.1–7(4)(1)].

Another shortcoming of the traditional method of staffing the military procurement function is that this bureaucratic routine attracts bureaucratically oriented people. The result is that many forward-looking reforms are lost in the paperwork maze. For example, the current bureaucratic interpretation of the Truth in Negotiations Act virtually guarantees a vast paper-shuffling exercise every time a contract is awarded. The law recognizes that competition is the best assurance that the government will pay fair and reasonable prices. When adequate price competition is found to exist, there is no statutory requirement for the submission of the elaborate cost and pricing data otherwise required. Sounds good?

Unfortunately, the bureaucrats have again fooled everyone. Unless the contract was awarded exclusively on the basis of the lowest evaluated price, *FAR* says that adequate price competition does not exist and all the special paperwork must be filled out. Even when adequate price competition is found to exist, the contractor must perform "cost realism analysis," which is almost as involved as in the uncompetitive case. Theoretically, then, as long as price is a substantial factor in the evaluation of competing proposals, the spirit of the law can be fully achieved by waiving the special paperwork requirements; however, the procurement bureaucrats who write the implementing rules take that as a defeat, and they are nothing if not tenacious.

Because the military's contracting personnel are outranked by their industry counterparts in terms of experience and training, Congress and the Defense Department have instituted procedural "safeguards" and intricate internal review processes. Programs proceed at a glacial pace as contractors and government purchasing personnel carry out the required reviews and audits. Authority (mainly to say no) is dispersed widely among program managers, contract officers, senior military executives, auditors, and inspectors.[26] Accountability is diluted, and all of this is extremely costly.

Approximately forty line and staff officials have veto power over some part of the efforts of the program managers. One can insist that they use certain designated military specifications in awarding the contracts, another can impose specific reliability requirements, and yet another can impose small business and minority business requirements. Of course, none of these "second guessers" has any responsibility for the success of the program. Program managers typically spend 50–70 percent of their time "selling" or "defending" their programs at higher levels. Some report that they have to go to forty meetings to get any significant decisions made on a single program.[27]

In those cases where good people are attracted to military procurement work, the do-it-by-the-numbers approach imbedded in *DAR* and other procurement regulations diminishes their effectiveness—and encourages them to leave for more challenging assignments. A RAND report on this subject concluded that the imposition of detailed requirements erodes the program manager's authority and reduces the ability to conduct the procurement program efficiently.[28]

Impacts of Bureaucratic Rule Making

The regulations themselves—cumbersome as they may be—are only "intermediate" products. They merely guide the placement of individual contracts for specific weapons and equipment. The administration of the contract award system is even more detailed. Because the distribution of the military's requests for proposals is limited, secondary sources must be relied on to provide insights into the actual workings of the process. One industry veteran has offered the following description:

> Requests for proposals of big-ticket systems are massive—hundreds or thousands of pages that spell out performance requirements, timetables for development and delivery, contractor qualifications, deadlines for submissions, prospective contract-award data . . . [29]

For a design and technical competition, a Request for Proposal is often 1,000–2,000 pages long. For sugar cookies, specifications run to fifteen pages; for whistles, nineteen. The fourteen pages covering the requirements for fruitcake are designed to ensure that the presence of vanilla flavoring shall be "organoleptically detected, but not to a pronounced degree."[30]

Unlike the negotiating of commercial contracts, defense contractors have virtually nothing to say about the provisions in a government contract. They are handed—on a "take it or leave it" basis—a mass of small print ("boilerplate," as it is often called) written by the government. Even worse, if the military procurement regulations require a clause to be in a contract and it is not physically there, then the contractor is still bound as if it were written in so many words.[31]

The military's requests for proposals for weapon systems result in even more detailed proposals on the part of perspective contractors. Typically three or four firms respond to a request for proposals, often with submissions that range from 20,000 to 40,000 pages each. Five competitors for the C-5A cargo plane wrote a total of 240,000 pages of material. Along with supporting documents, the submissions weighed three and a half tons and took several trucks to deliver. All that did not prevent major cost overruns on the C-5A program.

The cumulative effect of imposing virtually an endless array of bureaucratic requirements on the private enterprises that provide goods and services to the military establishment is to force them to adopt the thought processes of government arsenals. In the process, we lose the benefits of risk-taking, initiative, and innovation, which are the key reasons for using private business in the first case.

For example, at the leading manufacturer of shotgun ammunition, its civilian factory line requires one employee to supervise three machines, each of which produces 240 rounds per minute. However, the military product—which is identical—must be manufactured using antiquated processes involving a dozen machines, each manned separately and producing only one-fourth as much.[32]

Companies go to fascinating lengths to avoid the burdens of the military procurement system: one electronics company has two divisions, one producing defense components and the other making microchips for civilian markets. When the defense division needs some microchips, the civilian division gives it to them without charge—in order to avoid the oversight and regulatory burdens associated with defense business. The chips are worth about $200 each.[33]

Many contractors insulate their defense work from their mainstream commercial activities. Such action minimizes criticism by government auditors of the allocation of overhead costs and so forth. It also ensures that the commercial divisions will not be "contaminated" by the bureaucratic environment of the military procurement process and thus forget what they know about cost control and fast-market response.[34] Such insulation also makes it less likely that the govern-

ment will benefit from the rapid rate of technological innovation occurring in the companies' commercial research laboratories.

In a 1989 report on the defense technology base, the OTA concluded that the defense acquisition system is "a major contributor" to
the long delays in getting new technology into the field. There are
formidable barriers to exploiting technology developed in the civilian
sector. OTA noted that, "While Congress did not intend the system to
be slow, cumbersome, and inefficient, laws passed to foster goals other
than efficient procurement have made it so."[35]

Although it is difficult to quantify the cost of meeting the numerous
regulatory requirements imposed on military procurement, researchers at the RAND Corporation did identify some influences that
could be measured: the increase in the number of congressional staff
who work on procurement issues; the increase in the restrictions that
Congress adds to the annual defense authorization and appropriation
bills; the increase in administrative obstacles prevents acquisition personnel from accomplishing their program objectives in a timely and
efficient manner. There was widespread frustration among project-
level personnel who believe they could do their job more rapidly and
at less cost with fewer controls. The RAND researchers, however,
found almost no evidence that regulatory activity had affected the
performance or quality of the final product, either favorably or ad-
versely.[36]

REFORMING THE PROCUREMENT PROCESS

Over the years, there has been no shortage of proposals to revise the
way that the Department of Defense makes its purchases and indeed
many changes have been made. The recurrent dissatisfaction with the
status quo is hardly of recent vintage. In the course of the French and
Indian Wars, there were frequent complaints about high prices and
inferior goods. In 1861, Congress established a select committee to
inquire into allegations of waste and corruption involving military
contracts.[37] After World War I, the Nye Committee held highly publicized hearings on the same subject. During World War II, the Truman Committee focused on shortcomings in the war production effort.

Perhaps the most fundamental obstacle to improvement is the absence of a single central problem that plagues the defense procurement process. Consequently, there is no single panacea, no single
action that will eliminate all or even most of the shortcomings in the
military procurement process.

Some of the obstacles to carrying out reforms of the military procurement system may be intractable. Perhaps foremost is bureaucra-

cy's inherent resistance to change. In addition, there are the intricacies and uncertainties associated with military planning, acquisition, and operations that inhibit any systematic change in the process. Furthermore, the political character of many defense debates cannot be ignored.[38] Under the circumstances, it will take at least three major types of changes to truly reform military procurement.

The first category of reform is to streamline the regulations themselves, eliminating counterproductive restrictions and stripping out nonessential detail. The second is to upgrade the calibre of the people in the Department of Defense who administer the regulations and carry out the procurement process. The third involves the people and organizations who actually produce the equipment.

Streamlining the Regulations

A sweeping overhaul of the entire government procurement process is the only effective remedy for the unrestrained proliferation of bureaucratic detail and trivia. Richard Stubbing, a Duke University professor who worked on the military budget for many years, urges the replacement of the current 30,000 pages of military procurement regulations with "some short, simple regs . . . say 100 pages or less . . . "[39] That means eliminating all the socioeconomic provisions as well as all the restrictive "micromanagement" provisions that have been added more recently.

Simplifying the entire military procurement procedure is also the most cost-effective way of responding to the perennial complaints of small firms that they are scared away from defense work because of the complexity of the procurement process.[40]

Comprehensive reform also requires dividing military procurement into two broad categories: items that can be purchased readily from the private sector, and weapons acquisition. The great majority of all procurement actions and a substantial, albeit smaller proportion of the dollar volume of military contracting are for items available from the civilian sector. These should be bought via sealed bids, without the currently detailed military specifications. In addition, there should be a $25,000 minimum for contracts to which the various socioeconomic requirements are imposed. That single action would simplify the 70 percent or more of all defense contracts that are below $25,000.

For the second category—weapons acquisition—selection should be made on the basis of prototypes produced by two or more competing firms. The winner of the "fly-off" competition would receive the majority of the production business. The runner up would get a smaller contract, but large enough to keep its production line going. After the first production batch from each of the two contractors, the military service could alter the proportion awarded to each. Thus competition would continue throughout the production process.[41]

The Packard Commission and others have repeatedly warned that the only consistently reliable means of getting the information needed to evaluate a proposed military system is to build prototypes and to test them. This is the "fly before you buy" policy that David Packard initiated in the early 1970s when he was deputy secretary of defense. Given the repeated shortcomings resulting from rushing weapon systems to premature production, we can brush aside the counterargument that prototypes are costly and time-consuming to build.

Yet for the period 1984–1988, the navy relied entirely on computer modeling, simulation studies, and other "paper" analyses before starting full-scale development work on most new military systems.[42] In only three cases out of ten did it rely on actual operational testing before putting a new program into initial production. This reluctance is not entirely irrational. It reflects the dangers of "stop-and-go" military cycles. Given the vagaries of military budgeting, it is understandable that the military service developing a new weapon system is anxious to rush it into production even without adequate testing to avoid a new wave of budget austerity. A system in production is less likely to fall to the budget axe than one merely in the R&D stage. The cancellation of the navy's A-12 aircraft program in early 1991 after large cost overruns provides a striking case in point.

A simple and straightforward explanation of why the bureaucracy resists streamlining is that "Less regulation means less work [for government employees]; jobs will be lost, turf will vanish . . . "[43] Even more basic is the contrast between the governmental (or legal) approach and the business (or economic) approach to purchasing. The prevailing government/legal attitude is to regulate the process so closely that no "errors" occur. Business executives and economists, in contrast, look at costs as well as benefits of rule making. As noted by defense executive Jacques Gansler, "Trying to prevent *almost all* mistakes would be more efficient."[44] The practical problem that arises in the public arena is that, writing 15 million new contracts each year, the Department of Defense would commit more than 1,500 errors, even if its actions were 99.99 perfect.

Upgrading the People

Not only must the calibre of procurement officials be raised, but the authority of the manager of each weapon system should be increased commensurate with the responsibility of the job. Virtually everyone who has examined the military procurement process has focused on the crucial role of the people who award and administer contracts. In testimony before the Senate Armed Services Committee, David Packard described examples of good acquisition practice:

> [S]mall teams of highly competent people . . . were given the responsibility and the authority to do the job, and they were left alone.[45]

Packard cited the Minuteman and the Polaris strategic missile programs as two successful examples of the preferred approach. In companion testimony, R. James Woolsey, former navy undersecretary, made a similar point. Describing procurement programs that work, he said that they centered around a strong program manager with the ability to trade off costs, schedules, and performance. "We need to free up the scientists and engineers and military users at the front end of the process to talk to one another, interact with one another, and experiment some," Woolsey concluded.[46]

At present, the military's managers of new weapon systems have limited authority and few tools to manage their programs. They often function as little more than briefing specialists and marketing representatives, spending much of their time seeking additional funds and continued support for their programs. J. Ronald Fox, a former assistant secretary of the army, recommends that the officers assigned to supervise weapon production be persons experienced in industrial management. They should also possess the authority needed to accomplish their jobs, be well compensated, and be accountable for the results.[47]

Fox's recommendations sound so simple as to border on the naïve, but they are right on target. At two major military procurement offices with thousands of personnel, about half the officers are only lieutenants. One defense contractor responds to this situation in a cynical fashion:

> The government invites contractors to play games by assigning inexperienced government managers to key positions, and then changing them every two or three years.[48]

It is essential to improve the training of the officers responsible for making multimillion (or billion) dollar decisions. Such investments in "human resources" are long overdue. The very notion of upgrading the personnel assigned to the staff function of acquisition, however, flies in the face of the traditional focus of the military establishment on line management and combat responsibilities. The viewpoint of the modern military officer needs to be broadened substantially in order to carry out the multifaceted role of conducting national security programs in a rapidly changing, high-tech, global environment (the next chapter develops this theme).

Secretary of Defense Dick Cheney announced in 1989 that he intends to establish a corps of officers in each of the military services who will make full-time careers of procurement. If the plan is carried out, the officers would be assigned to acquisition positions and have the opportunity to be promoted to the highest ranks of general and admiral.[49] This change would be a positive response to the problems described here.

In truth, however, it is more than a matter of education and training. The cumbersome staffing structure of the military procurement process must also be overhauled and streamlined. A substantial reduction should be made in the total number of acquisition personnel, bringing it closer to the levels of comparable commercial business. Military program managers are usually separated from the senior acquisition executive in the Office of the Secretary of Defense (the undersecretary for acquisition) by five or six administrative levels. Each layer demands a right to review all progress reports and major proposals for change. Some of these layers have an extensive horizontal structure, so that the views of several different officers must be accommodated in order to pass through a particular layer or "gate."[50]

An examination of the "turnaround" that has occurred in large private corporations would be useful. In recent years, many companies have changed entrenched institutional cultures so as to enhance decision making, stimulate innovation, increase accountability for success and failure, and reduce overhead costs.

In striking contrast, many if not most of the procurement reforms enacted in the military in recent years have been counterproductive. In the words of one observer, what was "impossibly cumbersome" in 1988 (using the words of the Packard Commission) has become "ever more labyrinthine and intractable" following the burst of reform legislation since.[51]

More Incentives for Performance

Reforming regulations and upgrading procurement personnel, however necessary, are only preludes to the main act, which is doing a better job of designing and producing the critical items for this nation's military arsenal. It is often too easy to dismiss the concern over the high cost of military procurement with the assertion that the process needs to give competition a greater role. In purchasing standard items—desks, chairs, pencils, paper—contracts have almost always been awarded to the responsible bidder who asked for the lowest price. That is not the problem.

The real challenge occurs in buying items that are so advanced that they do not yet exist—aircraft, missiles, and space vehicles. Ideally, the award should go to the company that will provide the optimum combination of high-quality, low-cost, timely delivery, and ready maintainability. To place an order with a contractor who wants the business so badly that he will underestimate cost is hardly good management. Nor is it a bargain to go with a low-cost producer who will sacrifice quality, time, and readiness in order to minimize price.

For these reasons, in making the initial award, military contracting officers should take more fully into account the bidder's past performance on defense contracts, and the contracts should provide larger profits for successful technical and cost performance and, conversely, more severe penalties for poor performance.[52] Under the existing system, given the essentially cost-plus nature of so much of military procurement, poor performance may at times be rewarded.

One would have to be extremely naïve to believe that political pressures play no role in awarding defense contracts. Office of Management and Budget alumnus Stubbing notes the example of Boeing over a period of two decades, a company he describes in an understated way as having "a fairly successful commercial business." He mentions six cases where Boeing was a finalist in the competition and, in several of the cases, was the first choice of the military service. According to Stubbing, "In every case they lost to a company who either was in deep financial trouble or whose business was fast eroding and they needed business bad . . . "[53]

Under David Packard's policy of "fly before you buy," competing contractors were required to build and thoroughly test working prototypes before the major production contracts were awarded. This approach yielded the F-16 fighter and A-10 attack plane, two of the most successful procurement projects of the postwar era in terms of both performance and cost. Packard's approach was largely abandoned when he left the Pentagon.

One recurrent proposal is for the Department of Defense to retain two contractors throughout the life of the procurement program. Each year the contractor that produces the better product at the lower cost would get a larger share of next year's buy. Poor performance would be penalized with a smaller share.[54] As shown in Table 8-2, the savings from dual sourcing are significant, although not overwhelming, on the average 16 percent from the sole-source cost. The savings do substantially exceed the cost of starting up a second production line.[55]

A more pervasive change relates to the entire legislative process rather than to military procurement specifically. The typical congressional reaction to a "scandal" or horrible example of "waste" is to focus on the most dramatic aspect. The resultant headlines serve two politically useful purposes: they propel the legislator's name to public attention, and they show constituents that the Senate or House member is actively doing something.

Table 8-2   Savings from Competition for Major Weapon Systems

Weapon System	Annual Production Rate	Second Sole-Source Cost ($M)	Source Start-up Cost ($M)	Dual-Source Savings ($M)
Standard Missile	1,500	2,270	110.0	420
Standard Missile Motor	1,500	710	2.5	170
Tomahawk	400	3,720	88.0	550
Cruisers	5	9,800	110.0	1,810
Landing Ships	2	1,390	5.2	390
Oilers	2	1,870	47.0	140
Air Cushion Landing Craft	12	1,820	*	90
Missile Launchers	12	1,830	9.3	290

Source: Yale Journal of Regulation, Summer 1989.

*Start-up costs not separately identified.

Very little attention is given to actually writing the legislation needed to change existing policy or even to serious analysis of the underlying situation that gave rise to the waste or scandal. Specifically, there are many hastily written statutes, often drafted with little attention to their relationship to the existing body of law and regulation.

Two cogent examples of the shortcomings of the legislative process are the Drug Free Workplace Act of 1988 and the ethics provisions of the Office of Federal Procurement Policy Authorization Act of 1988. Both laws impose ambiguous and far-reaching obligations in sensitive areas upon the Department of Defense and its suppliers. A search of the legislative histories of these measures yielded no sign that Congress seriously considered what it would cost to put them into effect.[56] Until the political benefits of serious legislative work are enhanced, the status quo will continue.

This book does not deal directly with the subject of scandals and the episodes of fraud in defense work that so frequently make headlines, but simplifying the maze of procurement laws and regulations will encourage both compliance and enforcement. In contrast, setting up elaborate programs of "ethical education" are of very limited value. The case of Teledyne is instructive.

The company is one of the major defense contractors to sign the Defense Industry Initiative established in 1986. The Initiative prescribes a detailed program of ethical education and self-policing. Thousands of Teledyne's defense employees were sent to seminars on how to do their jobs ethically and legally.

Ethics handbooks were distributed. "Hot lines" were set up to enable "whistleblowers" to report potential wrongdoings. Ethics supervisors fanned out around the company to answer questions and investigate possible infractions of the law. None of that activity prevented the conviction of two Teledyne employees in 1989 as part of the federal government's "ill wind" investigation of defense contractors. There is no need, however, to focus on Teledyne. In 1988, more than 1,000 defense contractors were banned at some point from conducting defense business for violations ranging from bribery and bid rigging to making shoddy products and overcharging.[57]

Winning a large contract often means the difference between feast and famine for the competing companies. The pressures to market hard, bid low, and make unrealistic promises are very substantial— and likely will worsen as the military budget shrinks. Aside from avoiding enactment of unrealistic requirements, the basic point is that there is no effective substitute for punishing those who break the law. Enforcement of the military procurement laws has been vigorous. In March 1990, the Pentagon's inspector general testified that the efforts of the Defense Criminal Investigative Service, during the previous two years, resulted in more than 600 indictments, 500 convictions, and $500 million in monetary recoveries.[58]

Finally, there is the problem first noted in Chapter 1—the high costs of the peak and valley approach to military budgeting. Norman Augustine, chairman and CEO of Martin Marietta Corporation, urges eliminating program turbulence by making it more difficult to start the production of new weapon systems. Once Congress approves a new military project, however, it should fund the complete program, or at least an entire program phrase, rather than doling out the money for a missile or aircraft production program one year at a time. In an indirect swipe at the traditional Pentagon approach of "getting it while the getting is good," Augustine says, "We should be realistic about how many programs we can adequately fund."[59]

NOTES

1. U.S. Senate Committee on Armed Services, *Defense Acquisition Process* (Washington, D.C.: U.S. Government Printing Office, 1989), p. 136.

2. Cited in Richard Stubbing and Richard Mendel, "How to Save $50 Billion a Year," *Atlantic Monthly*, June 1989, p. 53.

3. James Blackwell, *Deterrence in Decay: The Future of the U.S. Defense Industrial Base* (Washington, D.C.: Center for Strategic and International Studies, 1989), p. 1.

4. William H. Gregory, *The Defense Procurement Mess* (Lexington, Mass.: Lexington Books, 1989), pp. xii, 191.

5. Bruce Stokes, "Come Fly With Me," *National Journal*, March 31, 1990, p. 781.

6. "Foreword," *Federal Acquisition Regulation* (consolidated reprint), February 1, 1987 (Washington, D.C.: U.S. Government Printing Office, 1987).

7. *CODSIA Response to DMR Regulatory Review* (Washington, D.C.: Council of Defense and Space Industry Associations, 1989), pp. 17–18.

8. Richard Danzig, *Reforming the Pentagon: The Knowledge Gap*, A Report to the Analytic Sciences Corp., under contract to the Ford Foundation, Washington, D.C., June 1989 (processed), p. 43.

9. According to the U.S. Office of Federal Procurement Policy, as reported in *Federal Acquisition Report*, April 1990, p. 1.

10. John F. Lehman, Jr., *Command of the Seas* (New York: Charles Scribner's Sons, 1989), p. 191.

11. U.S. Office of Management and Budget, *Procurement Regulatory Activity Report* (Washington, D.C.: U.S. Government Printing Office, 1989), p. 9.

12. G. K. Smith et al., *A Preliminary Perspective on Regulatory Activities and Effects in Weapons Acquisition* (Santa Monica, Calif.: RAND Corporation, 1988), pp. 157–58.

13. George Sammet, Jr., and David Green, *Defense Acquisition Management* (Boca Raton: Florida Atlantic University Press, 1990), p. 88.

14. Blue Ribbon Defense Panel, *Report to the President and the Secretary of Defense on the Department of Defense* (Washington, D.C.: U.S. Government Printing Office, 1970), p. 92.

15. William E. Kovacic, "The Sorcerer's Apprentice: Public Regulation of the Weapons Acquisition Process," in Robert Higgs, ed., *Arms, Politics, and the Economy* (New York: Holmes & Meier, 1990), pp. 104–31.

16. Molly Moore, "The Pentagon's Faulty Buyer-Protection Plans," *Washington Post Weekly*, October 30, 1989, p. 34.

17. "Congress's Paper Trail," *Wall Street Journal*, August 15, 1989, p. A10.

18. Gregory, *Defense Procurement Mess*, p. xi.

19. U.S. House of Representatives, Committee on Armed Services, *Defense Acquisition: Major U.S. Commission Reports 1949–1988*, Vol. 1 (Washington, D.C.: U.S. Government Printing Office, 1988), pp. 508–9.

20. Jacques S. Gansler, *Affording Defense* (Cambridge: MIT Press, 1989), p. 118.

21. Eric Weiner, "Grumman Is Girding for Arms Cuts," *The New York Times*, December 12, 1989, p. 34.

22. Dick Cheney, *Defense Management: Report to the President* (Washington, D.C.: U.S. Department of Defense, 1989), p. 27.

23. *Task Force Report on the Office of the Secretary of Defense* (Washington, D.C.: President's Private Sector Survey on Cost Control, 1983), p. 151; also see testimony of J. Ronald Fox in U.S. Senate, Committee on Armed Services, *Defense Acquisition Process* (Washington, D.C.: U.S. Government Printing Office 1988), pp. 194–200.

24. *DOD Acquisition: Capabilities of Key DOD Personnel in Systems Acquisition* (Washington, D.C.: U.S. General Accounting Office, 1986).

25. Cheney, *Defense Management*, p. 12.

26. Kovacic, "Sorcerer's Apprentice," pp. 104–31.

27. Gansler, *Affording Defense*, p. 212.

28. Smith et al., *Regulatory Activities and Weapons Acquisition*, pp. viii–ix.

29. Gregory, *Defense Procurement Mess*, p. 66.

30. Military Specification MIL-F-1499F. For a contrary view, see Gansler, *Affording Defense*.

31. F. Trowbridge vom Baur, "Differences Between Commercial Contracts and Government Contracts," *American Bar Association Journal*, March 1967, p. 249.

32. Blackwell, *Deterrence in Decay*, p. 46.

33. Ibid., p. 45.

34. "Rethinking the Military's Role in the Economy: An Interview with Harvey Brooks and Lewis Branscomb," *Technology Review*, August/September 1989, p. 60.

35. Quoted in Cheney, *Defense Management*, p. 26.

36. Smith et al., *Regulatory Activities and Weapons Acquisition*, pp. vii–viii.

37. David Lockwood et al., "Defense Acquisition," in U.S. House of Representatives Committee on Armed Services," *Defense Acquisition: Major U.S. Commission Reports* (Washington, D.C.: U.S. Government Printing Office, 1988), p. 2.

38. Danzig, *Reforming the Pentagon*, p. 6; see also *Acquisition Reform: DOD's Efforts to Streamline Its Acquisition System and Reduce Personnel* (Washington, D.C.: U.S. General Accounting Office, 1989).

39. Testimony of Richard Stubbing, *Defense Acquisition Process*, p. 226.

40. Lee E. Koppelman and Pearl M. Kamer, *Maximizing the Potential of Long Island's Defense Sector in an Era of Change* (New York: Long Island Regional Planning Board, 1988), p. 117.

41. Ibid., pp. 226–27.

42. U.S. General Accounting Office, *Navy Weapons Testing* (Washington, D.C.: GAO, 1989), pp. 1–19.

43. Gregory, *Military Procurement Mess*, p. 81.

44. Jacques S. Gansler, *The Defense Industry* (Cambridge: MIT Press, 1980), p. 258.

45. Testimony of David Packard, in *Defense Acquisition Process*, p. 136.

46. Testimony of R. James Woolsey, in ibid., pp. 165, 178.

47. Testimony of J. Ronald Fox, in ibid., p. 194.

48. Cited in ibid., p. 200.

49. Cheney, *Defense Management*, p. 14.

50. Smith and others, *Regulatory Activities and Weapons Acquisition*, p. 18.

51. See Kovacic, "Sorcerer's Apprentice," p. 106.

52. Testimony of Richard Stubbing, *Defense Acquisition Process*, p. 231.

53. Ibid., p. 222.

54. Murray Weidenbaum, *Rendezvous With Reality: The American Economy After Reagan* (New York: Basic Books, 1988), p. 82; Stubbing and Mendel, "How to Save $50 Billion a Year," p. 56.

55. Everett Pyatt, "Procurement Competition at Work: The Navy's Experience," *Yale Journal on Regulation*, Summer 1989, p. 325.

56. Kovacic, "Sorcerer's Apprentice," pp. 120–21.

57. Robert Wrubel, "Addicted to Fraud?" *Financial World,* June 27, 1989, p. 58.

58. Statement of Paul F. Math, General Accounting Office, before the Senate Committee on Armed Services, Washington, D.C., May 14, 1990, p. 5.

59. Norman Augustine, "Defense: A Case of Too Many Cooks," *Fortune,* December 15, 1988, p. 219.

CHAPTER 9

Recognizing the People Factor in the Armed Forces

Recent experience has shown that the challenge to military personnel policy can rapidly shift from how to attract enough qualified people to how to manage a large cutback in numbers—and back again. The longer-term outlook continues to envision a smaller military force structure.

In the haste to reduce the headcount during periods of military cutbacks, it is important to avoid damaging the morale of those who stay—and to ensure the right distribution of skills and experience in the remaining members of the armed services. Ironically, some of the same people who received bonuses to reenlist in the 1980s are being offered financial inducements to leave before their terms of enlistment expire in the early 1990s.

To compound the challenge to military personnel policy, the Department of Defense is simultaneously faced with the need to broaden the knowledge base as well as the perspective of its top management in order to work effectively in the post–Cold War environment.

In considering the policy alternatives, civilian decision makers must render obsolete the traditional image of American servicemen as semiliterate but courageous "grunts." As of September 30, 1988, more than 98 percent of all commissioned officers were college graduates, many with advanced degrees. As for enlisted personnel, 97 percent were high school graduates and 23 percent had completed some college work.[1] These ratios are significantly higher than for comparable positions in civilian life.

That is the good news. In the absence of the draft, the military establishment has been able to recruit and retain a well-educated segment of the nation's younger people. The share of the military budget devoted to personnel declined from 38 percent in 1975 to 27 percent in 1988. This reflects less an economy in personnel costs than the very substantial effort by the Reagan administration to shift funds to modernize equipment.

The bad news is that this personnel effort has been very expensive in an absolute sense. In 1975, the bill for maintaining 2.1 million servicemen and women came to $32 billion. In 1988, it cost $76 billion. The dollar increase was far more rapid than inflation due to the higher cost of a volunteer military force and the increasingly technical nature of the job.

R&D and procurement costs are a more flexible part of the military budget than personnel, which is more like a fixed cost, especially in the short run. To be sure, the annual cost-of-living pay increases may be reduced or even eliminated, but any change in the basic pay scales is likely to be upward. In contrast, it is much easier to postpone placing a new weapon system into production or to reduce either the rate of production, or the total numbers to be procured. The really large savings in personnel costs arise from reducing substantially the numbers of men and women in uniform.

The total annual bill for military compensation is substantial. In fiscal year 1986, for example, it was $84 billion. Of that, only $33 billion (39 percent) was actual pay. Another $13 billion (16 percent) covered the value of housing and subsistence, both cash and in kind. Other benefits, notably retirement, required $38 billion (or 45 percent) of the total (see Table 9-1).

Substantial increases in pay and allowances in the early 1980s enabled the military establishment to meet its personnel needs on both a

Table 9-1 Compensation of Military Personnel
Fiscal Year 1986

Item	Amount ($billions)	Percentage
Regular compensation		
Basic pay	31	37
Incentive pay	2	2
Housing	7	8
Subsistence	3	4
Tax advantage	3	4
Subtotal	46	55
Benefits		
Retirement	16	19
Medical care, etc.	22	26
Subtotal	38	45
Total	84	100

Source: U.S. General Accounting Office.

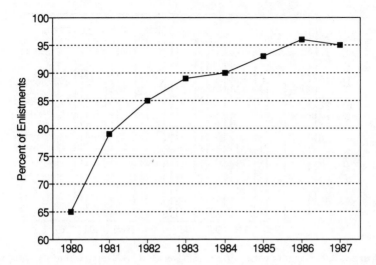

Figure 9-1. Recruits in Top Three Test Categories. (*Source:* U.S. Department of Defense.)

quantitative and qualitative basis. Consequently, those personnel now
are able to use more complex weapons, while real outlays for training
have come down. Today's recruits generally score better on the stan-
dardized military entrance test than do the general youth population,
and they are more likely to have graduated from high school. As
measured by scores in the Armed Forces Qualifications Test (AFQT),
which the Defense Department considers to be a good predictor of
success in military training, the quality of enlistments improved substantially in the 1980s. In 1980, 65 percent of new entrants into the
U.S. armed forces were in the top three quartiles of the AFQT. By
1988, the percentage was up to 95 percent. In the army, it went from
44 percent in 1980 to 96 percent in 1988 (see Figure 9-1).

There was also a significant upgrading in the educational backgrounds of new enlistments into the armed forces during the 1980s.
In 1980, 68 percent were high school graduates; in 1988, this rose to
93 percent. Again, the army experienced the greatest improvement
during the period, from 54 percent to 93 percent (see Figure 9-2).
High unemployment rates in the civilian economy surely helped recruitment and retention.

By the late 1980s, however, military pay increases had become less
generous, the economy had strengthened, and the military found it
harder to enlist young people with high school diplomas and good
scores on aptitude tests. For the period October 1988–March 1989,
the army and the Marine Corps missed their overall recruiting goal,
for the first time in ten years. The recent shift toward a smaller

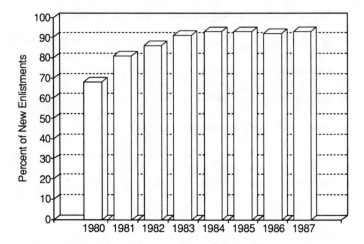

Figure 9-2. Recruits with Diplomas. (*Source:* U.S. Department of Defense.)

military force has somewhat mitigated the concern that would usually
accompany these trends.

The news on reenlistment rates is basically good. Overall reenlistment rates rose substantially after the generous pay increases of the
early 1980s—from 53 percent in the fiscal year 1979 to 68 percent in
1982, declining to 65 percent by 1987 (see Figure 9-3). The air force
continues to enjoy the most success in retaining its personnel, while
the Marine Corps rate remains substantially below the average of the

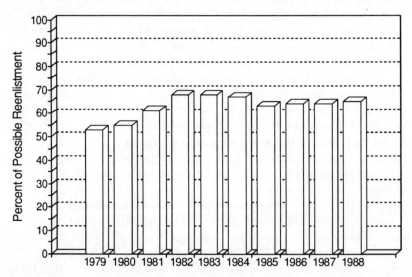

Figure 9-3. U.S. Military Reenlistment Rates. (*Source:* U.S. Department of
Defense.)

other services. All in all, about one-half of all enlisted personnel had more than four years of service in 1988, compared with 42 percent in 1980.[2]

Simultaneously, the pool of youths has been shrinking. For example, in 1980, 2.1 million young men turned eighteen, in 1985 this fell to 1.8 million, and for 1990 the estimate is 1.7 million. That would ordinarily mean that the armed services would have to attract a rising share of young high school graduates just to get a constant flow of new recruits. In the last few years, however, the total number of men and women in uniform has declined slightly from 2.2 million in 1987 to 2.1 million in 1989.[3] As noted, the outlook is for more substantial reductions in the 1990s, making the recruitment task for the early 1990s a little less challenging.

Clearly, many factors other than economic influences are involved in attracting and especially in keeping qualified military personnel. National attitudes toward national defense exert a key influence, and education is important. "High-quality" recruits (high school graduates scoring above the fiftieth percentile on the AFQT) experience attrition rates one-half of that of low-quality recruits. That relationship was an important factor in the justification for upgrading the educational and intelligence level of new recruits.[4]

TWO VIEWS OF THE MILITARY PAY GAP

Pay is likely to continue to be the main draw in attracting and maintaining the career people that the military services will need in the years ahead.

Shortfalls in military pay are usually cited as the primary reason for difficulties in recruiting and retaining military personnel. There are at least two views on this subject, military and civilian, and, not surprisingly, they differ substantially. The Department of Defense believes that military pay has steadily fallen further behind civilian pay scales. By comparing the change in the Department of Labor's Employment Cost Index (used as a measure of private sector pay raises) to military pay raises for the period since 1983, the Department of Defense shows that, by 1988, the shortfall was 11 percent[5] (see Figure 9-4).

In contrast, the General Accounting Office (GAO), using a different statistical approach, reported that in 1986 average compensation for the military was substantially greater than for the federal government's civilian workers. The GAO examined cash compensation for military personnel—including basic and incentive pay, nontaxable allowances for quarters and subsistence, and the imputed tax advantage, but not enlistment or reenlistment bonuses.

For male high school graduates, military and civilian workers were

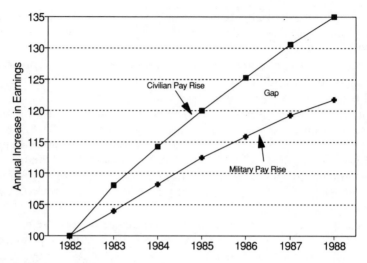

Figure 9-4. The Military's View of the Pay Gap. (*Source:* U.S. Department of Defense.)

paid approximately the same, with some slight variation by age group. For women, in each age group the military pay exceeded civilian pay. For college graduates of both sexes, military pay exceeded civilian pay for all age groups but was greater for women.

A very substantial change occurs in the comparison between military and civilian compensation when noncash benefits are included. In every case—male, female, high school graduate, college graduate, and for each age group—fringe benefits for military personnel are substantially higher than for the civilian work force. When cash and noncash compensation are aggregated, GAO finds that average military compensation in 1987 was 27 percent greater than that for a national sample of employed civilian workers.[6] In 1987, GAO obtained similar results in comparing military with federal civil service compensation, including both cash and retirement and health insurance benefits (see Table 9-2).[7]

Raw dollar comparison between military and civilian pay, however, can be misleading. Military compensation may be higher because the armed services have a "richer" (more demanding) mix of occupations than does the civilian work force. The military personnel may have greater responsibilities. In addition, it may be necessary to enhance military compensation by what is often termed an "X-factor"—to compensate for greater exposure to danger and for the liability for duty at all times without extra pay. Frequent moves also make it more difficult for spouses to establish careers at one location.

These disadvantages of service life are offset, at least in part, by

Table 9-2 The Civilian View of the Military Pay Gap: Comparison of Male High School Graduates, Selected Age Groups, 1988

Age	Cash Compensation			Benefits			Total Compensation		
	Military Personnel	Civil Service Personnel	Military as Percentage of Civil	Military Personnel	Civil Service Personnel	Military as Percentage of Civil	Military Personnel	Civil Service Personnel	Military as Percentage of Civil
19	$13,780	$13,227	104	$ 8,302	$5,329	156	$22,082	$18,556	119
24	18,555	18,444	101	9,997	6,883	145	28,552	25,327	113
29	22,110	20,564	108	11,259	7,515	150	33,369	28,079	119
34	25,493	22,149	115	12,460	7,987	156	37,953	30,136	126
39	29,235	23,948	122	13,788	8,524	162	43,023	32,472	132
44	33,339	25,211	132	15,245	8,900	171	48,584	34,111	142
Military as Percentage of Civil			106			150			118

Source: U.S. General Accounting Office.

greater job security, opportunities to learn a trade or skill, and adventure.[8] The changing nature of the national security threat facing the United States, however, may be altering significantly the perception of both the benefits and the dangers of service in the military. Moreover, studies of the impact of military service on subsequent civilian incomes are inconclusive. Although many show an enhancement of earning capacity, the most recent analysis concludes that Vietnam veterans suffered an earnings reduction equivalent to the loss of two years civilian labor market experience.[9]

APPROACHES TO MILITARY PERSONNEL POLICY

In addition to any significant pay differential that may exist, four other trends are adding to the difficulty of military recruitment and retention. First of all, advances in technology have transformed the occupational needs of the armed forces to include large numbers of specialists and technicians. Second, the "aging" of the U.S. population is having far-reaching implications for the armed forces.[10] Third, women significantly increased their participation in the nation's work force. Finally, the reserve forces are being relied upon to a much greater degree than in the past, as shown by the substantial call-up of reserve units for the Gulf action in 1990–1991.

The armed forces are the nation's largest single employer of young people. In a normal year, the military establishment is likely to "hire" more than 300,000 new recruits, most still in their teens. Conversely, about one-third of the civilian labor force is over forty-four years of age. Only a negligible 1 percent of enlisted personnel is in that age category. The median age for male military personnel has remained at twenty-three or twenty-four since 1920.[11]

According to Binkin and Kyriakopoulos of the Brookings Institution, the military's reliance on youth rather than experience is not providing the nation with the most effective armed forces possible at current budgetary levels. The high concentration of technicians and craftsmen in the military, and the training investment they represent, indicates a need for greater experience. Indeed, studies of specific military capabilities conclude that more experienced personnel can increase the operational effectiveness of a given unit very substantially.[12]

Added costs, however, are associated with an older work force. On average, they have more dependents, requiring higher medical, housing, travel, and other dependent-related costs. The older workers receive higher levels of pay and are more likely to become eligible for retirement pay. Offsetting that in part are lower outlays for recruiting, outfitting, and training. The reduction of tensions with the Soviet

Union should enable the military to cut the overall size of the armed forces and thus reduce the recruitment pressures in the years ahead.

It is proving more difficult to expand the role of women in the military, especially from office and other supporting positions to command and related operational duties. Although women are barred from active combat roles, the opportunities open to them have increased—albeit in an often arbitrary and uneven manner.

The air force has opened transport aircraft jobs to women. It also allows female pilots and crew members to participate in air-drop missions such as those conducted in the invasion of Panama. Although such missions may be conducted in a combat environment, these aircraft face a lesser risk than do fighter planes or other combat craft charged with attacking the enemy directly. Of the 4,848 pilots flying for the airlift command in early 1990, only 96 were female. Of the 4,838 enlisted air crew members, 111 were women.[13]

In contrast, the army has repeatedly postponed a decision on whether women will be allowed to remain in field artillery positions, one of the few combat-related fields open to them. In 1988, the army decided that some of the field jobs were too close to the front lines and closed them to women. As a result, the few slots remaining open sharply restrict chances to advance.

These developments reflect the political and social pressures faced by the military in defining the changing roles of men and women in today's armed forces. It is intriguing to note, however, that in practice the role of women expanded during recent U.S. military actions. For example, in Panama in December 1989, a platoon of military police led by a woman exchanged gunfire with Panamanian soldiers.[14]

For Operation Desert Storm in 1990, President Bush authorized the call-up of almost 50,000 reservists, including a high percentage of women. The president's action underscored the growing reliance on the reserves to provide combat support for active-duty U.S. military. Current reserve and national guard units perform functions not available in the active forces in sufficient quantity—ranging from cargo handling to water purification. Moreover, maintaining an army reservist, for example, costs about one-third of the expense incurred for a full-time soldier.[15] Thus, an effective corps of reservists can be a cost-effective way of stretching a tight military budget, with *effective*, of course, being the key.

Returning to the Draft

Some people advocate returning to the draft, either to save money or to generate a service force that is more representative of the national population. Moreover, the recent rash of involuntary departures from the armed services—temporarily halted by the Persian Gulf operation—may make future recruitment more difficult. Discussions about the desirability of returning to conscription have receded in view of the impending military cutbacks, but, given the longer view taken in this book, we should consider the possibility of another upturn in the pace of U.S. military activities. Reflecting on a return to the draft can be viewed as a form of contingency planning.

It is unlikely, however, and probably also undesirable, for the armed forces ever to become a statistical cross-section of the population. Conscientious objectors, persons with criminal records, and even those who score in the bottom tenth on the military entrance examination are excused or barred from military service.

In addition, unless volunteering is sharply restricted by either law or regulation, the number of draftees needed at current force sizes would not be sufficient to change the social composition of the armed forces markedly. Moreover, the higher turnover of draftees might offset the money saved by keeping military pay low. Any reduction in military pay would presumably occur by rigidly limiting pay increases, not by cutting current pay scales.

The discrepancy between military recruitment and the ideal statistical cross-section may not be as great as many people think. In 1987 (the latest year for which data are available), about 45 percent of active-duty recruits came from areas with above-average incomes; 55 percent from below-average areas.[16]

Prior to the currently contemplated cutbacks, the CBO estimates that a pay reduction on the order of 30–50 percent covering the first two years of military service might force the army to fill roughly half of its requirements with draftees. Because of the greater turnover among draftees, CBO figures that the army would have to raise its annual "accessions" from 112,000 to 160,000.[17] The other services would continue to rely on voluntary enlistments.

With a combination of draftees and enlistees, the armed forces would have a somewhat higher representation of whites and a lower representation of blacks and other minorities than they currently have. Young people with the fewest alternatives, which usually means those from less-advantaged backgrounds or who have limited access to civilian labor markets, are most likely to seek service in the military or to stay beyond the period for which they were drafted. At present, blacks reenlist at higher rates than do whites, and those from lower-income areas are more likely to reenlist than are those from higher-income areas.

The military needs to attract only about one in five of the young men reaching enlistment age each year. If the armed services' personnel needs remain that small—or smaller—then the case for bringing back the draft seems weak. The arguments that led to the elimination of conscription are surely as pertinent as ever. The draft is an unfair "tax" on those who serve, forcing many young people to perform services less valuable than their civilian occupations. The draft also means shifting a major cost of military activity from middle-income, older taxpayers to younger people who typically have less income and wealth. Moreover, the higher direct cost of military manpower forces the armed services to utilize their people more effectively than when they were almost "free goods."

Finally, it is ironic to think about reinstituting conscription in the United States at a time when the Soviet Union is beginning to move to a volunteer military. Their Ministry of Defense wants authority to begin contracting for skilled sailors who volunteer to serve three-year terms in the Soviet Navy. The volunteers would be paid more generously than are draftees and would serve longer.[18]

Using Competitive Pay Scales

Another far less disruptive approach to dealing with military personnel problems (should they be exacerbated) is to follow the practices of the civilian economy more closely—that is, offer higher pay for skills in short supply and lower pay (or at least lower increases) for skills in which the military has sufficient people.

While the lack of pay variation across occupation skills probably accounts for some of the retention problems among midcareer personnel, care must be taken in administering any new system. For example, some of the shortages may be temporary. The airline industry has experienced volatile swings in its demand for pilots and navigators; if pay for military pilots were permanently increased in response to a spurt in civilian demand, then they would probably be overpaid in the long run.

Most pay problems would be resolved under a military personnel system with compensation keyed to corresponding positions in the private sector. Flexibility in pay scales, however, would create a new uncertainty for military personnel, who presumably would demand higher pay in each period.[19] The introduction of pay variation within the same grades should therefore be phased in gradually, one branch of one service at a time, and the results should be monitored.

A variation of this approach is being considered by the army: asking or requiring some enlisted troops to retrain for occupational specialties that are suffering shortfalls; for instance an infantryman might become a logistics specialist.[20] However, the ability of the military services to "sandbag" an innovation they oppose should not be underestimated. A recently retired career officer, who served in various line and staff positions ranging from the Pentagon to Vietnam, concluded that "while the military is incapable of fundamentally reforming itself, it is supremely capable of preventing anyone else . . . from imposing reforms on it."[21]

Postpone Military Retirement Pay

Yet another suggestion for responding to the budgetary pressures on military personnel policy is to revamp the current very liberal retirement practice. Members of the armed forces can leave after twenty years of service and begin receiving retirement benefits equal to one-half of their previous pay (after 30 years of service, the retirement benefit rises to 75 percent). This generous treatment encourages relatively young able-bodied men and women (beginning at age thirty-eight) to leave the military. Several adverse effects can be noted.

First of all, the military establishment is deprived of experienced people in the prime of their working lives—although that is not now a pressing concern. Second, the government's outlay for retirement pay takes a rising share of the military budget—but the retirement benefit is an important part of the compensation package and a major attraction. Any reduction of retirement benefits can only be prospective; that is, it must be limited to new enlistees and cannot affect those who have been serving under another set of ground rules.

One specific change is to continue the practice of qualifying for retirement pay after twenty years of service (technically, the retirement benefits would "vest" after twenty years), but not beginning actual payments until the individual reaches a minimum age, say fifty-five. (Exceptions could be made for those with disabilities that prevent them from getting gainful civilian employment.) This one change, it has been estimated, would reduce military retirement obligations by approximately $10 billion a year. The revised practice would be much closer to industrial experience.

A more specialized response to early retirement is for the services to issue "minimum tenure assignment" contracts for selected officers with more than twenty years of service who are chosen for important positions requiring continuity to achieve effectiveness. One retired officer believes that this change would help to increase the readiness of the armed forces in terms of military operations.[22]

The need to attract and maintain an intelligent, educated, well-trained, and highly motivated volunteer military force structure requires taking a new and hard look at compensation practices. The likelihood of a sustained period of budget stringency makes that reform more urgent. Maintaining the morale and capability of the armed forces will remain a vital concern, regardless of the size of the future military establishment.

BROADENING THE HORIZONS OF TOP MANAGEMENT

Coincident with the substantial cutback occurring in the size of the armed forces, the senior generals and admirals are often hard pressed to keep pace with the rapid changes in the national security environment facing the United States and in the very concept of national power. Literally, the need is for a new and added layer of military education focusing on strategic decision making.

For example, the emerging redefinition of national power includes, at least to some extent, competitive strength in the global marketplace. That broader concept of power encompasses such varied factors as the availability of adequate energy and water supplies as well as the capability to marshall the support of other nations.

Strategic education must be broad but focused. As the United States found out during the Vietnam War, modern communications make it easy for citizens to "know" what is going on and difficult to maintain public support for an unpopular cause. More recently, the communist regimes of Eastern Europe learned that the ability to communicate rapidly can encourage the development of effective opposition forces.

In most large companies and in many nonprofit institutions, candidates for top management positions receive special, but not specialized, education to help prepare them for strategic decision making. The military establishment should be no exception to that practice, especially considering the tremendous responsibility given, for example, to the senior officers serving on the Joint Chiefs of Staff and their immediate deputies. Their intellectual horizons need to be expanded very substantially, considering the increasingly interagency nature of public policy decision making affecting national security. The typical "theater" of military activity, such as the Pacific Ocean, is interservice. Yet problems of coordination among the army, navy, air force, and Marine Corps are hardly novel.

That, however, is only the beginning. National security decision making is increasingly interdepartmental in nature, embracing civilian as well as military departments of the federal government. For example, the decision to permit General Dynamics Corporation to participate with the Japanese aerospace industry in building the FSX, the new advanced Japanese fighter aircraft, involved the Departments of Commerce, Defense, Energy, Labor, State, and Treasury, as well as NASA, the CIA, the NSC, the trade representative, and the president's science adviser.[23] In fact, the matter was ultimately resolved by the White House and the Congress. Senior military officers increasingly find themselves testifying before congressional committees and working with congressional staffs. These are very different relationships than the traditional line and staff allocation of functions in the armed forces.

Moreover, military representatives also find themselves involved in disputes or at least difficult relationships with private interest groups. The environmental impacts of military activities are often a friction point in dealing with local governments and private community organizations. Similarly, announcement of the closing of a military base quickly brings to a head all sorts of latent conflicts, the resolution of which requires knowledge of a variety of public issues and private concerns.

Compounding this extensive network of interrelationships between the military departments and the rest of the United States is the increasingly global nature of military and civilian activities. The ability to represent the Department of Defense in dealing with international organizations is now—or rather should be—part of the competence of a great many senior officers. These supranational bodies range from those well known to the military such as the North Atlantic Treaty Organization to the rising European Community institutions to specialized agencies of the United Nations.

Even more in the future than in the past, political skill will be a valuable asset to senior military officials. According to James W. Davis, the warrior model may be satisfactory for field commanders, but a high level of political sophistication will increasingly be required in Washington.[24]

Given the dynamic nature of the challenges to U.S. national security—and the changing character of the desirable responses—a major additional investment in the post-graduate education of senior military officers is surely a worthy undertaking.

NOTES

1. U.S. Department of Defense, *Selected Manpower Statistics, Fiscal Year 1988* (Washington, D.C.: U.S. Government Printing Office, 1988), pp. 98–99.

2. William A. Niskanen, *More Defense Spending for Smaller Forces* (Washington, D.C.: Cato Institute, 1988), p. 10.

3. Richard Halloran, "Military Recruiting Hurt by Tight Labor Market," *The New York Times*, August 1, 1989, p. 10.

4. U.S. Congressional Budget Office, *Quality Soldiers: Costs of Manning the Active Army* (Washington, D.C.: U.S. Government Printing Office, 1986), p. 23; R. Buddin, *Trends in Attrition of High-quality Military Recruits* (Santa Monica, Calif.: Rand Corporation, 1988).

5. "Prepared Statement by Honorable Grant S. Green, Jr., Assistant Secretary of Defense for Force Management and Personnel," in U.S. Senate, Committee on Armed Services, *Department of Defense Authorization for Appropri-*

ations for Fiscal Year 1989 (Washington, D.C.: U.S. Government Printing Office, 1988), p. 25.

6. *Military Compensation: Comparisons With Civilian Compensation and Related Issues* (Washington, D.C.: U.S. General Accounting Office, 1986), p. 12.

7. In a comparison between military and all civilian federal personnel, the General Accounting Office found a 6 percent gap in favor of the military in the case of male high school graduates aged 19–44; the gap widened to 18 percent when benefits were added. *Military Compensation: Comparison With Federal Civil Service Compensation* (Washington, D.C.: U.S. General Accounting Office, 1987), p. 11.

8. *Military Compensation*, 1986, p. 2.

9. Joshua D. Angrist, "Lifetime Earnings and the Vietnam Era Draft Lottery," *American Economic Review*, June 1990, p. 331; see also Sherwin Rosen and Paul Taubman, "Changes in Life Cycle Earnings," *Journal of Human Resources*, Summer 1982, pp. 321–38.

10. Martin Binkin and Irene Kyriakopoulos, *Youth or Experience? Manning the Modern Military* (Washington, D.C.: Brookings Institution, 1979), p. viii.

11. Ibid., p. 4.

12. Ibid., pp. 32–33.

13. Molly Moore, "Rethinking a Woman's Place," *Washington Post Weekly*, January 29, 1990, p. 32.

14. Beverly Ann Bendekgey, "Should Women Be Kept Out of Combat?" *GAO Review*, Summer 1990, p. 29.

15. Eric Schmitt, "Reserves Face the First Major Test of Their New, Broader Role," *The New York Times*, August 29, 1990, p. A8.

16. Richard L. Fernandez, "A Poor-Man's Military? Not at All," *Washington Post Weekly*, December 24, 1990, p. 29.

17. U.S. Congressional Budget Office, *Social Representation in the U.S. Military* (Washington, D.C.: U.S. Government Printing Office, 1989), p. 76.

18. John J. Fialka, "Soviet Defense Ministry Seeking Support for Shift Toward an All-Volunteer Force," *Wall Street Journal*, July 31, 1990, p. A10.

19. John P. White and James R. Hosek, "The Analysis of Military Manpower Issues," in American Assembly, *Military Service in the United States* (Englewood Cliffs, N.J.: Prentice Hall, 1982), pp. 74–75.

20. Peter Grier, "Shaving the Force," *Government Executive*, April 1990, p. 38.

21. William L. Hauser, "Manpower Procurement and Military Doctrine," in Gregory Foster, Alan Sabrosky, and William Taylor, Jr., eds., *The Strategic Dimension of Military Manpower* (Cambridge, Mass.: Ballinger Publishing Co., 1987), p. 119.

22. Ibid., p. 135.

23. Clyde V. Prestowitz, Jr., *Trading Places*, Paperback edition (New York: Basic Books, 1989), pp. 5–58.

24. James W. Davis, *The Defense Downsizing Debate*, a paper prepared for the annual meeting of the American Political Science Association, September 1990.

PART III

DEFENSE POLICY FOR THE FUTURE

CHAPTER 10

Planning for a World
of Lower Tensions

National policies for the 1990s—both for military and civilian needs—must be developed for a world facing vastly different challenges than those that decision makers encountered in the 1970s and 1980s. To begin with, it has become clear that decisions affecting war, peace, and the host of in-between positions cannot be made in isolation from domestic and international political, economic, and social factors.

Both the willingness and the ability of a nation to support a given level of military preparedness are determined by the complex interaction of these related dimensions. Just consider the different public responses to the Vietnam and Korean conflicts. As noted earlier, a far larger share of the nation's output was devoted to military purposes during the Korean War than during the Vietnam War, yet opposition to the U.S. role in Vietnam was far more intense.

Let us focus on the changes that flow from the end of the Cold War with the Soviet Union, but also take into account the developments in the Persian Gulf in 1990–1991. The recent past has seen four annual steps forward to smaller military budgets and one recent large step backward to a higher level of defense outlays. The net effect on the military–industrial complex is to force a significant downsizing.

The most sensible strategy for the United States is to pursue an understanding with the Soviets while we maintain overwhelming superiority over any third nation. The Iraqi invasion of Kuwait and its aftermath underscore the urgency of that simple proposition.

A step-by-step, incremental approach to arms reduction should be closely keyed to firm evidence of real change by the Soviets. Simultaneously, the United States must be constantly aware of potential threats from other nations. Hasty concessions to defense cutbacks

195

merely promised by the Soviet Union and not yet carried through are foolish; they could place the United States in a needlessly vulnerable position.[1] Indeed, the history of the past half century shows frequent, and wasteful, alternations of stop-and-go cycles of defense spending responding to short-term and poorly thought through changes in perceived threats to our national security.

It makes sense to cooperate with the Soviet leadership in serious efforts to cut back on the size of our respective military establishments. Such action both reduces international tensions and eases domestic budget difficulties. In the Persian Gulf, we have seen the benefits of cooperation with the Soviets on matters of mutual interest. Yet the United States should be prepared to reverse course if the Soviet government changes its mind or is replaced by a more aggressive group. The deterioration in the Soviet economy could worsen the ethnic strife now occurring in many of that nation's border republics. Such a development could lead the Red Army to play a larger political role in order to maintain order.

Should regional civil wars break out, the Soviet Union could become an area of great instability. The Pentagon's plans to withdraw most of our troops from Europe by 1995 might be jeopardized. The ability to maintain effective reversibility on the part of U.S. military policy thus requires a strong defense industrial base as well as alert and well-motivated reserve components. The dangerous world in which we live dictates maintaining a relatively large military establishment to prepare for the possibility of relatively small, limited wars.

THE GLOBAL MARKETPLACE

It is only in recent years that Americans have come to appreciate the civilian counterpart of the fundamental reality that pervades national defense planning—that the United States is an important factor in, but only a part of, a rapidly expanding global marketplace. The external economic environment is an important part of the context in which to set defense policies.

Recent discussions of foreign policy emphasize that national security has become far greater than mere military power and note the limitations of formal armed forces. This is not news to students of defense matters.

For many years, it has been apparent that the tremendous increase in the destructiveness of modern weapons, paradoxically, has resulted in sharp limits to raw military power as an effective instrument of national policy. Because of their awesomeness, nuclear weapons are reserved for use in an apocalyptic situation. All recent conflicts among nations have been resolved through conventional forces. Competition among the major nations in the 1990s will be severe, but it most likely will include nonviolent types of rivalry. Power relationships are very different from those that we have known in the past.

The center of national economic attention in the United States is increasingly on commercial competition from the Asian rim countries, especially Japan. The Cold War was a competition driven by the race for military superiority, but the new competition is a quest for economic and technological dominance.[2]

Focusing the domestic debate solely on Japan misses a more fundamental development. By the end of 1992, the European Community (EC) will be a huge internal market reserved in large part for European-based production. Even now, more than three-fifths of the foreign trade of the twelve member nations is carried on within the EC itself (up from two-fifths before the EC was established). That is a good statistical measure of an inward-looking area.

A single market of 320 million people with minimal internal regulatory barriers will allow the European companies to benefit from the economies of large-scale operations the same way that American companies have in our domestic market. Cost savings will be substantial, efficiency will be enhanced, and opportunities for innovation expanded. European companies will no longer have to make costly product variations to meet the standards of twelve different nations. The shipment of goods and the transfer of capital and labor across national boundaries will be much easier.

All this will encourage many of the remaining European nations to apply for membership in the EC, rather than staying on the outside and facing the increasingly protectionist restrictions being erected to keep out non-EC products. It would not be surprising if many of the former East Bloc nations wind up in some form of association with Western Europe. Even more likely is the entrance into the EC of one or more of the four Scandinavian countries not now members.

One strategic implication is clear: before the end of this century, the European Community will constitute the largest aggregation of market power in the world (their combined GNP already approximates that of the United States).[3] Simultaneously, Japan will be consolidating its position as a world economic superpower. The resultant trilateral relationship has great potential for generating cross rivalries and tensions around the globe. Perhaps the coming reality is best expressed by Jeane Kirkpatrick: "The arena of decision has shifted from bilateral U.S.–Soviet relations to multiple centers of decision making."[4]

IMPROVING THE DECISION-MAKING PROCESS

These global developments have important consequences for the U.S. government. Tax, trade, and environmental policies strongly influence the defense industrial and technological base—and vice versa. The high-tech defense industries (especially aerospace) are the brightest part of an otherwise dismal American foreign trade position.

At present, national security decisions and economic policy are made in two extremely different organizational structures, and respond to very different modes of thought. The growing interdependence of economic and security policies requires a much greater integration of decision making in these two now separate areas. For foreign policy and national security, the president is commander-in-chief as well as chief diplomat. In this area, secrecy is pervasive; most decisions involve very few key advisers.

In contrast, there are numerous players when it comes to economic issues. The role of Congress is fundamental, based on the power of the purse. The most powerful president cannot raise taxes—or lower them—and only the Federal Reserve System can really juggle the money supply. Moreover, since almost every decision has overt political motivations and obvious social consequences, citizens are as involved as experts in these matters. As a result, all government departments and private interest groups participate to some degree.

This fragmented structure of decision making, which is a reason that economic policymakers did not have a greater voice in the initial Vietnam buildup that led to rampant inflation, is one of the shortcomings of the status quo. Key questions, such as the role of technology, fall between the cracks. A streamlined yet coordinated approach is needed, one that does not create any new bureaucracy. The solution is to build on two existing high-level White House organizations, the National Security Council (NSC) and the Economic Policy Council (EPC). The integration of foreign and domestic policy can be achieved most readily by a simple organizational change: making the head of the EPC (the secretary of the treasury) a member of the NSC and putting the secretary of state or defense on EPC. That duality will provide automatic coordination from the top down. To be effective, that change also must be reflected in a broader composition of the subcommittees and working groups of both councils.

No system will work well if the secretary of defense looks only at the military threat and is oblivious to any civilian influences, or if the treasury secretary is solely preoccupied with budget deficits and fiscal policy. Moreover, the best-organized formal system will break down if the president tolerates frequent end runs by his key appointees. Surely vest-pocket diplomacy—whether it is by the secretary of state on "foreign" matters or the secretary of the treasury on international finance—is an anachronism in the modern global economy.

A group approach to the interconnected set of key security and economic policy issues is long overdue. No one federal agency has a monopoly on economic or strategic wisdom, or even the ability to see and understand all of the important connections between the domestic and national security structures of governmental decision making.

The comprehensive approach to policy development envisioned here can eliminate much of the waste and inefficiency inherent in a unilateral approach that invariably results in another "start-and-stop" cycle of military budgeting.

In the emerging international environment, economic hazards are more central than they were in earlier times. The collapse of financial markets, major debt repudiations, runaway inflations, or massive unemployment can unhinge political systems and lead them off in unpredictable directions.

The assured availability of energy sources can be more important than the precise number of ICBMs in place. Our military allies often become our economic rivals; Japan and Western Europe are two striking examples. In contrast, the Soviet Union has almost never challenged the United States for markets or investment opportunities.

The changing nature of international competition does not mean that the United States will lose its status as a major world power in the foreseeable future. It does require this nation to readjust its sights. No one country is likely to be "number one" across the entire spectrum of international competition. The Soviet Union is going through a similar, although far more difficult, transformation. Both nations have to adapt their policies and behavior to environments in which they have substantially diminished control and influence. As the Eastern European nations move toward democracy and market-oriented economies, the Soviet Union and the United States are not always going to be the key players. Germany, not a military superpower, is a more strategic participant in many of those events. In the Middle East, a nation still thought of as a "developing country," with a minimum of industrialization—Iraq—was able to challenge the major powers (although with devastating results).

The most constructive response to new developments is to improve American international competitiveness by increasing the efficiency with which we use our economic resources. This nation cannot afford to neglect the economic base on which both its political and military strength rests, nor can it ignore the fundamentals of national security. It is not, at heart, a choice between commercial and military considerations. The two are invariably interrelated. In view of the pressure to minimize federal spending, it becomes more important than ever to enhance the effectiveness with which the substantial amounts of resources devoted to the national security are used.

HOW TO ADJUST TO CHANGING LEVELS OF DEFENSE SPENDING

The possibility of a conflict breaking out of the magnitude of Korea or Vietnam underscores the need for contingency planning. Yet the most reasonable basis on which to plan for the period beyond the recent conflict in the Persian Gulf is the expectation of continued reductions in U.S. military spending.

Although the cutbacks may be as much as 5 percent a year in real terms, by all likelihood they will be far smaller than the 50 percent cumulative reductions urged during the euphoria of 1989 and early 1990 dominated by visions of large "peace dividends." Even the modest curtailments of defense outlays envisioned here, however, necessitate a variety of adjustments, some painful. Nevertheless, the changes involved would be much less than after the Korean or Vietnam Wars. Policy decisions need to be made in the following areas:

1. *Conform the military force structure to the reduced funding made available by Congress.*

To fit within fiscal reality, the president and the Pentagon leadership have to take those difficult actions that they have avoided since the mid-1980s—substantially reducing the number of aircraft, missiles, ships, and other weapons that the military buys. Just stretching out production schedules and squeezing contractor payments do not constitute a viable long-term alternative. The former raises unit costs, and the latter erodes the defense industrial base. The gap between the military's wishes and congressional appropriations can only be resolved in one way—by cutting military spending. Congress should not make this task more difficult by shielding pet programs from the pruning knife.

Coming to grips with the budgetary challenge will also reduce the great uncertainty that currently hangs over planning in the defense sector by business and individual employees and their families.

Some of the cuts that should be made are obvious; it is only bureaucratic inertia that blocks them. For example, the navy is still planning to spend $1 billion to build and outfit a series of additional "home ports" originally designed to support a 600-ship fleet. The current fleet is fewer than 550 ships and further reductions are very likely. Most of the money allocated to home ports could be saved by forgoing what we must label as an anachronism.[5] The major support for continuing this expensive and needless effort now comes from the cities where the new ports are scheduled to be built. We must be on our guard against born-again military enthusiasts. Local interest groups find it easy to confuse pork with patriotism. Taxpayers generally need to provide a countervailing pressure.

Many defense experts urge a basic downsizing and restructuring of each of the three military services. The result would be a smaller army with fewer forces on active duty. The reserves would be assigned the major portion of the task of defending Europe in a crisis, on the assumption that, once the Soviets have pulled back their armies beyond the Urals, they would be forced to provide many months of warning if they started to rebuild an offensive military structure. The 1990–1991 experience in the Middle East underscores the need for an adequate military posture.

A strong air force would remain, focusing on the continued responsibility for responding to potential strategic threats from the Soviet Union as well as in other regions. More oriented to airlift missions than at present, the air force would be smaller because of the reduced NATO defense responsibilities. The navy would shift more of its vessels to reserve status and would also reduce the number of aircraft carriers. It would focus on its traditional mission of control of the sea lanes, as well as its shared responsibility for the strategic mission.

This smaller U.S. military force—army, navy, and air force—would be based mainly in the continental United States. It would require much less infrastructure support than do the current armed forces.[6] It is vital, however, that the quality and morale of military personnel be maintained at high levels precisely because of the reduction in their overall size and budgets. This means that unit pay and perks need to be maintained at reasonable levels.

In voting lower appropriations for defense after the end of Operation Desert Storm, the Congress should avoid setting in motion a new stop-and-go cycle in military spending. While serious threats to the national security are changing in form, they surely continue, notably the proliferation of nuclear and conventional capability in the Third World. Future U.S. military prowess must be adequate to deal with that dangerous development.

Both Congress and the administration should plan on future levels of defense spending high enough to permit a ready transition to a more active international posture should that be required. Periodic visions of peace dividends should not obscure the long-term need to maintain an adequate corps of well-motivated and highly equipped professionals in the armed forces and key reserve units.

2. *Promptly adjust macroeconomic policy to compensate for the reduced military demand for goods and services.*

Recessions (albeit mild and short) followed the end of the Korean and Vietnam Wars and the decline in military procurement after the Reagan buildup. The microeconomic adjustments (see points 3–6 following) can occur more successfully in a growing economy in which job opportunities are expanding. Given the relatively modest nature of the anticipated future defense cutbacks, equal at most to a fraction of 1 percent of GNP in any one year, the nation should be able to rely on the Federal Reserve System to offset that economic void via its monetary policy decisions. The Fed, as recent experience demonstrates, is the most effective mechanism for influencing short-term economic developments. It does not have to go through the elaborate legislative process required for fiscal policy in order to shift course, nor is it subject to the same political pressures as elected officials in the Congress and the administration.

In large measure, the challenge facing the Fed is technical—to understand and respond promptly to the timing of the impact of changes in military purchases of goods and services. The obstacles are not overwhelming. They mainly involve knowing that, because of the way the GNP is calculated, the major effects of a defense cutback on production and employment show up before the formal measures of defense spending turn down. That occurs because the GNP records the government purchases at the time the completed weapon systems are delivered to the armed forces. The production and employment occur earlier, as likely do the layoffs.[7] The upshot is that the Fed should not hold its fire until it sees "the whites of their eyes" (or the red ink of federal spending).

The prosperity of the United States does not require any particular level of military activity. The productivity and competitiveness of the American economy will suffer if defense spending is used to prop up the prosperity of any region or industry. The real "peace dividend" in terms of a stronger American economy will come about by redirecting defense savings toward civilian R&D and greater investment in the industries in which the United States has a comparative advantage in the global marketplace. These civilian-oriented tasks are primarily the province of the private sector. Government cannot do them well. The main action required of the public sector is to reduce the tax and regulatory obstacles it has erected to the flow of innovation and private investment.

3. *Maintain the social safety net for laid-off defense workers and the affected communities.*

There is a great deal of uncertainty and considerable fear in many localities concerning the future of the employees at defense plants and military installations. Yet, the most likely outlook is for the great majority of the people involved to keep their current jobs. Defense spending is going to continue at historically high levels, even if lower than now. Nevertheless, significant increases in unemployment are occurring in centers of defense production and in locations where bases are being closed. More layoffs are expected.

The United States provides a great variety of help to people in need. Experience with previous defense cutbacks tells us that the knowledge that the government and particularly the community cares and is standing by to help is very important to the newly unemployed, whether defense-related or other.[8] Defense workers should be treated as generously as—but not more or less than—people who lose their jobs because of sluggish housing sales resulting from tight monetary policy or from reduced mining due to more stringent environmental regulations.

The scientists, engineers, and technicians that constitute a large fraction of defense payrolls do not really need federal "make work" programs. They are among the most mobile members of the labor force—geographically, industrially, and occupationally. As Gordon Adams, head of the Defense Budget Project, properly notes, while defense is a national problem, economic adjustment is largely local.[9] In any event, adjustment to defense cutbacks is best initiated in the private sector.

Many defense-oriented communities take the position that the nation owes them something special because of their "contributions" to national security. Their congressional representatives are prone to talk of them as "everyday heroes" and to extol their "sacrifices."[10] The vigorous lobbying efforts, however, made by those communities to get the base or the defense contract in the first place invalidate such obviously self-serving views.

Government decision makers must learn to refrain from jumping every time a constituent gripes. The experience at Fort Wolters in central Texas furnishes a cogent case in point. When the base closing was announced in 1973, the *Fort Worth Star-Telegram* headlined the story as "Economic Rape."[11] Later, after several thousand new jobs were created—over a period of years by a variety of businesses moving into the facility—the local reaction was very different. In 1990, the mayor of the nearby town, Mineral Wells, was quoted as saying, "That post couldn't be reactivated now. The people here wouldn't stand for it."[12]

4. *Provide adequate support for science and technology.*

A reduction in defense spending—because the military is such a large promoter of science and technology—almost automatically means a cutback in federal support for research and development. That downward pressure is also occurring in the defense portion of private industry, where a reduced military market is forcing cutbacks in all forms of discretionary spending including company-sponsored

R&D. The combination of public and private curtailment of investments in science and technology is troublesome for reasons that extend far beyond the military sector. Study after study shows that R&D is a major contributor to economic growth and rising living standards. Moreover, the high-tech industries, which in many cases are almost synonymous with the major defense contractors, account for many of the positive elements in U.S. competitiveness in world markets.

There are some sensible things that government can do within existing budget constraints to shore up the high-technology sectors. The Department of Defense should reduce the barriers it has erected between defense and commercial technology. Greater consolidation of military and industrial product specifications would be especially helpful. Increasing the procurement of commercially produced high-tech products will also strengthen the private sector base for innovation. These actions will enable both large and small firms to serve dual use markets in military and civilian spheres.

The Department of Defense should also liberalize its views on what types of contractor-initiated R&D can be reimbursed under the dollar ceilings established for independent research and development. Specifically, the contractors should be encouraged to do more work on dual technology applicable to both military and civilian products. The fact is that some defense technologies are ahead of the civilian counterpart (such as composite materials), while the commercial sector is increasingly ahead of defense with respect to others, notably semiconductors. The flow of technological discovery is unpredictable and can move back and forth between military and commercial activities.

This is not a plea to shield military R&D from the budgetary pruning knife, but to spend available funds more wisely. A defense cutback is the appropriate time for the Congress to reconsider its attitude toward tax incentives for R&D, which have always been grudgingly extended only a year or so at a time. Such tax measures generate benefits that are different from those that flow from direct federal subsidies. They keep the responsibility for initiating new R&D projects where it belongs—in the private sector; likewise, they ensure that the main financial risk stays with the firm sponsoring and doing the R&D.

The one area where some additional government spending is justified is research, especially basic research. It is rare that the firms doing and paying for the work can keep the rights to the knowledge being generated, and from which society as a whole benefits. Under the circumstances, universities and civilian government agencies need to be encouraged to fill the funding gap opened by defense budget reductions.

The continuing need for research, however, does not justify keeping military laboratories at their current levels of operation by assigning them civilian missions such as environmental research. It would make much more sense to transfer the people and equipment directly to the Environmental Protection Agency or, better yet, to set them up as a new national laboratory attached to a major university. The Jet Propulsion Laboratory of Cal Tech is a good example of the latter type of relationship. If the nation wants to convert military resources to civilian uses, the transfers should be made directly.

5. *Ensure an economic environment conducive to risk-bearing and entrepreneurship.*

Public policy requires a viable group of experienced companies and highly skilled people to meet current defense needs and to provide a base for expansion should international conditions change. The major defense prime contractors and subcontractors constitute a key part of this nation's capability for industrial innovation. That capability is best maintained by a competitive private enterprise economy in which governmental obstacles to entrepreneurship and innovation are kept to a minimum.

The sad fact is that American business, military and civilian, is faced with a major expansion of expensive and burdensome regulatory legislation and mandated benefits.[13] A major decline in the size of the military market is the proper time to administer a massive dose of deregulation to the entire military procurement process. Such long-overdue action would simultaneously reduce the overhead costs of defense contractors and increase their ability to transfer new technology between civilian and military products.

Efficiency can be served by stripping out the host of special provisions that require military contractors to act more like government bureaus doling out benefits to designated classes of beneficiaries than like private enterprises delivering innovation and technological progress.

Productivity can be enhanced by rooting out all the bureaucratic requirements imposed on government procurement personnel and private contractors. The nation pays for that bureaucratization in many ways, especially in the form of unnecessarily long lead times— notably the eight to twelve years now required to develop and produce a new weapon system. That great delay can and should be reduced. Simultaneously, more modern manufacturing technology and investment incentives should be introduced. The most compelling incentive, as noted, is to award major contracts to the firms that do well on earlier production programs rather than those that are skillful at drawing up proposals or merely "buying in" at initial low prices.

In one specialized but important area, there is a positive role for the federal government in dealing with the high-technology defense industry faced with a shrinking defense market—and it will not cost a cent. That role is to help open up markets in Eastern Europe, not through new subsidies, but through the opportunities that would spin off from deregulation. The benefits would extend beyond the defense companies directly affected and include reducing the nation's painfully large trade deficit.

Despite some recent liberalization, the United States continues to maintain the most vigorous export control system of any major industrialized nation. A relic of the Cold War, this labyrinthine system involves tens of thousands of annual licenses of items that could have possible military applications for the Soviets. The former satellites of the Soviet Union are still subject to many of the restraints imposed when the Warsaw Pact was alive.

Liberalizing the policies governing American exports is a cost-effective way to open new markets, especially for the high-tech firms that are bearing the brunt of the defense cutbacks. Simultaneously, such action would strengthen the economic condition of the Eastern European nations as they try to move to more market-oriented societies.[14]

Perhaps most important, the effectiveness of military procurement can be improved by removing the myriad of restraints and directives imposed by members of Congress anxious to protect the defense jobs located in their states or districts. Forcing the military to buy weapon systems they do not need is the most inefficient way of providing benefits to constituents.

6. *Downsize the defense companies perhaps to two-thirds of their 1990 level of operations in order to maintain their financial strength and thus enhance their ability to respond to future national security threats in a continually dangerous world.*

The large- and medium-sized defense contractors that constitute the membership of the Aerospace Industries Association experienced a reduction of 8 percent between 1987 and 1990 in their sales to the Department of Defense (a drop of 17 percent in real terms).[15]

Most economic conversion proposals are at best a diversion and, at worst, a dissipation of the remaining assets of defense contractors. As one who did not criticize defense companies when they earned substantial profits during the 1980s, I also see no reason for the government to provide them, or their employees, with any special assistance now that their military markets and contractor earnings are declining. Even business executives occasionally need to be reminded that private enterprise is truly a profit-and-loss system where stockholders, management, and employees all take risks, and the rewards are uncertain.

Trying to get commercial payoffs from military technology is an enticing concept, but the sad history of past attempts by major military contractors to enter the commercial marketplace underscores the need for government to refrain from subsidizing that process, as many are now urging.

Individual defense firms need to understand that, like companies in other industries, they have no particular claim to maintenance of their present size, or even to their continued existence—nor do their employees possess any special rights to the jobs now generated by defense spending. Most of these firms will find that a more modest scale of operations is also a more efficient scale in the decade ahead.

It is heartening to note that most defense industry leaders are declining to support proposals for government to "assist" them in converting to civilian markets. They are realistic enough to understand that, in the words of one company chief executive, "the best concept for conversion is to take the defense industry down slowly."[16] This advice is consistent with the response of the chairman of Martin Marietta when asked by the Soviets how to convert a tank plant into a refrigerator factory: tear down the tank plant and build a new refrigerator factory.[17]

Forcing defense contractors to try to penetrate markets that are alien to them is no favor to their employees—who would find themselves abruptly laid off when those ventures failed. Those now out of work are better advised to seek employment elsewhere. It is foolhardy to ignore the evidence. As a typical study of past experience concluded: "Detailed research has not identified even one successful product in our economy today which was developed through a military-to-civilian conversion approach."[18]

THE GEOGRAPHY OF DEFENSE EMPLOYMENT

If defense employment were spread evenly across the United States, the adjustment to large shifts in the size and composition of the military budget would be less painful. A relatively few states, however, contain the majority of defense workers and, likewise, only in a handful of states does defense employment loom large in proportional terms. As it turns out, there is some overlap between the two categories, but the two groups are not identical. This complicates the challenge of adjusting to large defense cutbacks.

The Big Ten

Ten states account for about two-thirds of all defense employment (see Table 10-1). The largest absolute concentrations are in California (more than 600,000 defense-related jobs), and Texas, New York, Mas-

Table 10-1   Major Centers of Defense
Employment in 1988

State	Number of Defense Jobs
1. California	657,868
2. Texas	246,473
3. New York	236,421
4. Massachusetts	214,299
5. Virginia	203,307
6. Missouri	147,417
7. Florida	145,219
8. Connecticut	134,018
9. Ohio	127,916
10. Maryland	117,206
Subtotal	2,230,144
Other 40 states	1,169,856
Total	3,400,000

Source: Joseph V. Cartwright, *Potential Defense Work Force Dislocations and U.S. Defense Budget Cuts* (Washington, D.C.: U.S. Department of Defense, Office of Economic Adjustment, 1990).

sachusetts, and Virginia (more than 200,000 in each). Reductions in aircraft orders primarily affect companies in California, Texas, and New York, while cutbacks in missile contracts hit Massachusetts especially hard. Military bases and offices account for most of the Virginia defense employment.

In most of these cases, the shock of the current military budget decline will be much less than the effects of the post-Vietnam cutback. In California, military spending now generates less than 5 percent of the state's jobs, down substantially from its dependence during the Vietnam War. Many Southern Californians, however, still recall the painful fact that their region suffered a much more severe postwar recession than did the rest of the country.

Unlike earlier periods, Washington State is absent from the list of vulnerable areas. Boeing remains the major industrial employer in the Pacific Northwest, but the company and consequently the region are currently more economically balanced than they once were. Boeing's sales are now primarily commercial, and the area itself is benefiting from the growing impact of international trade along the entire Pacific rim. As a result, defense employment generates only about 3 percent of Washington State employment.

The Big Six

Only six states, according to Defense Department economists, depend on military outlays for 5 percent or more of their jobs. In descending order of defense dependence, they are Connecticut (7.9 percent), Massachusetts (7.0 percent), Virginia (6.8 percent), Missouri (6.0 percent), Alaska (5.9 percent), and Maryland (5.0 percent)[19] (see Figure 10-1).

In the case of New England, the region with the most defense-oriented activity, the Federal Reserve Bank of Boston concludes that the budget cuts will have a noticeable negative effect on the region's output. Nondefense-related economic problems in New England will magnify the difficulty of adjustment.[20]

The future of defense activity in many regions will depend on decisions on individual weapon systems. Defense employment in Connecticut is primarily shipbuilding (Electric Boat Division of General Dynamics) and airplane engine production (Pratt & Whitney Division of United Technologies). Missile-producing Raytheon is a key Massachusetts contractor. Aircraft production at McDonnell Douglas accounts for the bulk of Missouri's defense employment.

In contrast, Virginia, Alaska, and Maryland are the locations for a great number of Defense Department installations, bases, and offices. Large shifts in their defense-generated employment will result from substantial changes in the size and composition of the armed forces.

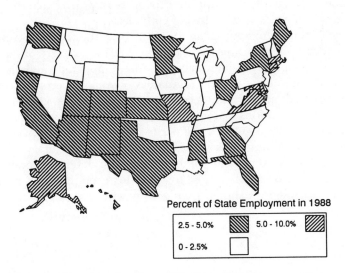

Figure 10-1. Relative Importance of Defense Employment. (*Source:* U.S. Department of Defense, Office of Economic Adjustment.)

Some of the individual adjustments will be difficult. Much of the initial impact of the 1990 cutbacks in defense industry employment occurred by not filling job vacancies, but increasingly the reduction is being achieved through outright layoffs. This is precisely the point at which defense workers and their families begin to reenter the civilian economy, with all its opportunity and uncertainty.

CONCLUSION

The prosperity of the United States does not require any special level of military activity. Our productivity and competitiveness will suffer if defense spending is used to prop up the prosperity of any region or industry. In contrast, reduced defense spending is a very direct way of bringing down the budget deficit.

The long-term needs of the nation require redirecting any defense savings away from government-supported consumption and toward the private sector, where civilian R&D and investment are best undertaken. That indeed is a compelling case for accompanying defense reductions with austerity in civilian government budgeting.

In an economy such as that of the United States, organized primarily along the lines of private enterprise, the basic responsibility for adjusting to unemployment or a reduced income falls on the individual. That person is then in a position to respond to the incentives (positive and negative) provided by the marketplace. The same fundamental approach is appropriate during periods of expansion in defense spending as well as during cutbacks.

The optimum national economic policy for the federal government is to focus on the important responsibilities that are uniquely its own—developing sensible macroeconomic monetary and fiscal policies and minimizing tax and regulatory obstacles to economic activity. Erecting that appropriate economic framework is challenging; it creates the conditions that make it possible to achieve a truly meaningful peace dividend—which will occur when individual workers, companies, and communities successfully shift from military to civilian activity. Once government combines reduced defense spending with revised policy priorities geared to a growing economy with expanding job opportunities, it should then get out of the way!

NOTES

1. See Abraham S. Becker and Arnold L. Horelick, *Managing U.S.–Soviet Relations in the 1990s* (Santa Monica, Calif.: RAND Corporation, 1989).

2. Shafiqul Islam, "Capitalism in Conflict," *Foreign Affairs*, Vol. 69, No. 1, 1990, p. 172.

3. Murray Weidenbaum and Mark Jensen, "American Business and the Global Marketplace," *Business in the Contemporary World*, Summer 1990, pp. 38–46.

4. "AEI Scholars Analyze Bush–Gorbachev Summit," *AEI Newsletter*, June 1990, p. 1.

5. Statement of Martin M. Ferber, National Security and International Affairs Division, General Accounting Office, to the House Committee on Armed Services, April 24, 1990, p. 17.

6. Gordon Adams, *Economic Adjustment to Lower Defense Spending*, Testimony to the Senate Armed Services Committee, May 4, 1990, p. 1; Sam Nunn, *Implementing a New Military Strategy*, a speech to the Senate, April 20, 1990, pp. 6–10.

7. See Murray L. Weidenbaum, "The Timing of the Economic Impact of Government Spending," *National Tax Journal*, March 1959, pp. 79–85.

8. *Economic Adjustment/Conversion*, Report Prepared by President's Economic Adjustment Committee and the Office of Economic Adjustment (Washington, D.C.: Office of the Assistant Secretary of Defense, Manpower, Installations and Logistics, July 1985), Chapter 5.

9. Adams, *Economic Adjustment*, p. 14.

10. See, for example, Richard A. Gephardt, "Displaced Workers Must Be Helped," *St. Louis Post-Dispatch*, July 22, 1990, p. 3B.

11. Quoted in *Communities in Transition* (Washington, D.C.: President's Economic Adjustment Committee, 1977), p. 28.

12. Quoted in Donald C. Bacon, "Closing a Base Opens Doors," *Nation's Business*, May 1990, p. 9.

13. See Murray Weidenbaum, *Rendezvous With Reality*, paperback edition (New York: Basic Books, 1990), pp. xxiv–xxvi.

14. Barnaby J. Feder, "U.S. Exporters Wary of Technology Accord," *The New York Times*, June 12, 1990, p. C2; Bruce Stokes, "Opening Eastern Gates," *National Journal*, June 23, 1990, pp. 1531–34.

15. The Aerospace Industries Association estimates that the sales of member companies may decline by 21 percent from 1987 to 1991 (a drop of 32 percent in real terms). See *1990 Year-End Review and Analysis* (Washington, D.C.: Aerospace Industries Association, 1991), Table II.

16. *Statement By Stanley C. Pace Before the Senate Armed Services Committee*, May 4, 1990, p. 5

17. Norman R. Augustine, "The Real Dividend Is Peace," *World Link*, May–June 1990, p. 22.

18. *Economic Adjustment/Conversion*, p. iv.

19. Joseph V. Cartwright, *Potential Defense Work Force Dislocations and U.S. Defense Budget Cuts* (Washington, D.C.: U.S. Department of Defense, Office of Economic Adjustment, 1990), p. 9.

20. Yolanda K. Henderson, "Defense Cutbacks and the New England Economy," *New England Economic Review*, July/August 1990, pp. 3–24.

Statistical Appendix

Table A-1   Major Defense Contractors in 1988

Rank Company	(1) Defense Contracts (millions $)	(2) Company Sales (millions $)	(3) (1)/(2) (%)
1. McDonnell Douglas	8,003	15,069	53.1
2. General Dynamics	6,522	9,551	68.3
3. General Electric	5,701	49,414	11.5
4. Tenneco	5,058	13,234	38.2
5. Raytheon	4,055	8,192	49.5
6. Martin Marietta	3,715	5,727	64.9
7. General Motors	3,550	120,387	2.9
8. Lockheed	3,538	10,590	33.4
9. United Technologies	3,508	18,000	19.5
10. Boeing	3,018	16,692	18.1
11. Grumman	2,848	3,591	79.3
12. Litton Industries	2,561	5,023	50.9
13. Westinghouse Electric	2,185	12,500	17.5
14. Rockwell International	2,184	11,946	18.3
15. Unisys	1,379	9,902	13.9
16. Honeywell	1,366	7,148	19.1
17. Textron	1,276	7,279	17.5
18. TRW	1,250	6,982	17.9
19. Texas Instruments	1,232	6,295	19.6
20. IBM	1,065	59,681	1.8
21. LTV Corporation	941	7,325	12.9
22. FMC Corporation	861	3,287	26.2
23. Ford Motor Company	790	92,446	0.8
24. Singer	785	2,140*	36.7
25. ITT Corporation	769	19,355	4.0
26. Allied Signal	711	11,909	6.0
28. Gencorp Inc.	639	1,891	33.8
29. Avondale Ind.	580	570	101.6
30. AT&T	565	35,210	1.6
32. Northrop Corp.	532	5,797	9.2
33. Hercules Inc.	499	2,802	17.8
34. Harsco Corp.	496	1,279	38.8
35. Loral Corp.	494	1,187	41.6
36. Teledyne Inc.	469	4,523	10.4
38. GTE	422	16,460	2.6
39. Dyncorp.	421	555	75.9
42. Thiokol	392	1,168	33.6
44. Motorola	381	8,250	4.6
45. Harris Corp.	371	2,214	16.8
46. Computer Sciences Corp.	368	1,304	28.2
49. PanAm	357	3,569	10.0

Table A-1 *(Continued)*

| | (1) Defense Contracts (millions $) | (2) Company Sales (millions $) | (3) (1)/(2) (%) |
Rank Company			
51. Science Applications Intl.	343	693	49.5
52. Olin Corp.	331	2,308	14.3
53. Penn Central	329	1,547	21.3
54. Chevron	328	25,196	1.3
55. Control Data Corp.	315	3,628	8.7
56. Atlantic Ritchfield	303	17,626	1.7
57. Mobil Corp.	302	48,198	0.6
59. Exxon	282	79,557	0.4
60. E-Systems Inc.	263	1,439	18.3
61. Forstmann Little & Co.	261	209	124.9
62. Oshkosh Truck	260	353	73.7
63. Emerson Electric	253	6,651	3.8
64. Black River Constructors (subs. of Armco Inc.)	251	3,227	7.8
65. Zenith Electronics	248	2,686	9.2
66. Contel Corp.	237	2,964	8.0
67. Sequa Corp.	220	1,713	12.9
68. Eaton Corp.	218	3,469	6.3
69. Coastal Corp.	213	8,186	2.6
70. Chrysler Corp.	210	35,473	0.6
75. Amoco Corp.	188	21,150	0.9
76. Eastman Kodak	186	17,034	1.1
78. Sundstrand Corp.	185	1,477	12.5
79. Kaman Corp.	184	767	24.0
80. Emhart Corp.	181	2,762	6.5
81. Digital Equipment	175	12,742	1.4
82. Morrison Knudsen	170	1,909	8.9
84. Arvin Industries	166	1,313	12.6
85. United Industrial	165	315	52.4
87. CSX Corp.	161	7,592	2.1
90. Hewlett-Packard	149	9,831	1.5
92. Tiger International	145	3,883	3.7
94. Phelps Inc.	141	5,385	2.6
97. EG&G Inc.	132	1,406	9.4
98. Texaco	131	33,554	0.4
100. Figgie International	129	1,200	10.8

Source: 100 Companies Receiving the Largest Dollar Volume of Prime Contract Awards, FY 1988, U.S. Department of Defense, Washington, D.C.; *Standard and Poor's Stock Reports (OTC), (AMEX), (NYSE), 1989,* Standard and Poor Corporation.
*Current data unavailable since company went private; figures shown are for 1986.
Note: Defense contracts awarded in a given year are often performed over a period of years. Thus, occasionally, contract values exceed annual sales volumes.

Table A-2   Importance of Defense Contracts in 1988

Percentage Range	Company	Defense Contracts as a Percentage of Sales
75–100	Forstmann Little & Co.	124.9
	Avondale Ind.	101.6
	Grumman	79.3
	Dyncorp.	75.9
50–75	Oshkosh Truck	73.7
	General Dynamics	68.3
	Martin Marietta	64.9
	McDonnell Douglas	53.1
	United Industrial	52.4
	Litton Industries	50.9
25–50	Science Applications Intl.	49.5
	Raytheon	49.5
	Loral Corp.	41.6
	Harsco Corp.	38.8
	Tenneco	38.2
	Singer Co.	36.7
	Gencorp Inc.	33.8
	Thiokol	33.6
	Lockheed Corp.	33.4
	Computer Sciences Corp.	28.2
	FMC Corp.	27.2
10–25	Kaman Corp.	24.0
	Penn Central	21.3
	Texas Instruments	19.6
	United Technologies	19.5
	Honeywell	19.1
	E-Systems Inc.	18.3
	Rockwell International	18.3
	Boeing	18.1
	TRW	17.9
	Hercules Inc.	17.8
	Textron	17.5
	Westinghouse Electric	17.5
	Harris Corp.	16.8
	Olin Corp.	14.3
	Unisys	13.9
	Sequa Corp.	12.9
	LTV Corp.	12.9
	Arvin Industries	12.6
	Sundstrand Corp.	12.5
	General Electric	11.5
	Figgie International	10.8
	Teledyne Inc.	10.4

Table A-2   (*Continued*)

Percentage Range	Company	Defense Contracts as a Percentage of Sales
0–10	Pan Am	10.0
	EG&G Inc.	9.4
	Zenith Electronics	9.2
	Northrop Corp.	9.2
	Morrison Knudsen	8.9
	Control Data Corp.	8.7
	Contel Corp.	8.0
	Armco Inc.	7.8
	Emhart Corp.	6.5
	Eaton Corp.	6.3
	Allied Signal	6.0
	Motorola	4.6
	ITT Corp.	4.0
	Emerson Electric	3.8
	Tiger International	3.7
	General Motors	2.9
	Coastal Corp.	2.6
	Phelps Inc.	2.6
	GTE	2.6
	CSX Corp.	2.1
	IBM	1.8
	Atlantic Ritchfield	1.7
	AT&T	1.6
	Hewlett-Packard	1.5
	Digital Equipment	1.4
	Chevron	1.3
	Eastman Kodak	1.1
	Amoco Corp.	0.9
	Ford Motor Co.	0.8
	Chrysler Corp.	0.6
	Mobil Corp.	0.6
	Texaco	0.4
	Exxon	0.4

Source: Moody's Industrial Manual (1988), *Moody's Transportation Manual* (1988), *Moody's OTC Industrial Manual* (1988), *Moody's Public Utilities Manual* (1988), Moody's Investor's Service, Inc., New York; *100 Companies Receiving the Largest Dollar Volume of Prime Contract Awards, FY 1988,* U.S. Department of Defense, Washington, D.C.; *Standard and Poor's Stock Reports (OTC), (AMEX), (NYSE), 1989,* Standard and Poor Corporation, New York.

Table A-3 Size Distribution of Major Defense Contractors in 1988

Range of Asset Size	Company	Asset Size (1988) (millions $)	Share of Total Defense Contracts (%)
$10 billion and over	General Motors	164,063	2.59
	Ford Motor Co.	143,366	0.57
	General Electric	110,865	4,15
	Exxon	74,293	0.20
	IBM	73,037	0.77
	Chrysler Corp.	48,567	0.15
	ITT Corp.	41,941	0.56
	AT&T	40,900	0.41
	Mobil Corp.	38,820	0.22
	Chevron	33,968	0.23
	GTE	31,104	0.30
	Amoco Corp.	29,919	0.13
	Texaco	26,337	0.09
	Eastman Kodak	22,964	0.13
	Atlantic Ritchfield	21,514	0.22
	Tenneco	17,376	3.69
	Westinghouse Electric	16,937	1.59
	CSX	13,026	0.11
	United Technologies	12,748	2.55
	Boeing	12,608	2.20
	Textron	12,554	0.93
	McDonnell Douglas	11,885	5.83
	Unisys	11,535	1.00
	Digital Equipment	10,112	0.12
	Allied Signal	10,005	0.51
$5–10 billion	Rockwell International	9,208	1.59
	Coastal Corp.	7,865	0.15
	Hewlett-Packard	7,497	0.10
	Motorola	6,710	0.27
	Lockheed Corp.	6,643	2.58
	Contel Corp.	6,479	0.17
	LTV Corp.	6,163	0.68
	General Dynamics	6,118	4.75
	Teledyne Inc.	5,125	0.34
	Honeywell	5,089	0.99
	Litton Industries	5,074	1.86
	Emerson Electric	5,027	0.18
$1–5 billion	Raytheon	4,740	2.95
	TRW	4,442	0.91
	Texas Instruments	4,427	0.89
	Hercules Inc.	3,325	0.36
	Martin Marietta	3,319	2.71

Table A-3 (*Continued*)

Range of Asset Size	Company	Asset Size (1988) (millions $)	Share of Total Defense Contracts (%)
$1–5 billion	Northrop Corp.	3,139	0.38
	Eaton Corp.	3,034	0.15
	Tiger International	3,009	0.10
	Armco Inc.	2,788	0.18
	Phelps Inc.	2,755	0.10
	FMC Corp.	2,749	0.62
	Grumman	2,566	2.07
	Control Data Corp.	2,534	0.23
	Emhart Inc.	2,426	0.13
	Penn Central	2,400	0.23
	Pan Am	2,149	0.26
	Sequa Corp.	1,959	0.16
	Olin Corp.	1,940	0.24
	Harris Corp.	1,644	0.27
	Sundstrand Corp.	1,567	0.13
	Zenith Electronics	1,428	0.18
	Loral Corp.	1,415	0.36
	Gencorp Inc.	1,230	0.46
	Arvin Industries	1,058	0.12
	Figgie International	1,022	0.09
$500 million–1 billion	Harsco Inc.	893	0.36
	E-Systems Inc.	758	0.19
	Morrison Knudsen	746	0.12
	Thiokol	729	0.28
	Computer Sciences Corp.	715	0.26
	EG&G Inc.	539	0.09
$250–500 million	Singer Co.	445	0.13
	Kaman Corp.	420	0.57
	Avondale Ind.	419	0.42
	Dyncorp.	347	0.30
	United Industrial	259	0.12
	Science Applications Intl.	256	0.25
Under $250 million	Forstmann Little & Co.	172	0.19
	Oshkosh Truck	164	0.18

Source: 100 Companies Receiving the Largest Dollar Volume of Prime Contract Awards, 1988 (U.S. Department of Defense, Washington, D.C.); *Standard and Poor's Stock Reports (OTC), (AMEX), (NYSE)* (Standard and Poor Corporation, New York, 1989), *Ford Motor Company Annual Report, FY 1988.*

Index